Crime Prevention, Migration Control and Surveillance Practices

EU expansion has stoked fears that criminals from the East may abuse freedom of movement to exploit the benefit systems of richer states. This book examines the way in which physical state borders are increasingly being replaced by internal border controls in the form of state bureaucracies as a means of regulating westward migration. The work examines the postmodern effect of globalisation and how ontological anxieties contribute to securitisation and social sorting in Western countries. It discusses the changes in control societies and how targeted surveillance as a geopolitical tool leads to new digitalised mechanisms of population selection. The book presents a casestudy of Roma migrants in the UK to examine the coping strategies adopted by those targeted. The book also critically evaluates the limitations of digitalised bureaucratic systems and the dangers of reliance on virtual data and selection methods.

Veronika Nagy, PhD, is an assistant professor of criminology at the Willem Pompe Institute at the Faculty of Law Governance and Economics, Utrecht University. Her research interests include surveillance, digital inequality with a focus on a broad connection between mobility and technology, securitisation of international migration, criminalisation and digital self-censorship. She conducted research on specific forms of ethnic mobility, human trafficking and digital profiling (exploitation of workers, forced criminal activities and trafficking of children).

Crime Prevention, Migration Control and Surveillance Practices

Welfare Bureaucracy as Mobility Deterrent

Veronika Nagy

Routledge
Taylor & Francis Group
LONDON AND NEW YORK

First published 2019
by Routledge
2 Park Square, Milton Park, Abingdon, Oxon OX14 4RN

and by Routledge
52 Vanderbilt Avenue, New York, NY 10017, USA

First issued in paperback 2020

Routledge is an imprint of the Taylor & Francis Group, an informa business

British Library Cataloguing-in-Publication Data
A catalogue record for this book is available from the British Library

Library of Congress Cataloging-in-Publication Data
Names: Nagy, Veronika, author.
Title: Crime prevention, migration control and surveillance practices : welfare bureaucracy as mobility deterrent / Veronika Nagy.
Description: First Edition. | New York : Routledge, 2019. | Includes bibliographical references.
Identifiers: LCCN 2018021607 | ISBN 9780815396666 (hbk) | ISBN 9781351181402 (ebk)
Subjects: LCSH: Crime prevention—Europe. | Emigration and immigration
law—Europe. | Border crossing—Europe. | Social security—Europe.
Classification: LCC HV7434.E85 N34 2019 | DDC 364.4/0456094—dc23
LC record available at https://lccn.loc.gov/2018021607

ISBN 13: 978-0-367-58624-9 (pbk)
ISBN 13: 978-0-8153-9666-6 (hbk)

Typeset in Galliard
by Apex CoVantage, LLC

Contents

Acronyms

CAB	Citizens Advice Bureau
CEE	Central Eastern Europe/European
DLA	*Disability Living Allowance*
DWP	Department of Work and Pension
HB	Housing Benefit
HMRC	Her Majesty's Revenue and Customs
IMF	International Monetary Fund
IS	Income Support
JCP	Job Centre Plus
JSA	Jobseeker's Allowance
JSA(IB)	Jobseeker's Allowance (Income-Based)
JSAPS	Jobseeker's Allowance Payment System
ERI	European Roma Institute
NHR	National Habitual Residence
OSCE	Organization for Security and Co-operation in Europe
PIP	Personal Independence Payment

Acknowledgements

This book is a milestone, a footprint of my first stept towards critical thinking in technology in the field of Criminology. In order to publish the first ideas of this development, I would like to express my gratitude to many of my collegues, friends and family for their support and assistance througout my research period and for fostering the development of my research interest in digital society. The topics of state control, exclusion and authority have always fascinated me in the Post-transitional context of Central Eastern Europe. However, this interest in securitisation and surveillance was strengthened when I became a migrant and a student of Professor Frank Bovenkerk. I thank him for guiding me toward criminology and sharing his critical view, which has informed my work in the last ten years.

My sincere thanks to my PhD supervisors, Professor Dina Siegel and Professor Klára Kerezsi; I cannot express my gratitude for the support, patience and encouragement I received to complete this study. During my fieldwork, they dismissed my defeatism when I felt exhausted and kept reminding me about the light at the end of the tunnel. I will never forget our heated discussions and late-night brainstorming sessions. My sincere thanks also to Mira and Danielle for helping me become a better writer. They read multiple drafts and continuously gave me advice on how to improve the manuscript. Without them, this work would have been much less clear and coherent.

I would also like to express my gratitude to all the families who hosted me in my fieldwork period, sharing their homes, food and cigarettes with me. I not only learned about their lives, but also about myself. I owe thanks to Maria, who cheered me up and held up a mirror to help me stay reflective.

I am particularly grateful for the support of Non-Governmental Organisations (NGOs), which are greatly important in the everyday lives of Roma migrants in London. I am thankful for their help in getting access to other organisations, policymakers and social services. Their experiences and recommendations helped shape my research objective throughout my fieldwork period.

I am greatly indebted to my Brazilian household, especially Paulinho, who offered me a "safe house" in the weekends and reminded me that there is a life beyond academia and 'I am no angel'.

This book would not have been possible without the encouragement, participation and support of my friends and colleagues Daan, Roos, Camille, Esteban, Alíz, Barna, Éva and many others who do not fit on a page of acknowledgements.

Furthermore, I thank all my fellow PhD candidates and the consortium of the Doctorate in Cultural and Global Criminology, in particular Dr Andrea Borbíró and Dr Damián Zaitch for supporting me in this programme. I would also like to express thanks for the hospitality of ELTE University and their flexibility and assistance in my administrative process.

Lastly, I want to lovingly thank my family and my godmother, who always encouraged me and believed in me, for their unconditional love.

Cornelis, please forgive me.

1 Introduction

Technological advances and data collection practices are hot topics in the daily news, as are discussions about the risks of digitalisation, self-learning algorithms and the marketisation of private information. Several studies have raised concerns about privacy, the threats posed by social media use and the consequences of the information society for local bureaucratic practices (Borja & Castells, 2013). New disciplines like digital humanities, internet governance, digital criminology, or studies on big data attempt to frame the social impacts of these technical advantages and their use in legal, social and economic spheres.

Digitisation has affected individuals since the era of machine-readable data began (Kistermann, 1991). Electronic data processing followed the emergence of electronic computing on both sides of the Atlantic around 1940. Within a decade, governments recognised that digitisation offered them an opportunity to create "national data systems" to consolidate data about people for use in governance tools and sociological research (e.g. the Metropolit projects in Sweden and Denmark; Osler et al., 2006). Digitisation created possibilities for faster, interrelated data processing at all governance levels, but it also led to the contemporary shift in the patterns of organisational behaviour, in which digitalised control practices like surveillance create unequal social structures (Taylor, 2017). This institutional digitalisation and the role of corporate actors in public services created a new academic discourse about digital inequality, such as the unequal distribution of risks and resources associated with online welfare practices.

Previous surveillance studies have generally stressed the risks and possible social implications of governmental data collection as it relates to privacy protection (Lyon, 2013). With the extension of digitalised service provisions, new surveillance practices are introduced by local authorities that increasing effect the life of newcomers. There has been unfortunately limited attention paid to the responses of those people who are subjected to such algorithmic control measures (Hannah-Moffat, 2018). Although qualitative studies are increasingly describing surveillance subjects' counteractions (McCahill & Finn, 2014), there has been limited research on the *asymmetries of digital surveillance*. Governments overestimate the objectivity and effectiveness of digital bureaucracies, in particular the relaibilty of surveillance practices. Moreover, the cumulative effects of surveillance awareness are underestimated in the field of welfare provisions, especially in the case of EU migrants.

This book aims to critically reflect on the relative efficiency of digital bureaucracies and the extent to which it might impact the everyday lives of groups subjected to financial risk profiling. Current securitisation of EU migrants increased the role of surveillance techniques in state bureaucracies of many old EU Member States and allows them to select and expose targeted groups, such as the Roma. This study explores the growing awareness of monitoring practices, how this leads to social distrust, increases fear and anxiety, and turns surveillance cities into ghost societies. By reflecting on social sorting mechanisms in the UK welfare system, I will explain how digitalised surveillance experiences of ethnic migrants lead to the amplification of self-censorship mechanisms, creating a sphere of confusion in the bureaucratic system that results in a spiral of securitisation and intensified surveillance practices.

By linking crime such as benefit fraud to intra-European mobility, political debates increased security concerns and scepticism about newcomers from Central Eastern Europe (CEE), in particular Roma (for a detailed explanation, see Duwell & Wollmer, 2009; O'Reilly, 2007a; Ringold, 2000). Governments have used these security concerns to justify new restrictive measures 'for profiling the bad foreign opportunist versus the good citizen who deserves state support and protection' (Erjavec, 2001, p. 670). Although the securitisation of Roma migrants is not a new phenomenon, the methods of targeting and selecting undesired citizens have been refined.

Recent convergences of once discrete control measures of newcomers have resulted in unexpected outcomes in governance practices. Data resources like social media are facilitating new surveillance practices that are used to classify, predict and prevent individual behaviour considered as social or economic risk. In this panoptic virtual society, governmental and business activities are intertwined in bureaucratic technologies, and population control is shifting from traditional policing methods to internal financial monitoring of suspected migrants.

This book presents the financial modalities of migration control and explains how welfare authorities screen and trace unattractive migrant groups that are associated with economic threat. Much of this book focuses on analysing the tactics used by securitised individuals, especially how they use identity management to challenge social sorting mechanisms in their interactions with social service organisations. This study provides an extended overview of coping strategies invented by one targeted population: Central European Roma. As an interdisciplinary, multi-sited research of welfare surveillance, this study addresses geopolitical incentives in the EU and how Roma migrants use calculated coping strategies to prevent exclusion from social services. The central question is: How does the interplay between digitalised bureaucracies of welfare providers of this book and the coping strategies of EU newcomers shape the social sorting of migrants in the United Kingdom?

1.1 Roma mobility in the EU

Based on the fifth EU Treaty, the coordination of social security systems (which was also revamped in 2004) was made more generous for people who move around the EU. This revision tightened the rules on non-discrimination and strengthened the right to use aggregate contributions made in different member states to calculate entitlements, including the right to export benefits to one's country of residence. After the last EU enlargement, like many other CEE families, Roma ethnic minorities have been trying to use their European citizenship to find better lives in Western Europe. However, the majority of Roma finds themselves excluded and marginalised by new administrative rules in their host countries justified by new welfare principles. Interestingly, the cause of the 'Roma flood' in the political discourse is frequently linked to the 'promising' welfare services of host countries, which has led local authorities to increase control strategies and limit access to social benefits claimed by CEE newcomers. The key argument for welfare restrictions is framed in a neoliberal approach to eligibility based on labour market participation. According to the underlying assumptions, these migrants are responsible for their marginal position and can consequently be legitimately excluded from any entitlement to governmental support (Goddard, 2012).

Shortly, many member states have questioned why they have to export 'their' social benefits to EU citizens who have acquired welfare rights in their state, in particular those migrants who are defined in terms of a security threat. Accordingly, neoliberal state recognition has been based on legal economic activity and social citizenship of newcomers rather than legal EU citizenship. This neoliberal principle also challenged the European integration framework, raising vigorous contestation about the meaning and extension of 'social rights'of EU citizens, how much they should be contingent on people's productive behaviour and who should be covered by the state. This contribution is measured in finalncial terms such as documented work and tax payment in the country of residence. Shortly, within the contemporary hierarchies of work, the functioning of borders has less to do with the geopolitical delineation of sovereign prerogatives (i.e. the power to exclude non-citizens from access to a state's territory) and more to do with the attempt to control, select and govern specific productive categories of people at a distance (De Giorgi, 2012). A key element of this selection is that citizenship is presented and wrapped up as a form of contract between the state and the responsible citizen who accepts the preconditions. Using the technique of a contract is often recognised as part of a neoliberal strategy, all the more in cases where the state also involves the (local) community or private parties in terms of sharing the responsibility for this process (Rose, 1999; Yeatman, 1998).

Recently, responsibilisation has been a key principle of this dominant neoliberal welfare approach to Western European surveillance incentives (Goddard, 2012). Therefore, it aims to identify particular groups who are seen as unwilling to integrate and participate in their societies. This participation is generally defined as labour market participation and is measured by the level of dependency on state funding, such as social benefits. To combat the perceived economic threat to national welfare, new security measures are intended to differentiate the good or productive citizens from the undesired, 'passive' citizens. As a result, social and spatial exclusion is based on financial determinants that serve as a functional realm that precludes inclusion of the unproductive others (Halfmann, 1998). Before we can explore how these welfare-service-based financial monitoring structures facilitate spatial population control, we need to understand how governing bodies in the EU are able to invent incentives that pressure undesired groups to voluntarily leave their territory.

Roma who are EU citizens cannot be ignored or sanctioned based on their migration status, but they might be dependent on government aid that enables them to settle down in a host country. When they are subjected to constant financial monitoring and benefit cuts, they can be forced to leave by restricting their entitlement to local welfare support. Therefore, the idea that certain countries are 'welfare magnets' has resulted in new monitoring-based restrictions and the securitisation of benefit claimants by social service providers, which is intended to enforce the mobility of unwanted migrants.

1.2 Social sorting as modality of governance power

By revealing social surveillance and selection mechanisms based on financial surveillance, I will show how crime politics infiltrates legislative areas (e.g. welfare provisions) by encouraging the use of new governance technologies in digitalised bureaucracies. This book provides empirical data on the mechanisms of surveillance strategies that promote efficiency and objectivity while justifying privatised practices of control and sanctions outside the field of crime control. Empirical data is used to describe the effects of businesslike values on welfare provisions and to identify the risk profiles of screening instruments used as social sorting tools. I will also examine how service-dependent migrants adapt their coping strategies to these constantly changing selection methods.

Virtual control measures not only reflect the values and categories of the host society but also how individual parameters are translated into risk categories. Welfare application systems, amongst others, use the narratives of political and academic stakeholders to shape these parameters by linking ethnic connotations to economic power. Although institutional discrimination is often described in terms of ethnicity and race, this book presents how EU migrants are subject to discrimination based on financial parameters instead of ethnic stigma. To better understand these selective surveillance mechanisms, I examine several actors (including professionals and activists) who might contribute to these mechanisms by linking poverty to ethnicity and thus shifting discriminatory notions based on visible parameters (e.g. skin colour, culture) towards less visible selection methods (e.g. credit checks).

Unlike studies that define transnational mobility in terms of migration categories, this analysis reveals the dynamics and constantly shifting nature of population flows. I explore how newcomers, stigmatised by financial inefficacy as an ethnic construct, adapt to rapidly changing circumstances by inventing coping strategies to circumvent the bureaucratic labyrinth of host societies. I challenge the underlying assumptions behind efficiency-oriented governance technologies and use selected empirical data to critically analyse the limitations of surveillance and control practices, and their implications for institutional distrust. The dynamic relationship between central European migrants and bureaucratic service providers in London provides an example of how neoliberal market values adapted in social provisions lead to discriminatory welfare services.

As it will be illustrated, social sorting and population control practices are shaped by the intersubjective construction of security (Burke, 2007). This securitisation 'enables, produces and constrains individuals within larger systems of power and institutional action' (Burke, 2007, p. 20) defined under different modalities of surveillance (Bigo & Walker, 2007; Jones & Newburn, 1998). Based on the Foucauldian concept of disciplinary power (1977), this panoptic modality in governing initiatives includes simultaneous control and behaviour-modifying mechanisms. As the following collected empirical data illustrates, enforcing mobility by financial restrictions is one of the most common goals deployed by authorities to channel and regulate their populations and control unwieldy flows of people. As Hyndman (2012) explains:

> The idea of migrants as a vector of insecurity prevailed, creating potent fear that could be used for draconian measures. The biometric management of 'insiders' and 'outsiders' with its assemblage of new laws, policies and control practices render geopolitics and biopolitics inseparable.
>
> (p. 245)

State incentives are coded in different panoptic modalities to guide people on the move. These include mapping, valuation, codification, enclosures and boundaries. Since these incentives are proactively trying to channel individual conduct, financial planning is one of the key means of managing (im)mobilities and access. This apparatus of control and surveillance, used as spatial disciplinary technology in the EU, might be even more central in the de- and re-territorialisation of people, since no visa regulations are in force for European citizens (Deleuze & Guattari, 1987). As a neoliberal incentive, border control is thus drawn out by the gaze of social economic surveillance.

Accordingly, social security and immigration policies are increasingly intertwined within the surveillance practices of member states, blurring the line between welfare and crime control measures. They introduce new geopolitical measures and local risk management strategies for tracing and screening mobile groups, such as Roma migrants. These monitoring practices, such as data analysis software, are taking new forms in technocratic bureaucracies and changing the means of interaction between newcomers and administrative bodies in host societies.

In order to understand how these welfare-service-based financial monitoring structures facilitate spatial population control, we need to understand how governing bodies are able to invent incentives that try to make undesired groups voluntarily leave their executive territory. This study uses a multi-sited ethnography to explore these asymmetries of surveillance within the virtual walls of Fortress Europe. In particular, this book uncovers coping strategies used by targeted populations and investigates how they reshape existing profiling strategies.

By following the critical surveillance paradigm, this study aims to analyse the growing challenge of expending digitalised bureaucracies as internal borders of EU member states by introducing the concept of a 'Welfare Ban-Opticon'. This refers to Bigo's social sorting mechanism (2008b) through digitalised social provisions.

By illustrating the dynamics of intra-European mobility control and the social construction of threat associated with foreign EU ethnic minorities, this study critically reflects on the use of digitalised surveillance methods and draws attention to the shifting parameters of bureaucratic selection measures, in particular those related to the financial capabilities of newcomers. By following the dialectic relationship between welfare providers and migrants, I reveal the dynamics of criminal and migration policies that are defined in terms of social and financial threat. These dynamics have also led to the expansion of selective control measures in other bureaucratic fields, such as social welfare.

The selected cases of Roma migrants are not presented to evaluate the label of 'benefit cheats' or to assess the extent to which Roma are involved in benefit fraud. Instead, they are used to illustrate the dynamics of targeted policing through digitalised bureaucratic welfare provisions, and to describe how financial parameters have become the new incentives of migration selection.

The methodology underpinning this study was intended to generate data about 1) how criminal politics and security measures are changing the role of welfare services; 2) how stakeholders such as academics and NGOs are framing migration management principles and 3) how Roma migrants labelled as 'benefit tourists' experience and anticipate interactions with social services in the UK. I collected data through observation and participation in private conversations, and through activities with civil servants, interpreters and advocacy workers. I then analysed many of these interactions through in-depth, semi-structured interviews with migrants, advocacy workers and civil servants.

1.3 The relevance of welfare surveillance studies

Although current changes in policymaking are targeting 'benefit shoppers', there is limited scholarly literature that explores the role of welfare policies in migration control within the EU. In the United Kingdom, social policies have been rapidly changing since 2006, causing confusion for service providers about entitlement changes and control measures. With increasing digitalisation and managerialist values in social service provision, the discretionary power of civil servants has decreased, raising concerns about efficiency-oriented normative approaches. By adapting surveillance techniques like profiling algorithms from corporate software producers, the UK government deemed the professionalism of civil servants to be unnecessary. Although these measures were invented to support the efficiency of service providers, according to recent conditions, they are only expected to decrease welfare costs based on annual targets (Harlow, 2003). The social and professional impacts of such changes in policy adaptations can only be evaluated by qualitative research methods. Therefore, I will assess practical implications and, especially, the extent to which professionals and service providers ignore restrictive policies.

The key objective of this study is to explore the shift in the purpose of welfare legislation concerning profiling practices, especially how restrictive social policy is used for migration control of newcomers in London. Contradictory objectives regarding intra-European migration and welfare restrictions between EU policy and local welfare measures are explored. In short, this book highlights how selective social policies trigger welfare claimants to modify their behaviour according to restricted welfare incentives.

Critical geopolitical studies are increasingly focusing on the relationship between space and identity in the context of the EU (Tuathail & Dalby, 1998). Most of them conceptualise biopolitical developments in Western societies, progressive technologies or the securitisation and exclusion of irregular migrants. However, these studies often avoid two aspects: the securitisation of minorities who are European citizens and the extent to which these surveillance subjects reshape governmental incentives that are manifested in bureaucratic registration procedures.

In summary, this study takes an interdisciplinary theoretical approach that interweaves recent critical studies in geopolitics, criminology, critical surveillance and minority studies. Theoretical objectives are used to reflect on digital surveillance mechanisms and to develop an interactive approach to the role of virtual identity management in the context of social service provision. Dataveillance and control of identification processes have created the illusions of objectivity and traceability. Following the Deleuzeian notion of the surveillance assemblage, this study explains how governance of mobility control turns into virtual social sorting of the poor in an intra-European mobility context. In short, this study contributes to better understanding of *virtual dialogues* and how service providers can be misled by targeted groups.

1.4 Overview of chapters

This book is divided into nine chapters. Chapter 1 is this introduction. It will be followed by a theoretical framework that places this study in a late modern context.

Chapter 2 integrates two main theoretical objectives. The first explains the digitalisation of information societies and how ontological anxieties contribute to securitisation and social sorting in Western societies. It is dedicated to redefine recent forms of exceptionalism in European citizenship rights, which have led to the latent securitisation of migrants in European legislation. The second objective is based on concepts introduced by Aas and Bosworth (2013), which rely on the critical surveillance paradigm. I will discuss the changes in control societies and how targeted surveillance as a geopolitical tool leads to new digitalised mechanisms of population selection. In addition, this chapter introduces Bigo's (2008b) concept of a 'Ban- Opticon', which refers to contemporary exclusionary monitoring practices in which surveillance subjects are directed into the funnel of expulsion. This theory enables a critical analysis of these selective policies, especially those in the bureaucratic field of financial surveillance that targets people on the move. Both approaches are concerned with encompassing practices of European population control elaborated in power relations.

Chapter 3 broadly discusses the situational construction of Roma identity and the methodological framework this study has been built upon. The coping mechanisms of Central European Roma minorities can only be understood through an in-depth knowledge of historically constructed prejudices and the recognition of Roma ethnic diversity. I will also present the selected empirical research methods that emphasise the relevance of different qualitative methods, such as digital ethnography as a research site in combination with institutional ethnography.

Following the cultural criminological tradition of qualitative data analyses, the selected research methodology is founded on a critical ethnographic approach. These research methods contain three pragmatic approaches (i.e. multi-sited ethnography, institutional ethnography and virtual ethnography) based on the three main contextual aspects of the research subject. Multi-sited ethnography was performed with various Roma communities to clarify their strategies for coping with control measures, such as contesting the digital monitoring techniques and trying to gain access to social services. Research techniques involved classical ethnographic tools of data collection such as respondent observation, interviews and shadowing. As a researcher, interpreter, housemate and 'advocacy worker', Considering research positioning, I adopted various, often conflicting roles to elicit specific information about the respondents' legal considerations.

Chapter 4 provides an extended analysis of recent social policy objectives in the UK welfare system and describes how they have become the new platform for social sorting. To facilitate the understanding of and differentiation between coping mechanisms used by Roma in the UK, I present current restrictions and control mechanisms that result from the technocratisation of local bureaucracies. I also address how neoliberal market values in the post-welfare period have shaped the targeted monitoring of migrants in this context. Next, I examine the shift in surveillance from borders to social services and the possible side effects of selective welfare measures in the context of the EU. Finally, I will discuss how managerialist shifts in government services and increasing institutional suspicion are changing the attitudes of service providers and service users.

This chapter also provides an overview of changes in benefit systems that shape the self-representation and self-identification of ethnic migrants, resulting in a discrepancy between surveillance data and real practices. Shortly, I will interpret welfare provision changes in the framework of increasing managerialism in the social service sector and summarise critical reflections about the businesslike structures of social provisions and the side effects of digitalisation in welfare services.

Chapter 5 explores the roles of professionals, Romani scholars, NGOs and interpreters who actively contribute to framing the Roma as a marginal ethnicity in Western countries. Although they are often excluded from policy studies, many stakeholders can affect the interaction between Roma newcomers and bureaucratic systems. The poverty narrative associated with Roma is strongly interrelated with discrimination experienced by Roma benefit applicants. This chapter includes reflections on the roles of professionals, academics and NGOs, and discusses how these stakeholders contribute to the securitisation of Roma in Europe. I argue that framing the Roma ethnicity with reference to its marginal position and welfare dependency might contribute to existing constructions of the 'benefit tourist' ethnic minority. Regarding the displacement of ethnic stigma, interpreters who are from the same sending countries might spread their prejudices to professionals in the host society, who are 'learning' and adopting the existing ethnic framing of Roma.

The last section of this book (Chapters 6, 7 and 8) presents coping mechanisms Roma newcomers use in their interactions (or lack thereof) with welfare services. The analysis is divided over three chapters to provide a better understanding of the fluid, situational, adaptive interactive nature of these digitalised bureaucratic relationships.

Chapter 6 describes the basic bureaucratic steps newcomers take and how different brokers and intermediaries anticipate the needs of new arrivals. These analyses give an overview of the barriers migrants face in their contacts with Job Centre Plus officers. Since these contacts are still partly face to face, they demand different tactics to ensure eligibility for basic benefit provisions than migrants use with the tax office.

Chapter 7 contains the central element of this study: it describes interactions between newcomers and case managers through a fully digitalised service provision system. This Orwellian insider view provides a critical reflection on the side effects of digitalisation. I assert that no individual parameters can determine migrants' coping mechanisms since these strategies, used in face-to-face meetings or online, are part of a constantly shifting dynamic with constantly changing eligibility provisions.

Finally, Chapter 8 critically evaluates the limitations of digitalised bureaucratic systems and the dangers of reliance on virtual data and selection methods. Based on the selected case studies, I suggest that ethnic Roma migrants are searching for existential safety but are instead facing new forms of discrimination based on labour history. Even though they have difficulties in accessing benefits, they take great risks and use innovative coping strategies to stay in a country that has limited knowledge about their identity. These strategies are not culturally defined, but their innovative aspects illustrate the growing awareness of surveillance mechanisms and the interactions of different minority groups in a foreign context. Finally, this chapter will evaluate how the digitalisation of service provisions creates a hypocritical system in which documented data are trusted more than the individuals they describe.

2 Critical theories – social sorting and surveillance in a digital welfare labyrinth

'Anxiety is the dizziness of freedom' states the famous quote of Kierkegaard (1844), referring to personal responsibilities, the discomfort of choices which become the driving force of the late modern Western society. Anxiety, as a conscious reflexivity raise the need of predictability in late modernity societies in order to reduce potential risks and increase ontological security. According to Security theories, this anxiety about the potentialities creates 'the urge to tame the uncertain at all cost' and by any means which relegate 'the other' to the category of cultural inferiority based on estimates and prejudices. 'This unease constitutes the basis for securitization'. In the EU mobilty discours Roma minorities are presented as a security threat by political leaders 'in order to push a social issue into the realm of security and legitimising this way urgent policy response' that otherwise are not possible (Lazaridis & Wadia, 2015, p. 211). However, this study intends to provide a more critical notion on the results of such securitisation processes. Based on the security narratives associated with particular migrant groups, it will be analysed how surveillance of individuals based on their financial capabilities expends the categories of threat, indicating new selection measures. Based on the case of Roma migrants in London, this chapter discuss such securitisation processes as late modern geopolitical control strategies.

Although theories about migration, exclusion and securitisation are regularly applied to conceptualise the situation of Roma migrants (Grill, 2011; Van Baar, 2014), little theoretical work has addressed the dynamics of intra-state exclusionary processes and the coping strategies of Roma with European citizenship. Securitisation of mobility has become a popular subject of different criminological theories, especially concerning correlations among ethnicity, crime and mobility.

In the following section, I give an overview of the theoretical background of this mobile ethnographic study. One key paradigm in this area is the recently growing field of financial surveillance, which provides the core theoretical outline of this study.

To understand the securitisation of Roma migrants, we first need to understand the correlations between mobility, surveillance and the new geopolitical incentives of host societies. I will first suggest that late modern European societies are developing a new understanding of control as a form of *social sorting* (Lyon, 2013) that leads to blurred lines between safety and social security in the EU.

The securitisation of Roma migrants must be understood within the larger context of neoliberal market tendencies that characterise the political landscape in contemporary Europe (Van Baar, 2011a). Neoliberalism is understood both as 'a set of policy programmes that deregulate political government' and as 'a conservative liberal political movement' that bases its ideas on neoclassical economics (Van Baar, 2012b, p. 9212). Based on Foucault's notion of governmentality, many scholars have evaluated neoliberalism in recent decades (Lemke, 2001; O'Malley, et al., 1997; Rose & Miller, 1992; Van Baar, 2012b). It can be understood as 'a way of explaining the establishment and exercise of political power, one in which the concept of government is broader than management by the state; it also involves the regulation of populations through multiple institutions and technologies in society' (Mitchell, 2006, p. 390). This governmentality concept has become the core of several securitisation theories that explain expulsion and selection of migrants in the European context. I introduce a critical adaption of the Foucauldian notion of governmentality, and its relevance in exploring transnational Roma mobility.

2.1 Securitisation and EU population control

In the late modern European arena, globalisation and restrictions in EU citizenship are increasing the securitisation of transnational mobility (Huysmans, 2000). Anti-immigration narratives are increasingly associating mobility with national threat and claiming extended control measures, which results in unconventional security policies and state-corporate cooperation beyond national borders (Broeders & Engbersen, 2013). First, let me explain how the definition of threat is linked to particular groups and how it leads to hidden security measures. Then I will relate the political use of securitisation to the concept of governmentality (Foucault, 1977). Current population control, legitimised by references to security threats, takes form through selected governmental incentives that are constructed by surveillance data. Hence, the securitisation of migrants and surveillance of mobility are shaped by a dialogue between the observer who selects the data and the observed surveillance subject. In this dynamic process, also called as a Panopticon effect (Foucault, 1977), those who are observed might be disciplined by this surveillance process. However, the subject of monitoring might also manipulate this data collection and therefore change those governance incentives that construct exclusionary practices to avoid 'the funnel of expulsion' (Aas & Bosworth, 2013, p. 258). Surveillance awareness of migrants and the social construction of threat are central dynamics in the mechanism of population control. This surveillance-based selection process of governmental bureacracies was predominantly theorised in the field of critical security studies.

In order to understand the current practices of social sorting, this epistemic field should be highlighted in a nutshell.

Although it has been criticised for its limitations, critical security approaches are strongly related to the Foucaultian interpretation of governance and the modalities of state power. Foucault (2007) introduced the notion of governmentality to explain how states govern their populations through biopolitical regulation. The concept of biopower as a power based on knowledge production played an important role in developing his concept of governmentality (Lemke, 2001). Foucault emphasised its importance in regulating modern societies at the level of populations rather than nationalised territories. Thus, governmentality is conceived as a form of power that intensively governs and manipulates people on different scales (Foucault, 1982, 1997a). Governmentality can generally be considered to be 'the mode of power concerned with the maintenance and control of bodies and persons, the production and regulation of persons and populations, and the circulation of goods insofar as they maintain and restrict the life of the population' (Butler, 2004, p. 52). Since Roma have recently been defined as a European minority, their governance becomes an interstate issue. As a result, their socio-economic position has become a matter of European population regulation and ethnic problematisation.

Foucault wanted to de-centre the state as the central power-arranging institution and apply a more general framework of government. In this sense, the state is considered to be a symptom of government, or to be a historically specific way in which the problem of government has been discursively and spatially articulated (Stenson, 2005). Thus, governmentality can be understood as

1. a way of explaining the establishment, and
2. exercising political power, a new perspective in which the concept of government is broader than management by the state. Foucault's concept is based on the hypothesis of the 'reciprocal constitution of power techniques and forms of knowledge' (Lemke, 2001, p. 190).

Governmentality's methodological principle involves the regulation of populations through multiple institutions and technologies in society, from the governing of others to the governing of the self (Foucault, 1997b; Mitchell, 2006, p. 389). As Lemke (2001) explains, 'the semantic linking of governing ("gouverner") and modes of thought ("mentalité") indicates that it is not possible to study the technologies of power without an analysis of the political rationality underpinning them' (p. 191). As he describes, Foucault used government in a comprehensive sense, indicating the link between power relations and processes of subjectification (Van Baar 2011a, p. 192). Shortly, Foucault's theory blurs the boundaries between the discursive and the technical by stressing that translation processes are materially embedded in the performance of government, which is how they make the 'activity of governing' possible (Van Baar, 2011a, pp. 37–41).

Accordingly, the problematisation of Roma migration in this security context evolved in a digitalised bureaucratic system, subjecting and selecting welfare applicants by an extended surveillance system.

Technological changes triggered critical voices in security studies, rejecting the notion of objective threat. Whereas realist security scholars argue that insecurity can be calculated by measuring military strength, social constructivists claim that threats to security are erected through intersubjective interaction in a context-specific dialogue or discourse. According to the constructivist Copenhagen School security and threat shall be interpreted based on speech acts (Wæver et al., 1993). Different contextual representations of threat have significant performative effects in population control (McDonald, 2013). Suspicion is a prominent feature that is strongly interconnected with Schmitt's notion of exceptionalism (Aradau, 2004; Williams, 2003). As it will be presented, suspecting migrants with welfare fraud reflects to political effects of such representations.

According to this vision, threats do not exist independently of our knowledge but are brought into being by processes such as political speeches (Vaughan-Williams, 2010, p. 5). Waever et al. (1993) suggests that securitisation refers to a linguistic representation that defines a certain concern as an existential threat. Later, he emphasised the importance of constituencies or audiences in 'backing up' speech acts (Buzan et al., 1998, pp. 26–33). Securitisation is thus also intersubjective in that the "audience" must accept or tolerate it for the act to be effective. 'The emphasis in the framework therefore arguably shifted from speech acts as product of security to speech act as one component of the inter-subjective construction of security' (McDonald, 2008, p. 3). Targeting undesired migrants, who are seen as a financial or security threat, leads to new selective mechanisms in the social policies of Western governments, who use this security narrative to justify their measures.

Such speech acts about the threatening migrants are applied to justify more elusive exclusionary measures. As recent securitisation of Roma migrants illustrates, the new movement of unwanted groups is securitised when it is 'presented as an existential threat, (. . .) not necessarily because a real existential threat exists but because the issue is presented as such a threat' (Buzan et al., 1998, p. 24). The process of securitisation usually conforms to the particular rhetorical structure in which the problem is equated with state survival and then given priority of action, 'because if the problem is not handled now it will be too late, and we will not exist to remedy our failure' (Buzan et al., 1998, p. 26). However, the real challenge of these processes begins when they become normalised in daily security politics, such as the threat of benefit tourism which has been legitimised by government propaganda. Although the relationship between securitisation and surveillance is often ignored (McDonald, 2008), there are many contemporary analyses of securitisation that include critical surveillance studies (e.g. Bigo & Walker, 2002; Sasse, 2005; Huysmans, 2006).

To understand the theoretical relevance of securitisation in the case of Roma migrants, three particular aspects of control shall be differentiated:

- The links between globalisation, sovereignty and governance of security, with a focus on policing and public institutions driven by risk-related surveillance methods (Ericson & Haggerty, 1997); shortly, it should be explained how the institutionalised performance of control includes surveillance as a population management to reshape contemporary European mobility.
- Social sorting as a governance modality of population control should be critically defined, and how this serves a new "managerialism" in digital

bureaucracies to control migrants by financial incentives (Jones & Newburn, 1998). This can only be understood through the mechanisms of social sorting facilitated by surveillance technics (Sassen, 2002). Hence, social sorting and population control takes form though the intersubjective construction of security as a political technology (Burke, 2002) that 'enables, produces and constrains individuals within larger systems of power and institutional action' (Mcdonald, 2013, p. 270). It is mutually constituted through elite knowledge, bureaucrats and individuals who conduct themselves concerning other groups (Bigo, 2008a; Huysmans, 2006).

- Anticipation of Roma migrants in control and selection mechanisms of routinised bureaucratic practices shall be explored.

2.2 Virtual Panopticon as migration control

The digitalised society normalised excessive control mechanisms in the bureaucratic system of nation states. Foucault's *Surveillir et Punir* (1975; translated as Discipline and Punish), which is used to explain population control by the administrative power, is considered as the touchstone of surveillance studies. In his analyses, Foucault represents Bentham's "Panopticon" as a key spatial symbol in the creation of modern subjectivity and control because its architecture symbolises the power relations of the modern disciplinary society. In short, the Panopticon figure's annular building is divided into different cells and a huge tower with windows in the middle that allows the supervisors in the tower to observe all the individuals in the cells without being seen themselves. Although not every inmate is observed continuously, the general assumption is that observation is possible anytime. Since the observed ones cannot see when they are monitored, all of them act as if they are under surveillance and therefore discipline themselves out of fear (Allmer, 2015, p. 77).

Similarly in the surveillance society, social control is created by the experience of uncertainty among the observed, who cannot view the observer. This asymmetrical power relationship creates an automatic functioning of power through the self-discipline of observed individuals. As Foucault (1979) steps beyond the physical Panopticon design, he elaborates this scheme into a new social order: the rise of 'disciplinary society' based on self-controlling mechanisms. Lyon elaborates on Foucault's concept of a 'disciplinary society' transforming into a mainly technology-based 'surveillance society' where governmental and privatised security services cooperate to 'discipline the mass' (Green, 1999, pp. 29–30). In neoliberal democracies, these sophisticated technical tools extend existing surveillance practices with electronic databases, enabling a new digital "bureaucracy" in favour of "national security" and "commercial competition" (Bauman, 2013; Lyon, 2003). Many administrative procedures have used panoptic sorting to invent "internal borders" against unwanted mobile groups. Risk management and profiling individuals defined as threats are increasingly becoming an economic type of classification, assessing the financial activities of individuals in neoliberal societies (Gandy, 1993). The power in surveillance is thus far more than observation. By individualising pathology through bureaucratic codification, such as unemployment, security risk is defined by individual characteristics and classified into risk categories of decision makers (Lyon, 2003, p. 250). In short, power relations can be traced through the identification and classification of individuals into specific databases in these bureaucratic systems.

After the digital turn, data collection has been extended to different levels of everyday life. Used across national borders and by privatised security agencies, it is technologically enabled to trace mundane activities of individuals for several purposes, in particular for risk assessments. As Lyon (2003) notes:

> Abstract data, now including video, biometric, and genetic as well as computerized administrative files, are manipulated to produce profiles and risk categories in a liquid, networked system. The point is to plan, predict, and prevent by classifying and assessing those profiles and risks.
>
> (p. 13)

The growing importance of transparency as collection of individual data is a tool of social sorting in managerialist bureaucratic surveillance practices. In Gandys' 'panoptic sort' concept, panoptic stands for 'the consideration of all information about an individual that may be useful in a production of intelligence of personal economic value. . . . It is a discriminatory technology because it is used to sort people into categories based upon these estimates' (Gandy, 1996, p. 133). As will be analysed later regarding profiling and the exclusion of welfare claimants, sorting personal information and using classified data enables exclusion and "targeting" of particular groups defined as a financial "threat". This late modern, economic-value-based risk management is a central analytical factor of this study.

Although social and personal categorisation is a common feature of every society, recent surveillance societies intend to influence and manage populations by social sorting along economic categories established by computer codes for personal data. Administrative surveillance not only rationalises but also automates this selection process. Lyon (2003) notes that 'codes, usually processed by computers, sort out transactions, interactions, visits, calls and other activities; they are the invisible doors that permit access to or exclude from participation in a multitude of events, experiences, and processes' (p. 13). This selection process has several phases, including identification by collection of personal information, sorting or classification of data and assessment of personal information (Lyon, 2003, p. 135). These are constantly redefined to manage the surveyed individuals and to indicate or preselect the choices of surveillance subjects.

This proactive selection of individuals is based on 'allocating their worth' in ways that have 'real effects on their life chances', such as accessing basic resources. 'In this discriminative process, individuals are sorted into categories based on estimates. These sorting practices are based on selected personal information like someone's economic value, which is defined by targeting guidelines such as those in commercial marketing practices' (Gandy, 1996, p. 133). When the registered identity of an individual and his or her classification has guided decisions about what kind of person he or she is, 'it is the process of assessment that determines whether this individual should be included in or excluded' (Gandy, 1996, p. 15).

In contrast to the classical notion of the Panopticon, the surveillant knows more than the subject in digital data surveillance systems (Marx, 2002, p. 29). One particular strategy, facilitated by electronic data collection methods, is a less expensive, increasingly popular automated system of "dataveillance". In this monitoring system, it is not the subject who is under control but rather the data about him or her. It is 'the systematic use of personal data systems in the investigation or monitoring of the actions or communications of one or more persons' (Clarke, 1999, p. 34). However, these databases become dated and do not always reflect the personal situations of the individuals they are indexing. Furthermore, the data is not always verifiable by those they are identifying, and individuals are therefore unsure about the content of the data collected about them. It is understandable that service users are suspicious: they never know if they are under the scope of an "inspector" and, if so, who it could be and how much access the inspector has to personal data. This invisible monitoring system is also called a "nonopticon", which refers to this unequal process of surveillance (Vaidhyanathan, 2008, p. 8). In these digital processes, the interactions of "virtual subjects" are tracked and controlled within the digital environment. As these dataveillance methods produce information about particular groups it enables to classify and profile them in order to develop new incentives of social sorting to select them and force them to on. These selection processes focus on particular groups defined as threats, so there are new theoretical challenges concerning the control of mobile populations.

In recent critical surveillance theories working on data justice and discrimination, the Foucauldian concept of disciplinary power refers to a panoptic modality that includes simultaneous control and behaviour-modifying mechanisms. These studies on surveillance and exclusion mostly focus on local populations from a normative approach, and dynamic aspects like securitisation of mobility have just recently been introduced in this field. Social sorting of mobile groups and migrants has become a popular subject of security studies, but an interactionalist approach is required to better understand social sorting effects by dataveillance. This analysis therefore includes the geopolitics of EU mobility, in particular how surveillance-based control incentives might impact trajectories of migrants. Population control is mainly associated with control of spaces and places by employing surveillance activities on several scales. As it will be argued, with increasing transnational mobility, new methods are adapted to control and manage people on the move.

2.3 The funnel of expulsion

Governmentality is commonly summarised as indirect control or the conduct of conduct. However, the control and selection of groups or individuals defined as a threat is also theorised by "governing through choice". Similar to Young, Aas and Bosworth (2013) also describe the exclusion of migrants by invisible governmental incentives. They call a different aspect of collective coercion and control "the funnel of expulsion".

This concept refers to an additional dynamic of control that forces migrants to make a seemingly free decision to leave. This dynamic cover those blurring boundaries I described earlier between the different forms of control and access (Aas & Bosworth, 2013, p. 264). They argue that the 'distinction between internal and external sovereignty becomes contested' and, instead of being deported, unwanted migrants are placed in a situation where they are expected to make the choice to leave themselves. Their actions are governed by establishing a life situation in which the only rational choice seems to be to leave. However, this assumption about the obedient individual may fail.

State organisations constitute the framework for the designed structure of exclusionary incentives. Interaction between these incentives and the selected group displays the dynamics of transnational mobility (Aas & Bosworth, 2013, p. 266). These are implemented in bureaucratic procedures that select and assess individuals, then classify them based on their personal data and, recently, their digital identities.

Recently, a participation-based neoliberal labour market approach has dominated Western European state incentives, targeting groups who are seen as unwilling to integrate and participate in their societies. This participation is generally measured in labour market participation and by the level of dependency on state funding such as social benefits (Woolford & Nelund, 2013). New security measures have been initiated to sort the good or productive citizens from the undesired, "passive" citizens, who are seen as an economic threat to national welfare. Social and spatial exclusion thus result from financial exclusion, as the major incentive against unattractive mobility of the poor (Halfmann, 1998). In practice, one can be structurally excluded from various systems, such as the labour market, the health system, the political system, the economy or the educational system.

Exclusion from one part of the system can have a snowball effect. Migrants who do not register at the council cannot obtain a legal certificate of roadworthiness for their cars, so they continue to drive with foreign registration plates. Migrants who know they are working informally are unwilling to become socially integrated in the host society, while those who are working in the marginal economy have no opportunity to integrate (O'Reilly, 2007b).

Many of these people on the move (ab)use the ambiguities of surveillance practice and enclosure by 'occupying a liminal space in flows', avoiding borders and challenging cultural and language differences (O'Reilly, 2007b, p. 292). This interaction between these individualised selection procedures and those who are defined as a security threat became the central subject for analysing mobility management strategies.

2.4 Surveillance and social sorting

Following the securitisation-based social sorting analyses of Lyon, Didier Bigo (2006) introduced the concept of a Ban-Opticon in critical securities studies to analyse structural governance of exclusion by 'the management of unease' (p. 6).

Similar to Aas and Bosworth, he defines those routines and technologies of professionals and politicians, the police and judges who restructure the legal state. Ban refers to the normalisation of exclusion which includes the predictable management of the future by control measures introduced in advance. This concept of a ban relies on the technical advantages of databases to define who might replace themselves to where and who should be immobile. A whole range of "risk management systems" should also be recognised. These include building special architectural features and structures (e.g. asylum centres and detention areas in airports) and introducing emergency laws or administrative measures (e.g. the regulation of "sans papiers" and agreements among governments about transportation in expulsion). They also play a role in the public discourse. Risk management attempts to define in advance who is a possible threat in the local context and why. Security no longer depends on immobilising authorities or on the permanent gaze of the guard. In Bigo's (2008a) words, 'This chart is not a panopticon projected on a global scale, it is what we – by combining the term "Ban", borrowed from Jean Luc Nancy and reworked by Giorgio Agamben, with Foucault's "optics" – called a Ban-opticon' (p. 10).

According to Agamben (1998), the term "Ban" refers both to exclusion from the community and to the power of the sovereign to eliminate the law. Labelling some people as "illegal", "criminal" or "terrorist" enables preventive measures in the post-September 11 context that normalised the permanent state of emergency in Western societies. As Bigo and Tsoukala (2008) suggest, 'this governmentality of unease is characterised by practices of exceptionalism, acts of profiling containing foreigners, and a normative imperative of mobility' (p. 10).

'The ban attempts to show how the role of routines and acceptance of everyday life protects some over others, or how the protection of these others against themselves is a profound structure that explains the "moment" of the declaration of exception' (Lyon, 2006, p. 47). It also attempts to reveal the judicial illusion that a specific moment declares the sovereign borders of the political. This view needs to be amended by a sociological stance that considers long-term social processes and public acceptance of the routines of surveillance (Bigo, 2005). As previously suggested, profiling in digitalised bureaucratic services becomes the key institutionalised risk management task of this system.

2.5 Managerialism and new borders in the bureaucratic field

Many studies have explored the management of citizen identity information from the perspective of government agencies in their public service relationships with citizens, while very few have explored citizens' attitudes toward the management of personal information with and across governments in the course of electronic public service provision. This contribution further explores scholarly thinking around the impact and implications of the use of new digital forms of citizen identity management in public service environments. In particular, it covers how the shift from face-to-face interactions to an anonymised digital arena has reshaped personal interaction in the European transnational context.

In this analysis, surveillance is used as an interactive social process, as 'symbolic material that can be stored by an agency or collective' and as 'the supervision of the activities of ordinates' (Giddens, 1985, p. 169). The disciplinary role of dataveillance reflects the means and strategies of authorities, managing citizen identity information in public service environments. Due to the digitalisation of these administrative practices, fundamental changes are taking place in the informational foundations of citizenship, government relationships, in particular regarding the "social contract" between the citizen and the state.

Increasing mobility and digitalisation have turned many aspects of the bureaucratic system upside down. Lipsky's (2010) 'Street-Level Bureaucracy' has changed into online applications and monitoring processes and interactions in which the distance between bureaucrats and individuals is driven by the functionalist principles of the neoliberal market. As a result, a managerialist paradigm is overruling recent governmental practices, resulting in local bureaucrats with decreasing autonomy, limited face-to-face contacts with their clients, reduced discretionary space in decision making and decreasing governmental transparency. These aspects of new bureaucratic systems are driven by target bases, cost-efficient systems with privatised governmental services and production targets in social policies. Service qualities are changing priorities of the welfare system with an increased focus on labour participation by citizens who depend on state aid. The lack of interpersonal communication is interpreted as an objective, fast and efficient processing, resulting in mutual transparency and selective risk management by digital data screening. Privatising social services, commodifying individual data and decreasing the transparency of authorities' bureaucratic procedures are socially accepted results of these digitalised processes.

This anonymity of service provision leads to new forms of interaction and social selection as part of a risk assessment. Individuals' detachment from their personal data and the selection of characteristics according to screening systems is resulting in a reality gap that increases governmental unease and suspicion of individuals and back-office bureaucrats. State transparency becomes vital because surveillance can negatively affect people's life chances via discrimination and sorting.

Individuals' financial positions have come to play a central organising and disciplinary role for governments and societies, although their social sorting power is still not fully acknowledged. Financial relations facilitate the reproduction of social order and selection of access in the context of inequalities, both within and across national spaces and along the overlapping lines of class, gender, race and nationality. Individual economic position, which means an inherently unequal and conflictual social position in society, mediates the social tensions of neoliberalism through both structural and direct power (Gill & Law, 1989; Strange, 1988) as a key aspect of social sorting. Dominant discourses of personal responsibility and morality have helped to further naturalise and depoliticise the growing indebtedness of population control, underpinned by a discourse on moralising, responsibility and securitisation of the poor that normalises social insecurity and the exclusion of "undeserving ones" based on economic performance. States are acting in this process as collective commodifying agents or market actors who are increasingly 'caught up in and constrained by crosscutting global/transnational/domestic structural and conjunctural conditions' (Cerny, 2000, p. 34).

The model neoliberal citizen strategises for her or himself among various social, political and economic options, instead of striving with others to alter or organise these options. A fully realised neoliberal citizenry would be the opposite of public-minded; indeed, it would barely exist as a public. In this surveillance system, a good neoliberal citizen is active and responsible, is capable of self-management, self-governance and making reasonable choices, and is not reliant on government or social services for survival; instead, she or he is an autonomous and empowered agent (Clarke, 2005; Ilcan et al., 2007; Schild, 2007). An entrepreneurial spirit is thus embraced alongside self-presentations of autonomy and active work to communicate a sense of self that is largely consistent with the neoliberal citizen. In short, successful economic participation is the key to social and legal acceptance, as well as to accessing legal services.

Legal borders for population selection are thus intertwined with an internal selection based on labour participation, and with avoiding and expelling the unemployed, welfare-dependent newcomer. The coercion of mobility flow is therefore streamed by economic priorities in the global context. This process presupposes financial surveillance of people on the move as a central aspect of welfare-dependent groups. Surveillance with the purpose of eliminating potential threats has resulted in restricted control and discipline of transnational movement of the poor in Europe. In such a harsh policy context, those who experience poverty are conceived of 'as "culpable actors" at risk of "moral hazard" (Mead, 1997, p. 19). The increasing stigmatisation and criminalisation of welfare claimants invokes the exclusionary process of "adiaphorisation". This stripping away of moral criteria proceeds to such an extent that the concept of "welfare" becomes loaded; not with compassion, but with fear and loathing of a criminally indolent welfare-dependent class for whom punishment and the withdrawal of benefits becomes a "firm but fair" course of policy action (Bauman, 1998, p. 80) to protect the goodly virtues of the "deserving" poor' (Dee, 2013 p. 275).

By analysing the bureaucratic field of welfare services, we can trace interactions in social service programmes that enable us to take a closer look into the operative logics of the monitoring processes that determine the contemporary politics of population control. The main hypothesis behind this analysis is that in place of accepting expulsive governing incentives, performances of mobile ethnic Roma 'are shaped to the symbolic conditions of the bureaucratic field and therefore are used to emulate the desired characteristics of neoliberal citizenship' (Woolford & Nelund 2013, p. 316). The question is what kind of strategies are invented to imitate those characteristics that ensure legal eligibility for government support.

The general claim of neoliberal welfare policies is that the adoption of production ideologies will force everyone into productive market relations through 'measurable technocratic procedures, managerial risk management, investigation strategies and intrusive surveillance practices' (Dee, 2013). These changes are distinguishable in the rolling back of social services and the rolling out of increased punitive controls that mix criminal and migration law.

Several shifts have converged to reorient selection and disciplinary practice in poverty governance today. An overt and muscular approach to welfare provision by surveillance uses penalties as therapeutic tools for transforming the subjectivities of the poor (Mead, 1997). Welfare programmes have also been restructured to 'serve as arenas of labour commodification that are continuous with local markets' (Pykett, 2013, p. 125). Furthermore, 'administration and management systems have been redesigned to enhance the scope of lower-level discretion and, as a corollary, to ensure that social-service personnel (embedded in new contractual and performance-based systems) will be self-disciplined in their uses of discretion' (Pykett, 2013, p. 125).

In his comparative research, Marx (2013) describes how different forms of interactions with bureaucrats in cases of ethnic groups act to coerce aid from specific parties. However, since the forms and priorities of interaction in the bureaucratic field have increasingly changed, there are some problematic assumptions regarding these concepts. With the digitalisation of governmental services, online screening instruments have changed the nature of communication and transparency between civilians and civil servants. We therefore need to stress the differences and flows between the responses and strategies of migrants to managerial, selective measures, not just from an interactional but also from a situational approach. Local circumstances and the contextually changing limits of individuals and their economic opportunities play a key role in response to host societies.

The following analyses challenge and analyse this top-down approach to determine the extent to which claimants' strategies reshape incentives at the top. The analysis explores the sources and operations of disciplinary practice under contemporary welfare reform by investigating the systems that structure practice for frontline workers and welfare clients. It challenges assumptions about the power and limits of new administrative systems and the limitations of managerialist strategies that should operate on the edge of normative guidelines.

The individual awareness and anticipation of monitoring mechanisms is increasingly important, as they are key dynamics of digitalised postmodern societies, in particular of mobility control. As a symbol of individual anticipation in surveillance, ethnic migrants represent the unpredictable innovative nature of surveillance objects, who embody resistance and the individual ability to anticipate incentives created by digitalised power structures that are supposed to determine individuals' behaviour. By observing the European surveillance strategies on local and transnational levels, we can discover the dynamics of interactions between mobile groups and governmental monitoring systems that employ profiling. The question is how these interactions shape the mobility of those who are anticipating these risk-assessment-based profiling mechanisms.

2.6 Conclusion

In short, individualisation and risk management objectives enable the surveillance of the "threatening other" by digitalised control measures. In this liquid database-oriented surveillance process, control and discipline go hand in hand, targeting the perceived threat projected on individuals with selected characteristics (Lyon, 2006). The implementation of profiling is based on selected data collected in a new digitalised interactive bureaucratic field. Due to technical changes, not only has the nature of transparency changed, but also the level of interaction between civil servants and citizens. These changes are implemented according to neoliberal principles, creating a new social sorting mechanism through a Welfare Ban-Opticon. The following chapter addresses the contextual and methodological challenges implicated by such a digital managerialism in the field of welfare surveillance.

3 Roma, a global ethnic minority

This chapter provides a detailed contextual background of Roma migrants from the Czech Republic, Hungary, Poland and Slovakia (known as the V4 countries) that outlines the research methods of this study. Roma ethnic minorities were selected as case studies for a number of reasons. Firstly, studying the policing of Roma migrants in the Intra-European context can be seen as a litmus test of the European Union's (EU's) free mobility principle, challenging the notion of an equal EU citizenship. Secondly, these cases reflect the dynamics of the sophisticated security measures used by EU member states and how these shape the mobility patterns of 'unwanted' groups on European territory. Thirdly, these cases illustrate not only mechanisms of geographic population control, but also the unforeseen effects that are hidden from those who make and enforce immigration policy. Because Roma minorities have decades of experience with bureaucratic strategies, including structural harassment and spatial control strategies (Van Baar 2014), their experience in this context is particularly informative.

As will be presented, the intra-European securitisation of mobility – that is, shifting the question of immigration to a matter of public safety and national security – arose as a result of contradictory policy developments of control and integration (Koczé & Rövid, 2017). After 2006, by decreasing the role of intra-European borders, the EU's top-down policies have indirectly motivated individual nation states to increase their internal security directives with ambiguous social sorting practices. As the OSCE report describes, there have been explicit governmental actions taken against these newcomers. For instance,

> The Blair government (i) instructed border officials to subject a number of ethnic groups, including Roma, to more stringent border checks than others; (ii) placed officials at Prague Airport to conduct the preclearance screening of persons boarding aircraft bound for the UK; (iii) pressed for an arrangement whereby German and Czech authorities would identify particular groups of persons travelling in buses over land and subject them to rigorous checks.
>
> (OSCE, 2010, p. 38)[1]

1 Casually derogatory headlines have prevailed across the media spectrum and have included "Gypsies Invade Dover, Hoping for a Handout" and "Gyro Czechs Arrive", playing on

In Central and Eastern Europe, ethno-nationalism has become a cornerstone of post-Soviet politics, leading to societal schisms in which Roma, as the biggest ethnic minority without a nation state, have been increasingly marginalised. On the other hand, in the security narrative of Northern and Western European states, state sovereignty has been replaced by societal insecurity, justifying restrictive measures against the inflow of poor migrants. Both processes are redefining the risk associated with the "other" and pushing mobility to the top of the political agenda (Waever et al., 1993, p. 221). European member states are increasingly extending their security approaches in order to protect their ethno-national identity from "threats" associated with newcomers. In short, the erasure of national borders between EU member states has led to security measures which tend to see transnational mobility as a markedly *national* risk, in which Roma migrants, who are defined as a criminal, cultural and economic threat, are the main focus of prevention strategies (Cahn & Guild, 2010; Vidra, 2013b; Grill, 2012). In order to understand the geopolitical effects of these measures, this chapter looks at how the interplays between societal insecurity and increasing ethno-nationalism, determine which groups are defined as a "threat".

Yet, it is necessary to begin by discussing the definitional difficulties of the concept of "Roma ethnicity". To understand the commonalities and differences of the Roma groups moving towards EU Member States, this chapter reflects on the socio-economic situation of Roma groups in their home countries, as well as their motivation to relocate to, as well as their expectations from, their host societies, particularly the UK. A brief introduction to Roma life in London, as well as an explanation of the local conditions is provided to shed light on the diverse mobility patterns among Roma ethnic subgroups. This overview facilitates an understanding of national and ethnic differences in migration patterns and expectations of the host society among the various Roma groups.

3.1 The hidden dynamics of ethnic identities

The first concern regarding the securitisation of Roma mobility is how to define ethnicity. Following this definitional conundrum, the question is whether there are any implications of Roma ethnic identity within the migration context. Ethnic classification is a frequent topic in the social sciences and there are several reasons why it is extremely problematic in the case of Roma. Firstly, there is no reliable statistical data on who should be considered an ethnic Roma. Although ethnic registration is a sensitive subject for Roma minorities, it is often claimed that ethnic statistics are needed in order to develop targeted support for Roma on local and national levels. Consequently, local authorities try to collect data via social services and multiple-choice surveys based on self-identification. However, most Roma refuse to be formally identified due to fears that such identification

stereotypes of Gypsies out to rip off the system. An overview of panic-driven media in the United Kingdom is provided in the Open Society Foundation (2004) *Who Is Afraid of Migrating Roma?* EU Accession Monitoring Programme, available at: www.eumap.org/journal/features/2004/migration/pt2/whoafraid (accessed 28 September 2008).

would feed negative stereotyping. Although there is common agreement among academics that observer-derived measures of race and ethnicity should be eliminated, how to identify Roma and represent their diversity in different contexts is an ongoing discussion.

Besides the difficulties in defining ethnicity, completing research based on the selection of ethnicity is a challenge, as there are no geographical limits on the scope of such research on Roma. Michael Stewart argues that, in the case of Roma, ethnicity as a research subject of ethnographic inquiry is particularly difficult to explain, because of their incompatibility with the Radcliffe-Brownian notion that 'anthropologists studied "societies" as naturally existing entities or bounded sociocultural systems with a quasi-organic unity in a particular territory (and not one arbitrarily imposed by the observer)' (Stewart, 2013, p. 417). Therefore, we need to take a different approach, one that steps over this static territorial connotation, as suggested by Urry (2012), who introduced a new understanding of mobility.

The uniqueness of the Roma lies in their transnational, non-territorially based nature, which means that they have no state to provide a haven or extend protection to them. Although there are other minorities with similar attributes, like the Kurds, most of them have distinct territorial affiliations. 'Roma disparity and marginalisation can be explained by their geographic distribution across many nation states and cultural and religious diversity. This has resulted in the condition of being subordinated to or excluded by others' (Bárány, 2002, p. 2), which is the central aspect of shared Roma experience. Although the collective name "Roma" is being increasingly used in European politics, this name does not represent many of those who claim to have the same identity; indeed, several subgroups that are seen as Roma, such as Sinti, Beash, Kale and others, distinguish themselves from a strictly Roma identity. Nonetheless, most of these groups, regardless of their diverse ethnic, religious or linguistic characteristics, share the same exclusionary experiences with the majority Roma group.

From the arrival of the Roma in Europe, the magnitude of Roma exclusion has 'varied at different times and in different states. Although political systems and their policies towards the Roma have changed, these variations have had little apparent effect' on the social construction of Roma (ibid., p. 2). In policy framing, as will be presented in the fourth chapter, this ethnic group is presented as homogeneous, poor and welfare dependent – thus ignoring the social, economic and cultural diversity of different Roma subgroups. 'As a vicious cycle, this seemingly interminable nature of the Roma identity is also used as an explaination of the continual marginal status devoted to CEE [Central Eastern European] Roma popualtions' (Marushiakova Popov, 2015, p. 19). At the same time, however, some Roma groups are resisting recurrent attempts at homogenisation and assimilation by dominant groups. These attempts deconstruct generalisations about Roma ethnicity and challenge negative cultural perceptions of Roma ethnicity. Nonetheless, even in academic circles, Roma ethnicity is generally associated with groups without a homeland, with a proportionally small population in different states, and who have no significant recources or political power (Bárány, 2002, p. 2). What is missing from the genral discourse is the diversity of Roma ethnic groups, as is the role of internal dynamics between the groups, and how they reshape the connotations around Roma.

Taking into account the different approaches mentioned previously, in this study ethnic identity is understood as situationally, socially and politically constructed, with constantly changing identity markers along different interactions. These attributes also play an important role in inter-ethnic relations, which have significant implications for the mobility mechanisms and their interchangeability in different contexts. As will be illustrated in the fifth chapter, when different Roma groups interact in a foreign setting, it has structural implications for their self-representation and interactions with the local authorities. These interrelationships among Roma groups are also fundamentally affected by direct interactions with non-Roma, and, often obtaining pertinent information for increased self-advocacy. Stereotypes, foreign media outlets, politicians, academics and of course a given Roma community's internal value system all have an effect on that community's interrelations (Szuhay, 2002, p. 10).

As Barth argues, 'ethnic relations are maintained in the boundaries between different groups even though their cultures might be indistinguishable and even though individuals and groups might switch from one side of the boundary to the other' (Barth, 1969, in Wimmer, 2008b, p. 971). Ethnicity is thus 'the product of a social process rather than a cultural given, made and remade rather than taken for granted, chosen depending on circumstances rather than ascribed through birth' (Wimmer, 2008b, p. 971). Accordingly, the situational coping strategies of Roma families in the last century have been defined based on two controversial and contradictory approaches. The first approach argues that the Roma way of life is the cause of their marginal position. The second sees economic and social integration into host societies as an example of "ethnic success", i.e. as evidence of Roma persistence and adaptability. 'Arguments for ethnic success suggest that Roma are remarkably flexible in adjusting their economic strategies and activities to changing circumstances and due to their attributes of promptness and dynamism with which they adapt to the changes in their environment' (Kováts, 2002, p. 47). According to these cultural explanations, Roma groups employ very efficient methods of conforming to the transformations of the local economy, and they do the same when their own community changes internally when moving to a place with new circumstances (ibid.).

Even though Roma live in a semi-isolated fashion among majority populations who generally look down on them, in Central Europe, Roma groups who are familiar with the social and cultural context around them, even in segregation, seem to be able to 'reproduce their communities with apparent ease; and they do so without shared religion, without any form of ritual or political leadership, and without overarching or underpinning political organization' of a host society (Stewart, 2013, p. 418). Several explanations have been offered for these techniques of social preservation. Firstly, there are historical explanations, which focus on the distinct origins of Roma groups and treat them as an unassimilated foreign ethnic group with a distinct ethos. Secondly, there are structural explanations, which are based on the division of labour and which locate the persistence of Gypsy and Roma populations in the way they have occupied particular niches within the changing European market. A subset of these are the structuralist approaches, which adopt the Foucault-inspired position that stresses the effects of labelling strategies used by state institutions. Thirdly, there are culturalist explanations, which consider the internal coherence of Roma value systems in a self-declared holistic approach. Each of these explanations comes up against the limits of the notion of ethnicity drawn from a model of autonomous and quasi-autonomous nation states (Stewart, 2013, p. 418) and claim that Roma do everything possible under the given circumstances to engage in economic activities independent of the given environment (Okely, 1983, pp. 53–56).

Many of these ethnic connotations are associated in relation or in opposition with non-Roma economic strategies and as an explanation for Roma exclusion. Regarding the mobility of Roma ethnic groups, the controversial tendencies of marginalisation mentioned earlier, and economic adaptation ascribed to Roma can only be understood from a situational perspective that sheds light on the institutional and social interactions of individual actors in different geographic contexts. Therefore, we have to adopt a pragmatic approach in order to analyse ethnic boundary-making in a transnational context. Wimmer introduces, in an attempt 'to understand how these characteristics are generated and transformed over time', a multi-level process theory:

> The theory assumes that ethnic boundaries are the outcome of the classificatory struggles and negotiations between actors situated in a social field. Three characteristics of a field – the institutional order, distribution of power, and political networks – determine which actors will adopt which strategy of ethnic boundary making.
>
> (2008b, p. 970)

Shortly, by accounting for the various matrices in which ethnic identities are constructed, we can attempt to see such identities as inherently complex and multifaceted. When it comes to Roma in Central Europe, we need to distinguish three major approaches: everyday classifications, administrative and scientific classifications, and the internal classifications of Roma groups. If these approaches were visualised on a horizontal axis, we would see the two extreme points – that is, the everyday perception and the perception of Roma groups themselves. These are the most contradictory classification types. While the common perception could be considered as undifferentiated or merging, Roma themselves separate the different subgroups in which direct and actively functioning inter-group relations are at the forefront. Administrative approaches are mainly characterised by more selective and judgmental attitudes (Szuhay, 2002, p. 11). Considering these differences in classification approaches, in order to explain the complexity of the situational aspects of ethnicity and nationality in the lives of different Roma groups, I will briefly describe the recent historical changes that have shaped Roma mobility in Europe.

3.2 Contextual roots of Roma ethnic classification

In the last decennia debates about the efficiency of Roma integration strategies and the role of international institutions illustrate the complexity of the ethnic framing of Roma in the European context. Due to the paradoxical integration and security policies, Roma mobility has received increasing attention in EU politics, in particular the institutionalisation of Roma governance. While there was an ongoing discussion about the legitimacy of the recently established European Roma Institute, the role of the Roma Decade program and other transnational top-down initiatives, there has been a growing number of reports published by the United Nations Development Programme (UNDP), World Bank and Organization for Security and Co-operation in Europe (OSCE) problematising the situation of Roma communities in the EU.

Definitional challenges of the Roma ethnic identity are also represented in the linguistic approach, which differentiates Roma by their Romani language dialects. Some Roma speak a Romani dialect and their national language, while others, such as the Hungarian Romungro Roma, speak the national language of their parents. Some Roma, such as Hungarian Roma in Slovakia, speak only their national language and others speak their national language together with second languages, such as English. According to the OSCE, 'common unifying features in reference to Roma – to the extent that they may exist – include common identification as members of the "communities of fate" regarded as "Gypsies" in Europe' (2000, p. 13). Likewise, 'the occasional or frequent experience of being "outed" as a "Gypsy" often results in negative treatment, or at least in suspicion' (ibid., p. 13). This is not the only difficulty, however. The term Roma cannot be linked to a particular area. Several subgroups may live in the same city or country, but their identity is not defined by their geographic or linguistic location. Hungarian Roma are living in Slovakia, Slovak Roma are living in the Czech Republic and Russian Roma groups are living in Poland. For a brief clarification, in the following sections I will give a short overview of Central European Roma, as the selected population group researched in this study, and their historical self-definition in ethnic and national terms.

Although there are Roma communities everywhere in the world, this study focuses on Roma from Central European countries; this is primarily because of shared political and economic backgrounds and migration patterns towards the West. In addition, Roma communities in these countries are sufficiently diverse in terms of their proportion of the overall population, number of distinct subgroups, and differences in socio-economic position to provide a broad cross section of their experiences. Referring to the historical selection by Bárány, we can conclude that all of the selected sending countries share the many historical similarities, such as the disadvantages related to the post-democratic transition period (Bárány, 2002). These countries are also unified under the umbrella of the so-called Visegrad Group, or V4, consisting of Czech Republic, Hungary, Poland and Slovakia.

Based on the different histories of the various Roma subgroups, I will differentiate between three major contemporary Roma migration flows in the European

Union. The first flow, which originated from each of the V4 countries, was when Roma claimed asylum before the dissolution of the Eastern Bloc. The Roma networks that settled in other countries (e.g. Germany, the Netherlands and the UK) and their asylum process provide the key transnational links to the later mobility flows by the same ethnic subgroups. After 1989, when the V4 countries had made the transition to democracy, a second flow can be identified: those claiming EU citizenship rights in host countries based on the law of free movement. Most of these Roma already had networks in the host countries or had tried to claim asylum there before. The third flow took place in the 2000s mainly following the path of economic migrants from their home countries. Movements from CEE countries, following the democratic transition, took the form of asylum seeking in other EU countries and in Canada. Examples include attempts by Roma from Poland and the Baltic states to settle in Great Britain during the second half of the 1990s; the emigration of Roma from the Czech Republic and Slovakia to Canada, which increased after 1997 (Vidra 2013a; see also Tóth, 2013; Vasecka & Vasecka, 2003; Matras, 2003; Grill, 2011; Kováts, 2002; Humphris, 2013); the arrival of Roma migrants from the Czech Republic and Slovakia in Great Britain in 1997 and later; the wave of refugees from Slovakia to Belgium and Finland from 1999 to 2000 (Sobotka, 2003); and the arrival of Roma from the Czech Republic and Hungary in Canada in 2009. All of these movements triggered different policy restrictions which contributed to current monitoring practices of Roma newcomers.

As most of these migration flows has been associated with Central and East European Roma, it is relevant here to introduce the Visegrad Group of countries. The Visegrad Group is a cooperation scheme in the Central European region between the Czech Republic, Hungary, Poland and Slovakia, active in fields of common interest in all-European integration (Visegrad.info, 2010). These countries have always shared 'cultural and intellectual values and common roots in diverse religious traditions, which they wish to preserve and further strengthen' (Bárány, 2002, p. 7). All of the V4 countries aspired to become members of the European Union, through mutual support that they attained on 1 May 2004. As the initiative suggests, the Visegrad Group was not created as an alternative to the all-European integration efforts, nor does it try to compete with existing Central European structures. Instead, it encourages optimum collaboration with all countries in the region, in particular with V4 neighbours. Due to attempts to join the EU acquis the Visegrad Group member states became the most important region of Roma out-migration/asylum seeking in the 1990s and 2000s.

According to the Migration Policy Institute, 'between 1997 and 2005, approximately 12,000 to 15,000 Roma left Central Eastern Europe. The first post-transition flow was mainly related to asylum claims and guest workers trying to retain the social economic position that they had established in their home countries' (Tanner, 2005, p. 3). The first post-accession Roma to file asylum claims in EU countries were Slovakian and Czech Roma, followed by Polish, Bulgarian and Romanian Roma. Besides EU states (particularly the UK), Roma applied for asylum in Switzerland, Norway and Canada. 'Most Roma arrived in

Canada from the Czech Republic and Hungary, and fewer from Slovakia. CEE state governments saw Roma asylum seeking as an impediment to their EU accession' (Vidra, 2013a, p. 530). This process explains the geopolitical circumstance of the westward flow of the Roma that shapes their current social position in the UK. Unemployment rates soared during the post-democratic transition period in the V4 countries. Roma became the most disadvantaged population group in the region, driving them to seek a better life abroad. 'After the transition, urban, but especially rural, rationalisation programmes targeting unemployment and segregation problems (in preparation for the EU acquis) started integration projects to convince the EU about integrated Roma politics' (Staniewicz, 2011, p. 261).

Social reforms such as privatisation and the 'restructuring of industries resulted in many previously family-managed small agricultural holdings being no longer economically viable' (Džambazovič – Jurásková, 2003). Since the transition, the Roma population in Hungary and Slovakia is over-represented in the unemployment rates of peripheral regions, primarily in the northeast and southwest of Hungary and Eastern Slovakia where industrial activities were taking place (Kertesi, 2000). Due to this process, ethnicisation of the poverty rate is rising (Kligman, 2001) and there are increasing stereotypes of ethnic "othering" (Kligman, 2001). As Vidra summarised, the official public and political discourses of immigrant countries following the "asylum crisis" of the 1990s were dominated by right-wing politicians and conjured up images of welfare states being "swamped" and national identities being undermined by mass movements of impoverished people from East to West and South to North. As she stated, the main argument was that emigrating Roma were "bogus" refugees and in fact 'merely economic immigrants attempting to take advantage of the welfare systems in their host countries' (Vidra, 2013b, p. 530).

As it was concluded in the research on Roma migration in 2002, the dynamics of mobility in case of CEE Roma migrants seem to be controversial. It has been argued that increasing numbers of Roma see emigration as a way to sort out their problems is not independent from their economic deprivation and the discrimination to which they are exposed (Kováts, 2012). Not having any special qualities or skills to offer on the labour market,

> most of them see a refugee status as the only chance for a residence permit in the target country and the disadvantages suffered in their country of origin become their primary 'social capital' that can be converted into some other kind of benefit. The underprivileged position of the Hungarian Roma on the labour market and the social ladder is likely to assert itself in their chances of acquiring temporary jobs abroad. It is not only in Hungary that the unskilled worker who is difficult to mobilise is the employer's last choice.
>
> (Kováts, 2002, pp. 11–12)

Refugee claims in Canada and in other EU states provided Roma with essential experiences with foreign bureaucratic systems, which have recently been exploited by newcomers in the UK. However, temporary work overseas or in

Western Europe has no specifically Roma or non-Roma characteristics. In addition, regarding the role of identity in the choice of mobility, Vidra states that

> the chances of getting a job are predominantly shaped by supply and demand and being an Eastern European is more important to the Western employer than being (or not being) a Roma (Wizner, 2000). This ethnic element is a key aspect in the motivation of CEE Roma to leave their countries for an environment in which Roma identity has limited implications for their social economic position. Although Slovak and Czech Roma have regularly been in the media, Hungarian Roma mobility is one of the most invisible in many host countries.
>
> (Vidra, 2013b)

As discussed in the following section, the recent existential deprivation of Roma has been politicised, partly fuelled by their westward mobility. Negative media attention given to Romani migrants has been extensive in countries of origin, especially regarding refugee claims. The Slovak media, for instance, citing high-level government officials, has spoken extensively of "ethno-tourism" by way of stigmatising Romani migrants and asylum seekers from Slovakia in Western Europe (Russell, 2008). Romani migration has become further emboldened what are already high levels of anti-Romani sentiment. As a result, many Roma report increased levels of discrimination in their home countries, which is forcing Roma minorities into situations of increasing deprivation.

3.3 Politicising marginalisation – the criminalisation of Roma

The situation in Central Eastern European countries after the democratic transition is summarised by Pogonyi (2013):

> After the economic shocks of the early transition years, east-central European economies grew. Since 2008, however, economic growth has again slowed down. Welfare cuts and austerity packages have been introduced throughout Europe. Unemployment rates are growing. As for the economic malaise, the current economic crisis may not have as big an impact on welfare as the transition to the market economy in the early 1990s. The context in east-central Europe is, however, different from that of two decades ago. In the early 1990s, the prospect of joining the prosperous club of Western Europe counterbalanced the decline in welfare. Today the context is far less favourable for democracy, since there are no similar external factors which could strengthen the legitimacy of fragile democratic institutions.
>
> (nb)

Euroscepticism, lack of solidarity, distrust of collective action and many other signs suggests that 'social transition still lags behind institutional transition. While institutions, thanks to EU accession, have been democratised, democratic values are still not entrenched in the political culture of east-central European populations' (ibid.).

The combination of a weak state apparatus, as well as increasing corruption and clientelistic relations, has eroded trust in political leadership. State crimes have been linked to privatisation and control over key resources and assets is increasingly in the hands of a privileged few. Corrupt political elites and administrative systems have allowed the spread of organised fraud, illegal border trafficking, bribery and money laundering, posing a direct threat to fragile democratic institutions (Swank & Betz, 2003). Socio-economic instabilities and experiences with exploitative hyper-capitalists have resulted in existential anxiety, new dependency relations and the experience of deprivation by the middle class, which in turn has led to an increase in conservative political ideas, nationalism and xenophobia. Extremism as a political force in Central and Eastern Europe has, in many cases, been able to penetrate mainstream politics and its ideological discourse has infiltrated wider social mentalities.

As a response to far right extremist developments, human rights issues have been raised by local NGOs and brought under the umbrella of social Europe, claiming socio-economic rights for marginalised and discriminated minorities. This socially oriented politics focuses people's attention to exclusion, marginalisation and poverty in association with the Roma. This movement in turn contributes to a broader political-economic transition, wherein a shift from defining Roma as a "transnational European minority" to conceiving them as a "European social problem" occurred at the turn of the century.

Also national Roma integration strategies have played a great role in situating issues of Roma poverty and social exclusion. These strategies have aimed at raising the awareness of all stakeholders to the gaps between Roma and the non-Roma population in all domains of life (Vermeersch, 2006). The national majorities of Member States, who blame the Roma for their socio-economic deprivation, have interpreted these integration narratives as "positive discrimination", which has resulted in decreasing local solidarity, economic exclusion, social deprivation and the "ghettoisation" of some Roma communities.

Through this marginalisation process, the Roma have become increasingly dependent on informal economies, driven by exclusion from the discriminative legal labour market in the home countries and geographic isolation (Bárány, 1998). These structures have exacerbated labour exploitation (locally and internationally), organised crime networks in identity fraud, prostitution and financial dependency on international migration networks. These aspects will be used later to explain some of the specific coping strategies applied by Roma in London. During these local developments, transnational ties became stronger through social media networks and online chatrooms. An increasing number of entrepreneurs have recruited Roma and facilitated housing and labour in Western Europe. After the first migration flow Roma mobility has become a highly politicised topic which raised diplomatic tensions even between the Member States. In short, there is a strong top-down European integration narrative that frames the inclusion of Roma and supports nation states in their local inclusion strategies, which contributes to the securitisation narratives adopted by the sending countries. These securitisation processes resulted from this EU narrative increasingly frame Roma ethnicity in terms of public disorder, economic parasitic behaviour and crime.

Hence, the recent criminalisation, exclusion and de facto segregation of Roma are the result of historical developments in the sending countries, which have created specific circumstances that have shaped and reshaped the mobility structures of Roma. In the case of the V4 states, political transition and changing bureaucratic apparatuses have resulted in the removal of many of the mechanisms that had previously helped keep anti-Romani sentiment under control.

> During the socialist era racist media invectives, whether directed against Roma or other national, ethnic or religious groups, could not be published. Paradoxically, the introduction of cosmopolitan law in the CEE region [. . .] was accompanied by a surge in racially motivated assaults on Roma, by stereotyping of Roma in the media.
>
> (OSCE, 2000)

'Roma became convenient scapegoats for societies experiencing economic pain and ideological dislocation in the transition to democracy and market' (Pogány, 2012, p. 16).

Communist administrations, as indicated earlier, transformed the socio-economic conditions of Roma by integrating them within the general workforce and giving them access to improved housing and public services.

> By discouraging and, in some cases, criminalising Roma entrepreneurialism and economic independence, as well as by creating welfare systems that provided an unprecedented degree of economic security for Roma, communist administrations suppressed Roma adaptive skills, encouraging a culture of dependency that is still much in evidence.
>
> (Pogány, 2006, pp. 337–341)

In addition, by proletarianising the Roma, i.e. by directing working-age Roma towards mostly unskilled or semi-skilled jobs in state-owned enterprises or in agricultural co-operatives (Bárány, 2002, pp. 137–140), the communist authorities were at least partially responsible for the fact that Roma generally lacked the formal qualifications necessary to find regular employment in the economic environment that emerged in the 1990s. As a result, the anti-Roma sentiment in the CEE area is more intense now than in either the socialist or inter-war periods (Bárány, 2002, p. 98; Mirga, 2009).

Writing about the Bulgarian Roma, Dimitar Panchev claims that Roma are disproportionately targeted by the police and are often used as a scapegoat based on stereotypes that emphasise their 'criminal nature' (Gounev et al., 2006 in

Panchev, 2013). Panchev says that 'the emphasis [is] on the "otherness" of the Roma, making a "distinction" between the law-abiding majority and the socially disadvantaged, who "lack the necessary cultural capital in order to be integrated" into the mainstream (Borjas, 1999)' (Panchev, 2013).

As a reaction, by mobilising transnationally, activists are essentially demanding rights and privileges that transcend those of citizens of nation states.

'Since the 1970s, efforts to build Roma identity in the transnational political context occurred with a concerted move away from the exonym "Gypsy" towards the use of the endonym "Roma", an umbrella term which harbours a highly diverse community'; however, 'Mirga and Gheorghe (1997, p. 22) cautiously warn against the danger of constructing Roma identity beyond the state as a stateless nation, because it reinforces the idea that Roma are not constitutive of the dominant nation and are not full citizens of the states in which they reside' (McGarry, 2011, p. 286). Thus, disagreements from within and without the Roma community about nomenclature, ethnicity, statehood and belonging and other factors crucial to constructing and maintaining an "identity" have led not only to confusion, but a measurable disadvantage for Roma and their political allies who seek to advocate on behalf of the Roma people as a whole.

The intertwined failure of national policies and international human rights claims have resulted in a new mobility wave in the EU and new forms of the criminalisation of migrants.

> Bridget Anderson (2013) has historicised the migration challenge, charting the development of state control and the criminalisation of, first, poor people within the territorial boundaries of a realm, then later of non-citizens outside the state. This historical perspective is useful, in that it contextualises assumptions concerning sovereignty, citizenship and the state and highlights the necessity for any analysis of the criminalisation of migration to consider questions of socio-economic status and the organisation of labour. [. . .] Indeed, when examining the discursive aspects covering the criminalisation of migration, the boundaries between migration, race and ethnicity are often highly blurred.
>
> (Parkin, 2013, p. 12)

Accordingly, I offer a short description of the situation of V4 Roma minorities in the post-transitional context and highlight their aspirations to move to London.

Beginning in the 1990s and continuing to the present day, many tens of thousands of Roma from the Czech Republic, Slovakia, Poland, the Baltics, Romania and elsewhere have gone to the United Kingdom, initially as persons seeking (and often receiving) refugee status, and currently as persons exercising EU free movement rights. Immigration into the UK, which resulted from the entry of V4 countries into the EU, was different from previous immigration to the UK due to high employment rates among newcomers. In the UK,

A8[2] workers have been able to freely and legally take up employment since May 2004, as long as they are registered in the Worker Registration Scheme. The opening of the UK labour market to workers from these countries led to a surge in immigration. From 2004 to 2009, the net migration of A8 migrants to the UK was about 304,000 and A8 migrants accounted for about 25% of all net migration to the UK during that period. Until 2004, those born in the A8 countries working in the UK had employment rates well below those of UK-born citizens and those born in the other original EU member states. But employment rates are not the only difference between A8 workers and other migrants. The geographical dispersion of A8 migrants is very high in comparison to other migrants. A8 migrants are also relatively young and well educated, although they tend to find work in lower paid jobs. Their lack of fluency in English is a likely reason for their low earnings compared to their education (Vargas-Silva, 2011).

There are several reasons why Roma migrate to the UK. Some academics argue that it is purely an economic decision and that Roma

> are not unlike other temporary economic migrants: they are generally looking for short-term opportunities that will allow them to elevate their status at home to a level of minimum sustainability and ideally create a base (new business, ongoing investments) for further income generation. Unlike other economic migrants from the EU, however, Roma are likely to be significantly poorer, less skilled at higher-level jobs and desperate enough that they will go to extremes to secure even a meagre income. They are more likely to travel in groups and rely on existing networks of migrants whenever possible and, because of language limitations, much more vulnerable to abuses by other Roma 'handlers'.
>
> (Pusca, 2014)

According to a report by Salford University (Brown et al., 2013), Roma are moving (and settling) in different locations because they experience relatively low levels of discrimination in these new locations compared to in their countries of origin. That report, involving 104 Roma participants across 10 different locations, found that work was a key motivation for migration, with 58.7% indicating that they had moved to the UK for this reason. Following employment, the main reasons were 'a better life for children' (22.1%) and 'discrimination in country of origin' (15.4%). The majority of those surveyed (97.1%) said that their lives had improved since coming to England; however, the report raises the question as to whether or not Roma in general possess low expectations due to experiences in their country of origin (see European Dialogue, 2009, pp. 7–8). As will be discussed later in the chapter, most Roma enjoy the invisibility offered by the

2 The A8 countries joined the EU in 2004; they are Czech Republic, Estonia, Hungary, Latvia, Lithuania, Poland, Slovakia and Slovenia.

diversity of London, which provides socio-economic and existential perspectives for their whole family (Brown et al., 2013).

3.4 Mobility and ethnic history

Studies by Vidra (2013b) and Kováts (2002) apply a classical conceptual framework to the analysis of Roma migration, in which Roma are considered a combination of refugee and labour (or economic) migrant (Klimova & Pickup, 2003). In the following description, I take these notions as a starting point and, taking into account the three contemporary waves of Roma migration from Central Eastern European countries, I focus on the interrelationship between different categories of intra-European labour movements.

To understand how and why people migrate, we need to know 'why local livelihood qualities are rejected in favour of migration, and to evaluate the local migration culture, in the sense of conventions about who goes where when' (White, 2009, p. 7). Though concepts of "survival" or "coping" strategies are sometimes invoked to explain mobility in general, these do not fully explain migrants' motivations (Pickup & White, 2003). Therefore, this study applies a livelihood strategy approach to understanding mobility, in both the sending and receiving localities.

According to the existing data and confirmed by the preliminary findings of the MigRom research project by Manchester University (Matras et al., 2015) and the latest Roma SOURCE report by Salford University (Brown, 2012), Roma mobility is generally motivated by a lack of local economic and social security, as well as ethnic discrimination. Harsh economic conditions and poor welfare have generated relatively stable annual migration flows of Roma over time, but differences between countries of origin confirm the importance of income and job opportunities as key factors in relocation. Three major factors that are common to V4 countries reflect similar motivations among those who migrate: the level of welfare, the availability of job opportunities and a restructuring of the production base during the period of transition, with the latter factor having implications beyond just the shrinking of employment opportunities.

These three factors have an asymmetric impact on various populations, affecting certain working-age groups more than others and setting higher barriers for their reintegration into the workforce. Among the most affected are older workers, those ethnically different from the majority population and people with disabilities. One of the most affected groups is the Roma. They face difficulties in accessing basic services, including education and health, as well as jobs in their home countries, due to the discriminatory attitudes of service providers and employers. One hypothesis is that the motives for the migration of Roma from these countries do not differ considerably from the motives of millions of other migrants who have left their homelands in search of work and a better livelihood. However, due to increasing harassment and discrimination in the host countries, their opportunities are much more restricted than their peers among the local majority and other migrant populations. However, when we raise the question of why this subject has recently become so relevant, we need to consider other facilities that enable greater mobility for less advantaged groups.

It can generally be maintained that Roma who plan to migrate have up-to-date and relevant information about foreign opportunities and ways of obtaining legal status in the host country. However, the institutions and regulations involved in immigration and refugee affairs are rather complex. The Roma do not rely on official information given by governments or civil organisations. Even if they know about such information and about the reports in the press, they think that such sources are misleading, manipulated and unreliable. Instead, they rely on their practical everyday knowledge of the working mechanisms of immigration and refugee matters, which can be acquired from experience passed on personally by those who have been through the process. This helps them compile, edit and submit application forms (for refugee status, welfare claims, National Health Service registration etc.) that are likely to succeed, and also helps them to integrate into everyday life in the host society (Kováts, 2002, p. 21).

Modern means of communication, such as Facebook and Skype, provide a flow of information about employment opportunities and wages on the grey markets of Western European countries. This in turn stimulates and facilitates emigration, as will be described in the sixth chapter. Previous personal life and work experience gained abroad can also facilitate the decision to leave again for a foreign country. People with relatives and acquaintances abroad are more likely to migrate to join them. The larger the number of people from a particular area working abroad, the greater the likelihood that other people from the same neighbourhood will emigrate (Cherkezova & Tomova, 2013).

In migration studies it has been regularly stated that newcomers mobilise a network of relationships in order to secure the journey and their stay in a new location. For instance, newcomers can receive help from others with the sale of their movables and real property and with the acquisition of documents and tickets. Low education status and lack of language competence is not considered a problem in this case, as emigrants depend on their relatives and acquaintances for support (Cherkezova & Tomova, 2013, pp. 23–25).

Without contradicting the preceding, it can also be remarked that, by examining the principle upon which Roma communities are constructed, it becomes clear 'that factors other than those related to descent may play a vital part in fostering communal ties' (Prónai, 2006, p. 56). In fact, with the Free Movement policy after the last enlargement migration agencies which, for a fee, package housing, travel arrangements and employment, as well as bureaucratic support, started to play an increasing role in these processes. Also, it is essential to understand the legal changes in mobility agreements, changes in the socio-economic position of particular groups on the move, their information resources, and the formal or informal networks in sending and receiving countries to explore the different connections between those who stay at home and those who migrate, and to determine which elements are dominant, particularly in cases of network dependency (Ringold et al., 2005). In order to find particular patterns of mobility in relation to ethnicity in the EU context, we have to extend the existing concepts of intra-state policing practices that increasingly engage administrative service providers.

Focusing on pure legal and social categories of migration can lead to a static approach to mobility. Legislation around citizenship-based rights and the different terms or conditions for remaining in foreign countries are constantly shaped by international politics and trans-economic agreements. Therefore, we need to contextualise particular interrelations between different modes of mobility and law enforcement targeting particular groups.

In previous studies a strict differentiation was made between guest workers and migrants (Vidra, 2013a; Kováts, 2002) as well as between subgroups in the legal migration framework. Some of these are not included in this research due to their A2[3] nationality, as they were later included in the EU, and their subgroups are historically and culturally different from CEE Roma. However, these classifications often ignore highly educated Roma expats and professionals who are integrated into the high-middle classes in their host societies. As these Roma do not appear in the support systems of the host societies, they seem to be invisible in most studies on migration. Not surprising, however, is the visibility of Vlach or Olah Roma communities, who are willing to escape from their modest, but not hopeless, living standards and life prospects, or Romungro, who settle abroad. As is described in Chapter 8, these groups engage in casual physical work (predominantly unskilled jobs in the construction industry), or work for local authorities via employment agencies. Others try trading and operate at a low level of success due to a lack of capital and organisation.

Kováts explains:

> They [Roma] engage in commercial activities in between the host and sending countries as their commercial activity is bi-directional: by systematically monitoring market conditions they try to make the best possible profits on goods. For many, cross-border migration is part of an economic activity, which has a long tradition going back several generations, whose direction and intensity is regulated by the extent of foreseeable profit. Although they try to maintain good contacts with non-Roma, on the whole their community is rather closed and traditional.
>
> (Kováts, 2002, p. 28)

Roma is also problematised as an imposition on the labour market of receiving countries. These Roma migrants are described as a serious challenge to receiving countries (and later to their countries of origin) as they "put all their eggs in one basket". These newcomers are often seen as 'benefit tourists', who, in truth, if forced to return to from where they started, might end up in a much a worse social and economic position than before they left. It was with these emigrants that the strategy of 'fishing for benefits' is observed, i.e. shaping one's migration

3 A2 refers to Bulgaria and Romania, which joined the EU on 1 January 2007.

strategies according to the possibility of receiving social transfers, which is the sole survival resource (Vidra, 2013b, p. 31). Yet these migrants arrive, almost without exception, with valid passports and find employment in the informal sector of the economy, like painting and gardening.

Roma mobility has specific aspects – not necessarily due to cultural or ethnic characteristics, but because of socio-economic conditions in their home countries. When Roma are described in terms of poverty and dependency in governmental and EU reports, these parameters are dominating the discourse on Roma ethnic identity and ignoring other Roma who are educated and living upper middle class or middle class lives around the world. These financial, welfare-dependent parameters are associated with a lack of productivity and are seen as a social burden. As it will be illustrated in the last part of the study, these connotations are adapted in the social service provisions that are meant to sort out those who are "undeserving" according to neoliberal market values. According to such connotations Roma feel they are sorted out from the welfare provisions. Social sorting of Roma is thus constructed rather by financial parameters then ethnic connotations. Considering the complexities described above, this ethnographic study on surveillance is completed in a liquid research field based on the migration flow of CEE Roma networks.

3.5 Contextuality and the liquid research field

Since Roma migration is a dynamic movement of people across social and spatial borders, we need to identify research sites that are not limited to specific geographic locations but instead follow the flow of migration. In order to complete empirical research with this dynamic construction of space, a multi-sited methodological guideline is provided including three methodological subfields. Based on transnational networks of Roma migrants, the first empirical context defined is a multi-sited approach, borrowing the strategy from Marcus (1995) and Falzon (2012), who advocate multiple localities for observation and participation. Second, institutional ethnography will be adapted for observations of welfare surveillance and the interaction between bureaucrats, NGO workers and migrants. This institutional setting is one of the key platforms for analysing stigmatisation processes and the institutional framing of ethnic differentiation, selection and exclusion. Third, online interactions play a significant role in the experiences of migrants with authorities and in gaining access to public information. This virtual space is the third major research context where information exchange and observations are completed. When seen together, these three ethnographic sites enable a rigorous and expansive assessment of interrelations across space and ethnicity, allowing us to analyse marginalisation and exclusion in different contexts and from different vantage points. The situational construction of Roma identity and its bureaucratic consequences can only be understood through the assemblages of these ethnographic sites.

The interrelations of Roma ethnicity, culture and space are frequently conceptualised by romanticised ideas of a nomadic lifestyle. These assumptions often include ideas of spacelessness and intangibility that might lead to misconceptions about place and mobility. Central East European Roma migrants are European citizens (not nomads) who are moving westward due to economic pressure and socio-political exclusion in their home countries. Although many studies have dealt with the 'relation between Roma and space' (Kabachnik, 2010, p. 200) or the territorial monopolisation of certain economic activities in the niche markets that Roma occupy (Mirga, 1992; Piasere, 1992), most of these studies refer to one specific location or community. Although Roma do not have the same nationality or ethnic subgroup and do not speak the same languages, they reside in a shared location in the countries to which they emigrate. In this transnational context, their common daily experiences are shaped by local and international control measures and social policies. However, their narratives about their experiences and how they cope with legal restrictions change according to the place, time and social context and in particular according to the social position of those conducting research or otherwise documenting Roma narratives (Grill, 2005). By conducting multi-sited ethnographic fieldwork involving cross-cultural inquiry, we can avoid place-culture isomorphism (Dalakoglou & Harvey, 2012, p. 462) and analyse the mechanisms that shape the decision-making processes of Roma in different countries (Clifford, 1997).

Roma mobility presumes a field definition that replaces a static cultural area with a field that is a mobile cultural formation. As Falzon (2012) suggests, the field does not need to correspond to a place or space in order to find its boundaries. Based on his methodological approach, the research field can be seen as discontinuities in the networks within which we are collecting information, including the boundaries (p. 64). Ethnographic sites are not static and their uniqueness lies not in some essential identity but in the particular intersection of social relations, so history should be a part of global ethnography (Massey, 1994). Thus, we are penning up the possibilities of an 'unsited' field where fieldwork must not study the chosen sites but account for changes in the relations between them (Massey, 1994).

Mobility does not simply mean a physical form of displacement, but also an imaginative, virtual, communicative and corporeal travel, which includes several forms of social and spatial interrelations (Urry, 2008, pp. 101–102). By tracing the movements of our respondents in different settings, we can emphasise how decisions about movement are made and how these reflect individual priorities and considerations. Therefore, we need a research method "on the move". Multi-sited analyses as a model for mobile ethnography enables the tracking of people's movement, images, information and objects in various ways and allows us to be moved by, and to move with, research respondents (Sheller & Urry, 2006).

From a methodological aspect, interaction with bureaucrats has a particularly important role in the daily interaction of migrants and their experience with surveillance mechanisms. Roma's experiences in formal settings and the social imagination of civil servants about Roma as an ethnic minority has a mutual influence on their situational approach with real effects in processes of accessing social services.

There are two major access points where migrants try to gain access and are monitored in relation to welfare services. The first access point includes governmental service providers, which coordinate, screen, select and monitor the social coordinates of citizens. They decide about their eligibility, entitlements and administrative and financial obligations, such as HMRC, Job Centres and local councils. The second access point is the non-governmental sector where self-funded organisations aim to contribute to the full participation of ethnic migrants and support them with information, self-representation and access to governmental services. These organisations, like local charities, often adopt the role of mediators and collect case studies to draw more attention to particular problems that migrants are faced with. By following the interactions between these actors and how they become involved in the processes of claimants, we can trace bureaucratic dysfunctions and selectivity regarding the entitlement of ethnic migrants to welfare services.

The key advantage of institutional ethnography is that it is 'more concerned with political-economic contexts than most qualitative approaches' (Eastwood & Devault, 2001, p. 400). Compared to other organisation studies, this approach does not simply look at the structure and efficiency of an institution, but 'hooking on to activities and relations both horizontal and vertical, it is never confined to the very institution under investigation' (Widerberg, 2004, p. 180). Ferguson (2001) describes the embeddedness of certain images, such as those of the 'benefit thief', in the routine practices of state bureaucracies. The social practices of state bureaucrats construct an image of the state through metaphors in discursive representations that shape the ideas in the host society. Many of these presentations are implicit, unmarked, signifying practices (Ferguson & Gupta, 2002, p. 983).

Mobile ethnographic methods enable one to detect differentiations in bureaucratic practices and welfare services (Ferguson & Gupta, 2002, p. 984). This empirical method was adopted in different countries in a long-term shadowing process completed in London. Institutional ethnography was applied from three different angles. First, from the client's point of view, it was important to see who was interacting with the bureaucrats of the host country, As an interpreter and advocacy worker, I attended the personal appointments of Roma migrants, interpreted their telephone interviews, and took part in many follow-up conversations after applications were submitted. The second angle was the personal experience of civil servants. I interviewed civil servants in different councils, some of whom work specifically with Roma and others who work with different groups in addition to Roma. The last and most important approach was my experience with NGOs, where I worked as a volunteer advocacy worker. Over an eight-month period, I had the opportunity to see the attitudes of charity workers toward Roma clients, their interactions with social services and their support to empower Roma migrants to bolster their self-advocacy. These diverse perspectives highlight the role of international connections in welfare bureaucracies, the level of surveillance and data exchange between the different parties, and how Roma migrants try to find their way in a foreign bureaucratic system. These daily interactions, seen from the vantage point of a case study, demonstrate the changes during the observed period, following the dynamics of strengthening policies and migrants who develop their bureaucratic knowledge.

Research sites are also linked by cultural practices on computer-mediated spaces, most notably the internet. Dekker and Engbersen (2014) argue that social media plays a particular role in the transformation and facilitation of migration paths. With the increased availability of internet access and the increasingly common use of social media platforms, there are growing possibilities to maintain strong ties with one's family, friends and peers. These so-called virtual fields not only support existing relationships at a distance, but provide information on, and the organisation of, migration processes, such as bureaucratic requirements, practical knowledge about resources and cultural translation for newcomers. As Dekker and Engbersen (2014) note, 'this can be viewed as a democratization of knowledge for migrants and also as a form of silent resistance against restrictive immigration regimes' (p. 16). Ethnographic knowledge of the development of virtual infrastructures and how they facilitate insider information for potential migrants in a cost-efficient and convenient way should include virtual ethnographic methods.

The role of media technologies on mobility, exclusion and social formations is a debated subject in empirical studies (Hjorth, 2007). Virtual ethnography is included in this research to gain access to migrant networks and follow their traces online and offline, and to recruit research respondents. These routes mirror the changing patterns in the decision making of respondents and how it shapes their international social relations. However, it is also a mutual observation. In addition, the social movements of migrant groups, NGO activities, ethnic activism and anti-immigrant public discourses can be mapped in virtual environments.

Essentially, we cannot conceptualise sites with boundaries between online and offline communications, not just because these lines are vague and changing with the situations (Carter, 2004; Haythornthwaite & Kazmer, 2002; Beneito-Montagut, 2011, p. 717; Salaff, 2002), but also because people communicate simultaneously on different levels using multiple channels. An interpretation and translation of these multiple online and offline interactions refer to 'collective (cultural) understandings that are continually negotiated through linguistic and other symbolic practices' (Rabinow & Sullivan, 1979, p. 31). This cultural understanding reflects not only physical reality, but implicitly also transfers meanings and norms embodied in practices of shared behaviours and other social relations (Taylor, 1977, p. 119). Social media platforms such as Facebook serve as a key ethnographic site to trace actions and their meanings via multiple channels. Conducting ethnographic research with a mobile ethnic group reveals their practices in the visualised or written online context as a part of their culture, with a 'system of conceptions expressed in symbolic forms by means of which men communicate, perpetuate and develop their knowledge about attitudes towards life' (Geertz, 1973, p. 89).

Yet it's not only academic researchers who are collecting data about potential beneficiaries of social services online. Online surveillance strategies by governmental organs such as the police might cause deliberate online deception by migrants in an attempt to remain covert. Differences in self-representation between virtual space and reality can be clarified by the narratives of respondents who explain their online misrepresentations. Online spaces that offer opportunities for explicit self-representation provide new modes of visibility and presumed participation that do not always ensure the ideals of democratic involvement and equality. As it will be explained, these opportunities might legitimate new approaches justifying surveillance and adjudicating, resulting in the 'transgressive' criminalising practices of those institutions that were tasked with upholding the law (Lindlof & Shatzer, 1998).

In short, virtual ethnography is not independent from offline ethnography but as a subfield it is conducted on the internet, as Beneito-Montagut (2011) stated, as an 'expanded ethnography' in which virtual experiences are expanded enhancements of real relationships. That is to say, just like transnational (im) migrants themselves, the field becomes multi-sited.

3.6 Research process

This book is based on an ethnographic fieldwork in four Central East European EU member states of the Visegrad group and in the UK – between January 2013 and September 2014. That is where I first collected data from returnees in the sending countries and extended my network in the academic and NGO fields. Observations and interviews mainly took place in Hungarian-speaking settlements, in particular in Presov, Kocise, Moldava Bodvou, Bratislava, Prague and Brno. I conducted several interviews in Slovakia and the Czech Republic (e.g. people in need, MECEM, IOM, social workers, political leaders who are responsible for Roma integration projects) and observed the living circumstances of returnees. I developed new contacts with social workers and Roma integration project leaders which resulted in contacts with their clients who had returned from the UK. Several academics from different fields such as security studies, Romani studies and anthropology were involved in the theoretical development of this study.

From November 2014 onwards, I moved into a Romani household in East London and followed the mobility traces of their extended network. Moreover, by shadowing NGO workers who were supporting Roma with different issues, I gained more insight into the institutional barriers that Roma migrants face and how they respond to them in different circumstances. This NGO provided me with many opportunities to learn about the local bureaucratic structure and I was introduced to several partners of the organisation with whom it was beneficial to network. Roma clients regularly asked me for clarification regarding the contents of some correspondence, which gave me several opportunities to understand their knowledge about their local obligations toward councils, employees and landlords.

Furthermore, I attended several Roma activist meetings as an interpreter, where I could participate in the interaction between Roma migrants and local authorities. These meetings provided an opportunity to explore the power relations and cultural differences between Roma migrants and the host society. In addition, I developed contacts with several migrant families and built up a long-term relationship with Roma women who were organising financial issues in their households.

Sampling

During the first research phase information was collected from professionals, academics and activists working with Roma, and sampling frames were created for all the Visegrad countries in order to reflect the diversity of the Roma groups in terms of mobility patterns. The criteria used for the selection of localities were developed based on information collected during the background research. Using all available information from existing studies on Roma migration such as primary sampling units composed of municipalities, neighbourhoods and localities, fieldwork sited were identified. Importantly, in most of the sending localities NGOs or activists were needed to assist as interpreters or gatekeepers. Considering the limitations of the sample, regarding the community size and geographic distribution of the sample, this low-scale ethnographic fieldwork is unable to provide results that would be representative for the situation of Roma migrants. Also, the selected urban localities indicated by activists and NGOs as high concentration sending area, might indicate different mobility issues then smaller isolated localities. The relevance of the localities defined by professionals were in some cases already outdated since many migrants were involved in guest working mobility and were not interested in migration.

The most informative respondents were listed in Appendix A, working for non-governmental organisations. These respondents have intense contact with Roma migrants. Their experiences are not representative for all similar NGOs, but their view on and access to data was essential for a better understanding of surveillance dynamics in London. In addition, NGOs in sending countries were providing access to returnees and additional information on the historical and political background of some localities. Samples for NGOs lead to the first snowballing interviews with Roma in different localities. The central aim was to arrive at a random sample that provides reasonably good coverage of the target population given the time and resources available. This sample was not selecting Roma people who are benefit claimants or involved in welfare fraud, but who were willing to share their experiences and describe their coping strategies abroad, as a CEE Roma. Therefore, this sample is not relevant for any generalisation regarding the correlations of ethnicity and illegal activities. This study is not focusing on Roma as ethnic minority abroad, but Roma case studies are selected in order to analyse the effects of surveillance targets in which these cases provide better understanding of the social sorting dynamics. Shortly, cases of welfare fraud should not be correlated to ethnicity. In the preliminary phase of the research period, I collected secondary data to develop the right methodological and theoretical foundations for the operationalisation of the research project. First, I completed a literature review. Media analyses were included in the fieldwork process, related to different minority-targeting issues in the selected sending and receiving countries. The main goal of the pre-conceptualised research process was to follow and study Roma migrants in real time by means of a mobile ethnographic process and to document the formation and operation of their interaction with local authorities and social networks online and offline, as well as how they develop coping strategies to access welfare services. In the second phase, I completed fieldwork in three Central European countries and in one host country of CEE migrants.

Generated data was analysed based on cleaned-up transcripts of the interviews and field notes with transcription software (Express Scribe), and based on my observations at different meetings and analysed with qualitative data analysis software (Nvivo). The software was used to store and code the data with the help of three coding frames: one for emergent coding based on my perceptions, one based on literature and one based on a coding framework devised per location. However, coding systems are not analytically neutral. Text-based qualitative data analysis is a process of interpretation (Mason, 2002). In choosing or devising a particular system of coding data, certain assumptions are being made about the kinds of phenomena being coded and those that are not (Mason, 2002).

In order to ensure confidentiality of research respondents and organisations, different cases are mixed together and presented per coping strategy. Since many respondents know each other, respondents' names also have been changed to prevent their identification and removed from the publication version. The resulting transcripts were as accurate as possible, but did not document grammatical or phonetic mistakes or intonation and speech habits. When using quotations from the transcripts in this thesis, I have to some extent "cleaned up" the text and removed such features to make the content easier to read and to reduce the word count (unless I deemed the features important for the meaning being constructed).

Interviews

In a 14-month fieldwork, 98 interviews were completed. Of those, 56 were audio recorded, transcribed and analysed using Nvivo data analysing software. More than 50 interviews were completed with Roma migrants and returnees in different countries, 12 with social workers and advocacy workers, 4 with police officers, 6 with interpreters, 2 with lawyers, and 24 with civil servants such as integration officers, education officers and counsellors. More than 30 Roma respondents were women and 12 were men with an average age of 41.2 years (range = 21–62 years). Some were related to each other or living in the same household: they included 7 people born in Poland, 20 in Hungary and 6 in the Czech Republic or Slovakia.

In the first period, I interviewed Hungarian, Czech and Slovak returnees or the relatives of migrants in their home settings in order to understand the aspirations, expectations, dependency relations and reflections about living abroad. Most of these respondents were traced by social workers in Roma settlements or via Roma activists, NGO workers, politicians or friends and was followed in online conversations via Facebook. The extended overview of research respondents and the method of anonymisation is added in the tables as an Appendix. Respondents residing in London, Manchester, Leeds and other host cities in the UK, who were interviewed face-to-face or via Skype, were engaged by a snowballing recruitment strategy. One of the already included respondent introduced me via email or social media. If the person responded an appointment has been planned for an online or offline conversation. Interviews were planned after a few conversations. Trust of respondents and their awareness of the content of the research was a central reason to build up such relationships.

It was extremely difficult to guarantee total confidentiality, because most of the respondents knew each other, attended the same church, lived in or came from the same area and kept comparing themselves to others they thought I might know. Local NGOs and some civil servants were also frightened that I might know their clients or that they would divulge confidential information that would make them recognisable. These challenges are later described as limitations of the research methods.

Besides revealing important aspects of individual experiences with a foreign bureaucratic system, narrative in-depth interviews with Roma migrants were explored as primary sources concerning the complexity of identity formation in ethnically mixed boroughs. Furthermore, informal interviews were conducted with Roma to shed light on the overt and/or covert ethnic divisions and conflicts between different Roma migrant communities. The online behaviour of respondents was an important aspect of the interviews. I was observing and participating in online Romani networks and in the face-to-face interviews I also elicited reflections about internet use compared with my observations, such as the modes of connection and what kinds of relationships respondents maintain on the internet: work or study mates, friends, family, acquaintances and people known by face (Chen & Hinton, 1999; Kazmer & Xie, 2008).

The approaches of NGO leaders also revealed the deeper rationale of the prevailing local policies of integration and exclusion, as it is extensively discussed in Chapter 5. Additionally, semi-structured, face-to-face and in-depth Skype, phone and Viber interviews were completed with professionals like advocacy workers, lawyers, police officers and education officers to obtain a better understanding of their knowledge about Roma migrants, their attitudes toward Roma, and their insights, experiences, opinions, values and aspirations with regard to special support for Roma migrants. There was clear competition between different organisations, which tried to expropriate specific funding and projects on behalf of Roma migrant groups. This resulted in tensions between organisations. I wanted to be able to explore these tensions and differences of opinion, which emphasises the appropriateness of individual interviews.

Some professional respondents were extremely worried about their expressions, their eventual stigmatising notions about the Roma or the possible consequences of my study. The police and council social workers who interact with a high concentration of Roma migrants were extremely suspicious and reluctant to give their real opinions in an office setting and to evaluate different perspectives of stakeholders. To sum up, in order to capture the complexity of interpersonal relationships in particular settings, I used different techniques that each generated a particular set of data. This also cross-validates the study and triangulates the results.

Observations

An initial observation during an extended period of time offered knowledge about the interactions that take place in public spaces, in family settings and on the internet. In this phase, I visited different Facebook pages, read blogs and used instant messaging systems or email to make contact with people. It is important to point out that as a migrant from Central Europe myself and due to my engagement with the research population, I have partly become an insider in the Romani network (Adler & Adler, 1987). However, it is important to add that I was introducing myself as a researcher and the purpose of my presence was a common knowledge in the Roma networks, NGOs and also in the church communities.

After a short initial phase in the sending countries, I conducted several short-term respondent observations during which I followed migrant families. I was visiting my Facebook contacts in settlements, I followed instructions of local NGOs and social workers and visited settlements, while referred to some relatives abroad. In most cases one gatekeeper of the locality introduced me to the returnees or to their relatives. Also, some families called their family members on skype for me while I visited them. By visiting the same extended family networks in different countries, I collected extensive amounts of data about the contextual strategies of respondents. All of them were informed and gave their consent. After an initial online contact, I visited the families several times, invested in social contacts and after a few conversations I also conducted face-to-face interviews. Later I made contact online with the respondents via applications, websites and services that they use; so I had become a friend, a cultural mediator and a reader of their posts. Moreover, while moving around I interacted with them through email and Facebook Messenger during the data-gathering period. My private interactions (emails and chat conversations) with respondents were not registered due to ethical issues; however, they generated field notes.

My first strategy was to follow and observe users on social media and then offline in order to follow up on rapidly moving processes with the necessary reflexivity. This required signing in to the social networks that users belong to, selecting and approaching them through personal messages, emailing, chatting, reading their posts and sharing their photos. But it also meant paying attention to and locating the places from which the users connect. The internet has to be seen as a field of inquiry and is the social realm of respondents where decision making is being shaped. This implies a careful reflection about the research field and its accessibility. Consequently, methodology had to be designed, redesigned and derived as the research process unfolds, informing the data iteratively and generating a constant reflection on the research process. Following users in an expanded ethnographic approach requires flexibility.

The main features of this expanded ethnography mean that the real-virtual division is no longer sustainable. People use all the media at hand to communicate with others (Beneito-Montagut, 2011, p. 731), so links between online and offline modes of interaction have to be taken into account. In addition, as ethnography does not generate a predetermined setting for fieldwork, it is considered "expanded". It is individuals who compose the sample and determine the place where the ethnography takes place, thus the setting is flexible and potentially concerns all social communication and information systems on the internet, including a variety of multimedia data. As last, as a result of this fluid and dynamic field, the expanded ethnography approach requires a theoretical sample (Beneito-Montagut, 2011, p. 732).

For this I would like to use the individual narratives to replace the role of ethnicity with the local inter-ethnic power relationships from a diversity prospective (Barrett & Sigona, 2014). Since most of the cases I have collected are not particular strategies of the Romani migrant group(s), this project can give a better understanding of the local social strategies involving the positions of advocacy workers, local entrepreneurs and those who are using these newcomers for exploitation. It might reflect on the interracial interaction of migrants and how they learn these strategies from each other. It can offer a critical reflection about the role of EU citizenship and its similarities to illicit migrants who are experiencing a secondary citizenship. Observations of council employers in different boroughs, Roma events and court meetings, as well as suggestions from police officers, school assistants and interpreters for future observations were all subsequently included in the data collection process.

Participation

Participant observation took place continuously in the fieldwork period at different levels. From birthday parties to protests, festivals to formal meetings at council houses, I observed (and in some cases, assisted in) daily considerations of Roma life. Participation in the academic and activist networks working on Roma migration issues raised the key hypothesis of this study, reshaping the setting of the mobile fieldwork to East London and the sending countries for the UK migration to Central Eastern Europe. Online research participation facilitated contacts with migrants in different countries, who provided local connections in sending countries. Being an interpreter at several formal meetings and appointments with migrants at councils, Job Centres, hospitals, banks, schools and other government settings gave me the opportunity to collect data on interactions between these newcomers and civil servants. As a tenant in a Roma household, I had the opportunity to participate in the daily life of different Roma ethnic groups and to understand their relationships with their environments, both at home and abroad. At one point, the line between the role of the researcher and the advocacy worker was so blurred that I was forced to stop assisting the families I was working with. As an informal interpreter and advocacy worker of an NGO in London I had access to several interactions between civil servants and Roma clients at schools and Job Centres. These interactions concerned benefit and health care applications, payment agreements, HMRC applications or housing issues. Reciprocity was a central element of the data collection: I was expected to help with several bureaucratic issues and to interpret letters, phone calls and visits to local authorities. In addition to spending time with other advocacy workers, activists and artists in interviews and cultural events, I spent most of each interview day with different Roma families or with their relatives.

I developed regular contacts with civil servants on behalf of Roma families, to bridge their contact by providing support with school applications. My church attendance in London radically changed my position in the Roma network too. After a few weeks many families started to approach me with their dilemmas, which gave me the opportunity to understand and compare their decision-making processes. By supporting local training courses for teachers and interpreters about Roma, I had an opportunity to hear their knowledge and ideas about Roma migrants.

Shadowing and lurking

Daily participation at the office of the biggest NGO working with Roma in the UK not only provided me with contacts and a better understanding of bureaucratic procedures, but also with information about the relations between different local actors working with Roma migrants. I shadowed for eight months on a regular basis in the office and also in outdoor activities with advocacy workers and trainers focused on different functions of the NGO. It was also a great opportunity to gain access for interviews with clients, since I had obtained entry to the organisation and the agreement of trustees.

Shadowing NGOs and appointments in Job Centre Plus offices gave me a better understanding of self-management as a tactic used by ethnic migrants in a foreign setting. By using shadowing, an institutional research method that involves a researcher, I was able to closely follow the members of organisations over an extended period of time (McDonald, 2005, p. 457). These practices were combined with shadowing online activities of activist, academics and transnational migrant network.

To be able to understand the additional value of virtual ethnographic fieldwork, we have to clarify the relationship between online and offline fieldwork. Research fields are intersecting and constantly changing along with the daily interaction of respondents. Internet and social media networks are defined as important elements of data collection in a mobility study, not only for accessing respondents and following their activities, but also for understanding the role of social media in their decision-making processes. Due to their intensive but limited use of social media, Roma migrants are often unaware of the security and privacy risks related to internet use. However, social media helps to keep them in touch with core family members and their home environment. In transnational mobile networks, the real and the virtual are so strongly intertwined that we are unable to complete empirical research without devoting attention to these intersections (Matei & Ball-Rokeach, 2001).

Virtual fieldwork ensures transparency and provides a form of guarantee about the accessibility and location of the researcher. During my fieldwork, Roma activists passed my name to their friends on Facebook. They verified my background on Facebook page before the first contact and approached our common friends. However, Facebook page research involves the risk that respondents will not trust the ethnographer due to a lack of a verifiable background.

Second, not only migrants and their family networks but also activists, NGOs and anti-immigrant groups are mapped on social media. Professional networks are often in contact with NGOs and activists as respondents take part in the study. Interactions within various networks also offer many insights into the flow of information and perceptions of professionals that influence the individual decisions of migrants. Social media contacts with academic networks and project groups working on similar research are also a major source of online data. Observations online or, as it is often called, "suck" is a virtual research method that raises many ethical questions about the invisibility of researchers.

Third, social media is also a cost-effective platform for intimate conversations with relatives. Although internet literacy is not a common skill in the older members of immigrant communities, the minimal technical knowledge is quickly transferred as long as the family is not united in one geographic area. As it will be explained as identity-management strategies of Chapter 7, through observing conversations through Facebook chat and live simultaneously with Roma migrants, I had more of an opportunity to better understand the relationship between internal social relations and online self-presentations.

3.7 Ethical issues

Ethnographic methods face ambiguous ethical dilemmas in disseminating rich data in particular because of recent technical inventions that are changing the respondents' circumstances. With increasing digital data resources come increasing ethical dilemmas about the use of online data and about data ownership issues in digital spaces. Digital data-sharing methods are reconfiguring the landscape of research by redrawing boundaries and relationships between respondents and blurring boundaries between private and public spheres. This online communication and open data resource raised new dilemmas about ensuring the confidentiality and anonymity of respondents. This digital level of interaction involved new dilemmas about balance when conveying detailed, accurate accounts of the social world while simultaneously protecting the identities of the individuals. The official consent of respondent who are involved in such a study has been considered as problematic in Criminology. In such studies, researchers maintain considerable, potentially dangerous, influence over respondents due to their knowledge and perceived authority. This paradigm was presented in Milgram's classic obedience experiments which affirmed the power of situational forces on human behaviour (Jones, 2012, p. 1). However, in this study all the respondents were informed about their role in the research conducted.

Research consent varied between observations and participation in online groups. Many respondents or friends who were informed about my project were forwarding invitations to events and information about local events that were visible to everyone in my online network. Further, given the openness of many respondents about their individual data on social networks, online respondent observation theoretically allows a covert position (Fielding et al., 2008; Mann & Stewart, 2000). This was seen as problematic due to ethical concerns associated with the potentially unnoticed consequences of users' privacy, but it became clear that respondents were conscious about their self-presentation and aware of the risks and possibilities of monitoring online data. Respondents do not share personal data on their Facebook pages and they modify their location and affiliation presented on internet. For instance, most of the respondents are registered as an employee of Dolce and Gabbana or Armani and they register as a student of Oxford University. These online characteristics are also confirmed offline as fake in order to protect their real digital identity. In order to prevent any risk of confidentiality, this book contains no data that has been collected without consent.

4 Welfare policy and the new social sorting of Europe

'YOU pay for Roma Gypsy palaces', screamed the headline of an article in the British Sunday Express newspaper (Sheldrick, 2016). It quoted UKIP member of the European parliament Mike Hookem, who complained that the welfare state was being used to bankroll 'Gypsy Kings', who were 'building lavish palaces funded by people in the UK working on the minimum wage'. With a reference to Roma, this article called for restrictive measures against the flood of opportunist EU migrants.

After 2006, populist discourse on Roma mobility and welfare fraud began feeding anti-immigration policies (Galita & Bonta, 2013). The UK Department for Work and Pensions produced a targeted advertising campaign, one aim of which was 'to maintain public perception that benefit fraud is a crime and is taken seriously' (National Audit Office, 2008, p. 44). The state department promoted welfare fraud hotlines on billboards that accused migrants of exporting UK social benefits to their home countries (Figure 4.1).

As these governmental advertisements illustrate, not only were incoming migrants publicly associated with the suspicion of crime, but also UK civilians were being encouraged to identify and target these so-called benefit tourists. By linking crimes such as benefit fraud to intra-European mobility, political debates raised concerns and scepticism about newcomers from Central Eastern Europe (CEE), in particular Roma (for a detailed explanation, see Duwell & Wollmer, 2009; O'Reilly, 2007b; Ringold, 2000).

The immigration policy and practices of host countries in the EU can be better understood in the framework of a new governance philosophy in which traditional values of the welfare state have been replaced by new managerialist objectives. This shift from the equality-based social service principle towards and efficiency-oriented bureaucratic system has been legitimised by the advantages of digitalised services provisions. Roma migrants in the UK are engaged with such welfare service measures that classifies applicants according to these new managerial values.

EU welfare regulations have resulted in new processes of control and transparency techniques, redesigned bureaucratic incentives of member states and increased the role of entrepreneurial governments. This government philosophy strongly resembles profit companies, arguing that government institutions

Figure 4.1 DWP Billboards. Retrieved 11–10–2013.

should compete with for-profit businesses, non-profit agencies and other units of government. David Osborn and Ted Gaebler claim that it means a catalytic, 'steering rather than rowing', 'empowering rather than serving', competitive, results-oriented governance (1992: 32). As private companies these governments proliferate earning rather than spending and in their crime politics the core objectives are preventive rather than solution-oriented strategies.

Before describing these new articulations of managerialism in social service structures, I must stress some important issues regarding governmental aims. This study began with the hypothesis that different forms of control and sanctioning in the bureaucratic field are implemented with the purpose of high efficacy. Efficiency is generally defined as increased productivity, which is a problematic term in the field of social services, since the welfare system is supposed to refer to equal treatment of citizens and act on behalf of the population to protect individual rights and resources. To be able to recognise an increase in differentiation patterns related to practices guided by efficiency principles, we first need to understand the changing values behind social policies and the pragmatic guidelines of policy implications.

4.1 The new values in welfare management

As previously mentioned, neoliberal market mechanisms in the EU and the governmental responses to the growing mobility of citizens between different member states led to new businesslike structures in bureaucracy. Citizens' participation in the entrepreneurial governance structure creates shared authority and reduce the amount of power that is normally entrenched in government organs and thus allow citizens to become more influential in policy making. According to its proponents, the idea of increased citizen engagement would promote information sharing that is more transparent and efficient (Denhardt & Denhardt, 2000, p. 549). This privatisation has become the focus of strategic management through which citizens are defined as clients. It also uses innovative financial methods and creates competitive services, representing some of the reforms that Western governments have implemented in response to the New Public Service built on a management philosophy (Denhardt & Denhardt, 2000).

Accordingly, government agencies adopt practices that have been found useful in the private sector. The New Public Management philosophy takes this idea one step further, arguing that government should not only adopt the techniques of business administration, but adopt certain business values as well. This is often described as a form of public entrepreneurship or what Terry (1993, 1998) has called "neomanagerialism". These processes have taken place on several levels; key values of equality and solidarity in social policies have gradually been lost, laying the ground for social sorting practices.

As part of EU multi-level governance, supranational, sub-national governmental and non-governmental agencies negotiate over policy areas, causing contradictions in bureaucratic measures at different levels. According to Kaboolian (1998), bureaucratic structures increasingly simulate 'market-like arrangements such as competition within units of government and across government boundaries to the non-profit and for-profit sectors, performance bonuses and penalties (to) loosen the inefficient monopoly franchise of public agencies and public employees' (p. 190). This threatens to undermine democratic and constitutional values such as fairness, justice and representation. Above all, this arrangement system moves away from traditional modes of legitimising the public bureaucracy, such as procedural safeguards on administrative discretion, and toward 'trust in the market and private business methods . . . ideas . . . couched in the language of economic rationalism' (Kaboolian, 1998, p. 191). For instance, in Great Britain, the Conservative party imposed cuts on local authority costs and pushed them to shift their service provisions to contractors (Smith, 2010). These dysfunctions and the *social sorting* side effects of these measures are discussed in detail in the following chapter, as these are the key aspects of this study and have contributed to distrust, suspicion and criminalisation tendencies in local implementation.

This book aims to emphasise the role of this managerialist shifts that rely on digitalised normative services that cause harm and trigger illegal responses by social service clients.

Following this paradigm, the first managerial principle serves to homogenise every person who receives benefits and lives in a municipality, based on moralised dependency relations with authorities. These narratives enlarge the gap between "us" and "them", and juxtaposes the "hardworking taxpayer" and the "immoral scrounger". As White (2014) confirms:

> Those who work hard and pay taxes are constructed as having a superior ontology compared to those who do not work and receive benefits. Welfare benefits have been constructed definitively as a moral issue, which has served to construct those receiving benefits as morally inferior.
>
> (p. 3)

The second principle is strictly built on responsibilisation of the poor (Bauman, 1998). This involves a moral construction of work that implies that those who "choose" not to do their duties are "abnormal" and do not "deserve" support. The unemployed are constructed as the undeserving poor. These unrepresentative depictions of "welfare-guzzling layabouts" serve to denigrate welfare claimants and legitimise benefit cuts. Once the media and public discourse name benefit claimants as "scroungers", "skivers", "the feckless", "the idle", "cheats" and "social scum", negative associations arise.

The third and final principle is that the targeted groups are subject to discrimination. These three managerial principles and values have led local authorities to use different methods and tools in their administrative practices. These include the recently invented restrictions that will be described in the following UK case.

Recent public management, particularly its digitalised monitoring structure, has had significant impacts on the traditional organisational settlement of welfare provisions. This change has recently been coined "bureau-professionalism". As suggested earlier, this principle implies a shift in public professional organisations from public toward business values (Denhardt & Denhardt, 2000). These changes increase accountability procedures and bureaucratisation, limiting the focus of professional work to quantifiable and measurable outcomes (Diefenbach, 2009). In short, this conformism leads to more automatisation, online processes to submit a claim, new eligibility rules, less funding, more procedures and more tick boxes to standardise decisions about care planning and needs assessment.

Kirkpatrick summarised how recent developments have led to changes in the nature of professional work. Now more than ever, decision making is constrained by 'ever-increasing procedural instructions' (Postle, 2002, p. 343 cited in Kirkpatrick, 2006, p. 14). Service providers are facing high targets, more administration and intensified contact with clients, as well as competition with similar service provider branches. In addition, this form of bureau-professionalism requires the field of social services to focus more on collaborating with new types of stakeholders and professions (Van Berkel & Knies, 2013). As social services practices are subjected to 'proceduralisation and commodification of the social work labour processes, differences between practices have been increasing. Instead of performing well, many have become less effective than expected due to decentralised decision making' (Harris, 1998, p. 858, cited in Kirkpatrick, 2006).

As it will be proved by the following case studies, contracted social service providers in the UK need to be more cost efficient, and citizens need to be more responsible for their own role in the bureaucratic system. One of the major implications of welfare reform has been the cut of free aid in the UK for those who might rely on these services. Foreign client groups who were previously defined as vulnerable, like migrants or Romas, lost their special government-funded support as Roma support services at the local municipalities. Since the privatisation process sets competitive targets for local service providers, "unattractive" clients who might hinder the efficacy of these street-level bureaucrats now receive only limited information that would enable their claims. Frontline workers in these agencies have become responsible for promoting the employability and labour market participation of their clients, without much flexibility to consider individual conditions. These agencies' "core business" was the administration of income benefits, but this changed with the introduction of welfare-to-work or 'activation policies and programmes' (van Berkel & Knies, 2013, p. 4). The goal is simple: decrease benefit costs and increase clients' participation in the labour market. In other words, control and push.

After clients manage to get though the online application systems, they face other challenges. They have to deal with "sticks and carrots": they are sanctioned if they do not comply with the obligations related to social assistance, and they are rewarded with regular benefit payments if they cooperate, which usually means carrying out regular job search activities. The assessments that determine a client's compliance are not only impersonal due to the digitalisation of service provisions, but they are also restrictive toward foreigners who have extra limitations to participating in these bureaucratic channels, such as language barriers. Due to security procedures, mediation by friends is restricted; even interpreting is problematic when foreigners try to complete phone application procedures. When they call they need wait long till the call is answered. By control questions in order to prevent fraud, service provider restricts interpreters in giving suggestions or additional information for claimants. Although applicants are obliged to provide all kind of personal data, they are unable to access their own information registered at service providers' databases. However, when there is a miscommunication, or a claim is incomplete, the claimant is responsible for fixing it. Unfortunately, when a claimant needs to know which data or documents are missing, bureaucrats may not be transparent about the procedures, for fear of benefit fraud.

Clients were regularly receiving letters refusing their benefit claims with an argument that "The information provided does not match our (HMRC or JCP) records". When applicants phoned for additional information their requests were refused. Shortly, applicants are often not aware of the discrepancy between the data they provide, and the data collected by service providers about their circumstances. In the meantime, inspection of clients and assessments of their financial conditions are gradually increasing, with decreasing respect for privacy.

This example of surveillance and control in the UK is originated in the conception of the mixed welfare state that promotes participation in a market society and efficiency in bureaucratic mechanisms (Gilliom, 2001). Technological development enables an extended process of sorting, categorising and qualifying welfare recipients by checking and enhancing the information applicants provide. Judgements about qualifications for benefits, previously based on interviews or an occasional home visit, are now guided by information from a vast array of national law enforcement, property ownership, savings and court records. In his review of Gilliom, Munger emphasises that in this structure the clients are more directly subjected to the power of higher, more centralised, less flexible administration and screening methods. 'Technology increases control exercised through surveillance, for now the recipient and caseworker have far less space in which to negotiate the pre-emptive description of a recipient's identity presented by a database' (2003, p. 664).

These digitalised conformist systems not only screen claimants' data, but also define characteristics of groups, which could be used to invent restrictive legislations. As I illustrated in the beginning of this chapter, this entrepreneurial new bureaucracy is paired with the assumption that non-active foreign claimants might abuse access to cash-paid benefits and will move to host countries just to exploit them instead of contributing to the local economy. Surveillance methods and assessments are influenced by studies of this "welfare-magnet effect", "welfare tourism" or benefit temptation, which has led to targeted polices that reinforce dissimilarities between the "deserving" and "undeserving" poor. Because these programmes, like those of HMRC, are coded to treat foreign benefit claimants with specific traits as a suspect of freud, benefits are based on degrees of rectitude and submission to disciplinary measures intended to force recipients to work and to "responsibilise" their spending (see Rose, 1999).

4.2 The reality of welfare tourism

The welfare-magnet theory provides the key argument for digitalised social sorting mechanisms in social policies that advocate welfare restrictions for immigrants (Böcker & Havinga, 1998). Due to the perception of benefit tourism associated with unemployed newcomers, financial parameter becomes the core parameter of exclusion manifested in social policies. Borjas (1999) asserts that the choice of destination countries is mainly influenced by welfare provisions (Schulzek, 2012). However, coincidence, employment, security and social networks seem to be just as important in such a consideration. A contributing factor in the case of the Roma is the ethnic diversity in larger Western cities; it seems to provide a sense of invisibility and equality where Roma can avoid discrimination and harassment. Furthermore, other studies have argued that 'welfare generosity has an influence on immigration in the EU-15 – although this effect is considerably smaller than the effect of wage levels on migrants' choices of a destination country' (ICF GHK, 2013, p. 48). In addition, 'where some studies found evidence supporting the "welfare-magnet effect" hypothesis, the overall estimated effects are typically small or not statistically significant' (ICF GHK, 2013, p. 49).

Sociological research in Kent found no evidence of such instrumental motivation among these claimants (Clark & Campbell, 2000). Even if it were partially true, 'the underlying social and economic roots can nevertheless not be ignored' (Fenton & May, 2002, p. 68). The importance of local benefits in these movements was not irrelevant, but other factors remained mostly unstated in media coverage. As it has been explained before, the social and economic insecurity of CEE Roma in their home countries led to the migration – not the hope of temporary benefits, as it has been presented by the UK media. The motivation for the mobility of CEE Roma should be explained by their loss of ontological security, discrimination and economic deprivation in the new regime of Central European member states. Structural changes in the labour markets of post-transition countries led Roma migrants (as well as significant members of the national majority in their home countries) to try to find employment abroad (EU-LFS, 2008).[1]

Regardless of actual labour participation, UK state support for accessing welfare benefits has been increasingly restricted for newcomers from EU member states (Mcdonald, 2013). As one report concluded, the terms of eligibility for welfare support and the entitlement to access are shaped by the suspicion of illegitimacy. After the last EU expansion in 2014, tensions about the unintended effects of welfare attraction in their migration population have been increasing in Western states. Media outlets often fuel these welfare tourist stereotypes and offer oversimplified explanations for the migration and mobility of specific ethnic groups or nationalities. Many of these explanations are moralising and ignore the internal diversity of these groups and the historical and legal circumstances of their departures. In recent decades, the media has used two controversial approaches to explain Roma movements. On the one hand, the media has acknowledged the exclusion, hostility and racism against Roma in their home countries, describing them as victims who legitimately leave their homes to find a safe environment in other countries. On the other hand, as it was illustrated in the Introduction,

1 Work was by and large the main reason for EU nationals to move to the UK between 2002 and 2011. Figures from the Office of National Statistics (2011) show that 53% of migrants coming from other EU countries stated that they came to the UK for work (EU-LFS, 2008).

they describe Roma ethnic migrants as a financial threat, expressed in terms such as "Roma invasion". Their emigration is also framed as cultural opportunism in which Central European Roma are attracted toward Western states because of generous social services. These media narratives describe the Roma as "benefit tourists" or "welfare shoppers" who are unwilling to work and willing to abuse Directive 2004/38/EC, which guarantees the right to move and reside freely in the EU, to take advantage of eligibility differences between member states. Theories about chronic unemployment in Roma communities and their dependency on welfare as a cause of mobility can be seen as "zombie arguments": resistant to evidence and to social scientific efforts to eliminate them (MacDonald et al., 2014).

White (2014) describes such media discourses as key ideological tools the elite use to manipulate public views of welfare claimants, especially migrants. She argues that these messages legitimise political responses to welfare claimants and serve as 'propaganda to denigrate, exclude and stigmatise welfare claimants and cultivate animosity and a perception of "us" as being superior to "them"' (White, 2014, p. 3). These assumptions about 'welfare cheats' and 'dole scroungers' (Cohen, 2002, p. xviii) in the British treatment of welfare claimants as a socio-economic group have been used to offset them against the group of "hardworking taxpayers". This rigid polarisation of "benefit claimant" versus "hardworking taxpayer", which has been constructed for political ends, is oversimplified and stigmatising. The reality is much more fluid: some people who work and pay taxes also receive benefits, and some people move in and out of the labour market (White, 2014).

As will be shown in this chapter, austerity toward welfare claimants, used by managerialist bureaucracies as a key tool for welfare reforms, has been constructed to reduce costs and make foreign welfare claimants self-sustaining. While designing national policies for foreign welfare claimants is generally seen as a welfare-to-work strategy, these policies also serve as mechanisms of territorial control of different populations. Due to the lack of visa requirements, the surveillance practices and restrictive incentives of these welfare bureaucracies enable geopolitical reorganisation in the EU. However, these assessments and the way in which their incentives shape transnational mobility are deeply problematic.

This chapter aims to provide an overview of changes in social welfare services available for EU citizens in the UK. It will particularly focus on how migration and welfare are increasingly interwoven with criminalisation practices, and how the social division of welfare surveillance is applied in the managerialism of a national bureaucratic system. First, I will describe the reality of so-called welfare tourism by using an example of Roma mobility before the 2004 expansion of the EU. This case illustrates the development of the image of the "welfare tourist" and how this perspective changed the platform of migration control from border agencies to social services. I will present the rise of the welfare-migration-crime triangle, which shapes local and federal government administrations that aim to control the population inside national borders. Second, I will discuss specific bureaucratic approaches toward social rights regarding intra-European mobility. Third, I will describe recent EU legislation about welfare provisions and how national policies reject these incentives in the case of the UK. In the last decade, EU member states have adapted neoliberal principles related to welfare objectives. These new principles around social provisions have been changing the bureaucratic field into an entrepreneurial system, including the implementation of new methods for service providers. These restricted and broadly assessed services have created new structures for controlling and monitoring mobile groups. New restrictions, changes in eligibility and access to certain benefits, and sanctions will be reconstructed as the new social sorting of welfare in the UK.

4.3 Geopolitics through welfare regimes

In recent decades, welfare policy has taken a central place in immigration discourses, attracting the attention of academics and politicians across disciplines and party lines. Discussions about the harmonisation of European immigration policy among EU member states reinforce the general assumption that welfare is a pull-factor for immigration and a risk of poverty flow (Bank, 2000, p. 149). On the one hand, there is a discussion between member states about welfare eligibility based on citizens' different migration statuses; on the other hand, there is a discussion about the respective diversity related to eligibility for welfare services and the amount of benefits available in various EU member states. As Schulzek (2012) writes: 'In 1999, Jacques Chirac already noted that "the situation regarding welfare benefits is apt to break all the barriers that we could elevate against increases in immigration"' (p. 1). As a result, there are two major tendencies in European welfare policies: one is the general harmonisation of welfare regimes between different states and the other is a new welfare principle based on entrepreneurial governance. These inconsistencies resulted serious ambiguities between EU and local legislation policies to define welfare eligibility conditions and how to evaluate these by digitalised surveillance systems.

Real concerns about welfare policies started to arise after 2004, when citizens of A8 countries increasingly moved toward the West and began to use different governmental support programmes in their new host countries.

Harmonisation of social policies became an urgent issue with the introduction of the Treaty establishing a Constitution for Europe in 2004, which included 'the right to move and reside freely within the territory of all Member States'. That same year, EU Directive 2004/38/EC defined the right of EU citizens 'to reside in another member state for an initial period of three months'. This directive is supposed to regulate equal treatment regarding access to social assistance and the right of residence for non-active EU citizens other than jobseekers. Practically:

> Member States are free to regulate their own social security systems; however, for the past 50 years these systems have been subject to EU level coordination to ensure that people have social security coverage and do not lose rights when exercising their right to free movement in the EU. Regulation 883/2004, as amended by Regulation 465/2012, sought to modernise and simplify the rules on the coordination of social security systems at the EU level. It applies to certain branches of social security, ***but not to social assistance.***
>
> (ICF GHK, 2013, p. 1)

Shortly, member states have raised concerns about the entitlement which EU law gives to non-active EU migrants to claim access to health care and special non-contributory benefits in cash (ICF GHK, 2013, p. 7). Due to differentiation between human rights, social security and social assistance, several limitations were tagged in EU legislation. This has enabled different local interpretations and allowed individual member states to pass legislation that includes new control and selection mechanisms. Such welfare surveillance mechanisms operate to construct and categorise populations, and to unevenly inspect citizens in the seemingly routine processes of distributing services and resources (Gilliom, 2001).

Welfare providers need to deploy the power of surveillance to draw conclusions about recipients' behaviour, which requires detailed and intimate information about family and cohabitation, means of subsistence and personal needs. However, the introduction of computerised data aggregation has enormously increased the power exercised through surveillance in recent years, creating a new threat to individual autonomy (Munger, 2003, p. 661). These mechanisms are the central aspects of this study. Therefore, I define those cases of interaction where these counter-dynamics are manifested. In doing so, attention can be drawn to the unequal distribution of both burdens and benefits in the social relations of welfare, and to how clients are responding to it. As suggested earlier, the new policies are increasingly restrictive and redefine the methods and tools of social services to prevent service provision for undesired benefit claimants. These targeted restrictions are easy to follow on different levels of entitlement in the benefit system as well as in the bureaucratic management of service providers. These steps are introduced in the following section, based on cases from the UK.

These listed provisions are rapidly changing or even disappearing, such as with family credits or disability allowance. These descriptions should therefore be taken with caution as benefits are reconstructed or renamed regularly, even when changes take place gradually. For instance, Severe Disablement Allowance has been closed to new claims since 2001, but there are still thousands of recipients. And Income Support, which used to be one of the most important benefits, is going to be divided by transferring its functions to other benefits that have yet to be determined. These constant changes are difficult to follow, not just for clients, but also for bureaucrats who must try to apply and harmonise different legislations, claims and payments (Spicker, 2011). These changes also represent political guidelines implemented into policies: for instance, the harassment of newcomer benefit claimants and the subsequent restrictions of benefit rules are easily traceable to recent changes in welfare provisions. These changes have triggered new coping strategies for CEE migrants who are already settled in the UK.

First, I introduce the most recent changes that have had a serious impact on the living circumstances of EU transnational migrants. Then I reflect on the complexities that have increased due to these rapid legislative and managerialist shifts in social provisions. As part of this problem, I discuss the role of control in these monitoring procedures and how these selections and sanctions reshape the social division of welfare claimants.

4.4 Social sorting tools and restrictions

To become eligible for any government welfare provision in the United Kingdom, not only EU migrants but all EEA nationals have to meet certain special requirements that are not imposed on UK nationals. After a prospective foreign benefit claimant receives a National Insurance number based on their tenancy contract and bank account, he or she must also pass a National Habitual Residence (NHR) test.[2] The EU found this legislation to be discriminatory but, according to Prime Minister David Cameron, restrictive measures were necessary to stop 'rogue EU benefit claims' and the test was designed to 'stop people abusing Britain's benefit system' (Wintour, 2013). This approach was seen by some as an attempt "to rush through a block on EU migrants" access to benefits in response to the politically sensitive lifting of the restrictions on Romanians and Bulgarians working in the UK from 1 January 2014 (Rutledge, 2014a). This change in legislation radically affected EU migrants' access to benefits as jobseekers. These restrictions often had their intended effects on a national level, while simultaneously pushing those migrants toward other municipalities, where similar processes would be repeated with the same service providers. Although several social service databases are accessible from different boroughs, claimants experience differences in support from client managers and civil servants, which might impact the success of the claims.

After a foreigner passes the NHR test, different claims can be processed online. Although most of these claims belong to different government organs or to privatised services, entitlements are strongly interrelated and complex. Jobseeker's Allowance and Income Support are the most frequent benefit claims among immigrants from CEE, who often depend on irregular jobs from employment agencies that cannot provide them regular income.

These claims brought these foreign claimants, like any other UK claimant, in contact with Job Centre Plus (JCP) offices. Programmes such as 'Employment

2 This test was introduced in 1994 by the Tory government to limit the number of state handouts available to migrants. In order to apply for any government benefits, claimants first need to pass the test to prove that they are habitually resident in the Common Travel Area (the UK, the Channel Islands, the Isle of Man or the Republic of Ireland). They must also intend to remain in the UK for the time being and have actually resided there for an 'appreciable period'. That period was not originally fixed, so each case had to be decided on its facts. From 1 January 2014, based on a revised version of the test, entitlements cannot begin until the claimant has completed a three-month period of continuous residence within the Common Travel Area. EEA nationals who arrive in the UK to seek work are also subjected to this test to establish a link with the UK employment market.

The controversy of requirements centres on a second rule, called the "right to reside test", introduced by the Labour government in 2004 to prevent benefit tourism when the EU expanded to Eastern Europe. This rule states that economically inactive migrants, who are neither in work nor seeking work, must be self-sufficient if they want to live in the UK. They are banned from receiving Income Support, income-related Employment and Support Allowance, income-related Jobseeker's Allowance, pension credit, Housing Benefit or Child Benefit.

Zones' and 'Pathways to Work' were managed from these offices, sometimes by JCP. These offices regulated many aspects of unemployed people's lives by making job searching obligatory and sanctionable.

From 19 October 2012, all claimants applying for Jobseeker's Allowance are expected to look for work online, using the new Universal Jobmatch website, an online system accessible from a government portal and powered by Monster.com, a private company which also illustrates state-corporate relations in this neo-managerial welfare system. Jobseekers who do not possess the necessary computer skills are offered IT training. However, they often cannot even manage to arrange their online application to become JCP clients in the first place. Jobseekers are expected to spend 30 hours per week searching for jobs on top of the mandatory Work Programme, or to take part in community service.

Interaction with client managers is essential to the financial well-being of migrants, since other welfare implications depend on their JCP contract. Several barriers limit efficient communication between these offices and their clients. First, there is limited face-to-face contact and what little there is mostly consists of inspections of the claimants' situations and activities, but there is hardly any support of claimants. Second, many clients are not internet literate, so they cannot use online job search applications. This results in sanctions and further restrictions on their finances, which are controlled by case managers. Third, there is a high turnover among case managers and legislation changes frequently, so clients are often not up-to-date. Due to these issues, claimants' payments are often cut before they are able to understand that they are not fulfilling the obligations defined by JCP.

There is also a lack of transparency about case managers' activities, their targets and their system of sanctioning, which is often debated in the media. Both foreign claimants and UK nationals who are jobseekers feel like they are treated as criminals when their job search activity is tracked. If they do not appear to apply for enough vacancies, they can have their money halted. They are also sanctioned for voluntarily leaving work or refusing a notified vacancy: the first sanction period can be up to 13 weeks, the second up to 26 weeks and the third up to three years. This seriously impacts these families' housing situations due to the interrelationship between Housing Benefit and Jobseeker's Allowance (JSA) claims.

Transnational mobility of many migrants from CEE is defined by their access to resources in addition to their regular income from work. If they leave the country, they are losing their eligibility. The interdependency of additional benefits from welfare services plays a key role in their possibilities to settle down or to move to another borough, so I will give a short overview of these resources and how restricting access to them changes clients' mobility patterns.

Knowing the rules and administrative practices of the local eligibility system for welfare services plays a central role in claimants' decisions about intra-European mobility; not only because of its selective nature, but also because of its sanctions. In the case of the UK, after claimants from CEE have passed the NHR test, they are able to access various resources based on their position in the labour market. However, these are not regularly assessed. Therefore, if claimants leave the country and they keep receiving tax credits they might get into debts due to monthly overpayments. In addition, Housing Benefit claims, Jobseeker's Allowance, Employment and Support Allowance and Personal Independence Payment claims have implications for applicants' entitlement for council tax cuts, tax credit payments and housing benefits:[3] These eligibility rules and the structure of their

3 Housing Benefit is the most important financial support for welfare-dependent foreign citizens. It is a statutory instrument regulated by the Social Security Contributions and Benefits Act 1992 that reduces the level of rent payable by the tenant. It is only available to those who are liable to pay rent and have a permanent right to reside in the UK. Private tenants' benefit is paid to the claimant, who has the right to decide to whom payments are made (in some cases, to the landlord). The Department for Work and Pensions (DWP) pays local councils and administration grants, as well as various other cost factor adjustments to take into account the relative staff and accommodation costs.

Some elements of the subsidy claim are subject to penalty to encourage local authorities to control that element of expenditure. Overpayments of benefit are not fully funded in order to ensure that the local authority takes recovery actions where appropriate. Since the amount of Housing Benefit is the highest among all benefit payments, it has a major impact on the living condition of newcomers, particularly on their chances to settle down in the host society.

Jobseeker's Allowance (JSA) is a form of unemployment benefit for those who are actively seeking work. It is part of the security benefits system and is intended to cover living expenses while the claimant is out of work (during my fieldwork period in 2013 and 2014, it was £71 per week). It is administered by the Social Security Agency, an executive agency of the Department for Social Development. It is contribution-based or income-based; to be eligible for JSA, claimants must state that they are actively seeking work by filling in an agreement form and attending a New Jobseeker interview. They must also go to a JCP every two weeks to "sign on" (i.e. to certify that they are still actively seeking work). JSA claims are maintained by a legal computer system called JSAPS.

Employment and Support Allowance (ESA) is a state benefit introduced in 2008. It replaced Severe Disablement Allowance, later called Incapacity Benefit, which was paid in case of illness or disability. ESA can be either contributory or income-related. If a claimant meets National Insurance conditions, he or she can claim contributory ESA for up to one year (for the work-related activity component) or indefinitely (for the support component). Income-related ESA is subject to a means-test, but if claimants meet both sets of conditions, they can get contributory ESA topped up with income-related ESA.

Income Support is an income-related benefit in the UK for people with a low income who have less than £16,000 in savings. Claimants must be between 16 and state pension age, work fewer than 16 hours a week and have a reason why they are not actively seeking work (e.g. illness, disability or child care).

Tax credits involve payments from the central and local governments. Despite their name, tax credits should not be confused with tax credits linked to a person's tax bill. Unlike most other benefits, they are paid by Her Majesty's Revenue and Customs (HMRC). Two types of tax credit claims are important for migrants from CEE:

- Child tax credits (Guardian's Allowance or Carer's Allowance), available on top of Child Benefit for families with children that have an income below £32,200. The tax credit is "non-wasteable" (i.e. it is paid whether or not the family has a net tax liability) and is paid in or out of work. Higher rates are paid for disabled children.
- Working tax credit, for those who work and have a low income. It is part of the current system of refundable (or non-wasteable) tax credits introduced in April 2003 and is a means-tested benefit.

Personal Independence Payment (PIP) is a welfare benefit to help with costs caused by a health condition or disability. It is non-means tested, non-contributory and can be paid whether the recipient is employed or not. PIP is based upon the effects of a condition on a

implementation have major impacts on the lives of newcomers, who must try to stay up-to-date with legislative changes in order to keep their welfare eligibility.

4.5 Trapped in a loop – welfare restrictions as mobility control

As part of the political narratives of the Conservatives under the Prime Ministership of David Cameron, social benefits have been defined as a dangerous attractant for CEE migrants, who are portrayed as lazy, opportunistic free riders who live off the backs of hardworking UK taxpayers. These narratives have resulted in tougher NHR tests, less eligibility, stronger penalties for fraud (or error) and extensive assessments or investigations of data provided by claimants.

The first serious wave of restrictions started with the Welfare Reform Act of 2012. This act, enacted on 8 March 2012, changed the British social security system to restrict 'access to welfare benefits for new EU migrants including a six-month statutory habitual residency for benefits paid to jobseekers' (Rutledge, 2014a). Among the provisions of the act that came into force on 1 April 2013 were key changes related to accessing Housing Benefit, the Social Fund, child support, JSA, PIP and other benefits for CEE foreign nationals. The act abolished the discretionary social fund, community care grants and crisis loans. Instead, funding was given to local authorities to provide such assistance in their regions. Most of the measures implemented placed more responsibility on local authorities and pushed them toward intense monitoring of their clients. Local councils are already struggling with financial cut that makes them less willing to provide more payments for benefit claimants. In order to understand the restrictive implications of these social policies it should be considered how the most pervasive changes in Attendance Allowance and as a consequence of the The benefit cap or the so called 'bedroom tax' and later the introduction of Universal Credit influence the lives of EU transnational migrants.[4]

person. PIP was introduced in 2013 by the Welfare Reform Act 2012. It replaced the Disability Living Allowance as of 8 April 2013 for people aged 16 to 64 years and was phased in over the following years.

Attendance Allowance is a non-contributory social security benefit paid to disabled people over 65 years that was introduced in the National Insurance Act 1970. A claimant must show that they need help in connection with their bodily functions or need continual supervision. At night, supervision has to involve someone being awake to watch over the claimant. Claimants must have met the conditions for at least six months before they are entitled to the allowance, unless they are terminally ill.

4 The benefit cap was the first serious restriction. It was gradually introduced as a limit to the total amount of money available to social security claimants. The cap is set at the average (median) net earnings for a working household (e.g. total benefits paid to a single person may not now exceed £350 per week; the maximum available to families (single parents and couples with children) is £500 per week). The benefits limited by this new cap include most of those described in the previous paragraphs. It was strongly criticised by the national Housing Federation for its unintended side effects, which will be described in the next chapter.

The Under-occupancy penalty, referred to by its opponents as a "bedroom tax" or "spare room subsidy", reduces Housing Benefit by 14% for one extra room and by 25% for two or more extra bedrooms if claimants have too much living space. This new Housing Benefit criteria considers the number of rooms and number of people occupying a property and restricts

Iain Duncan Smith, the Work and Pension Secretary who sponsored the Welfare Reform Act 2012, argued that the new benefits system would encourage people to work and reduce social benefit costs (BBC, 2013a). His statement in an interview that it was possible to live on £53 per week attracted considerable media attention. He criticised the older system of disability benefits, which did not contain systematic checks to assess whether the claimant's condition had improved or worsened. Controversially, many non-governmental organisations raised their voices about the dangers of recently privatised screenings and assessment, as the criteria were flawed, caused undue hardship to disabled people and were too strongly focused on cutting welfare budgets (BBC, 2013b).

Private contractor Atos Health Care, who performed work capability assessments, was accused of unreasonably cutting the benefits of disabled clients, some of whom were driven to suicide by their experience. The report[5] notes that 'DWP currently investigates all deaths of benefit claimants "where suicide is

---

payment for the property they are renting. If it is estimated that there are too many rooms in a rented dwelling for the number of occupants, housing benefits are drastically reduced. The rule applies to tenants in local authority (council) and Housing Association accommodation, which stipulates that all children under 10 years of age are expected to share a room; children under 16 of the same gender are expected to share; and carers of disabled tenants who need to stay overnight are permitted to have one extra bedroom.

Universal Credit is meant to replace six of the main means-tested benefits and tax credits – JSA, Housing Benefit, Working Tax Credit, Child Tax Credit, ESA and Income Support – with a single monthly conditional means-tested payment for working people on a low income and the unemployed (Department for Work and Pensions, 2010). Its stated aims are to increase the incentive to work by making it easier for people who have temporary, low-paid work to move in and out of employment without losing benefits, and to simplify the benefits system by bringing together several benefits into a single payment. Due to complications in implementation, it has not replaced existing benefit payments.

Council Tax Benefit was replaced by a new system called Council Tax Support, offered under the Universal Credit scheme. Prior to this change, benefits, discounts, exemptions and reductions were paid by the central government to support claimants unable to pay council tax. Regulations, responsibility for assessment of claims and payments have now been shifted to local authorities paid by the central government, but the budget available has been reduced by 10%, requiring councils to limit support payments.

The Personal Independence Payment gradually replaced the Disability Living Allowance. An initial pilot began in selected areas of northwest and northeast England in April 2013, followed by a full roll-out across Great Britain through October 2015. Claimants are required to undergo assessments to prove their eligibility for the benefit. The tests must be passed three months prior to the claim and claimants must be able to satisfy the requirements of the test for a period of at least nine months after their claim. Payments are varied according to the severity of disability as determined by the tests and relate to the claimant's ability to carry out daily living activities and their level of mobility. Claimants are also required to undergo periodic reassessments to ensure ongoing eligibility for the benefit; depending on the type of disability, a person may be given a short award of up to two years or a longer PIP award, which lasts for up to five or 10 years. Responsibility for the tests has been outsourced by the DWP to private companies, like Atos Health care.

5 https://ico.org.uk/media/action-weve-taken/decision-notices/2015/1424160/fs_50557638.pdf

associated with DWP activity", and in other cases where the death of a vulnerable benefit claimant is brought to its attention, through a system of internal "peer reviews"'.

Since February 2012, DWP has carried out 49 peer reviews following the death of a benefit claimant. Although these cuts affected all welfare claimants in the UK, new additional measures explicitly targeted newcomers who might rely on state benefits.

An amendment to the Immigration (European Economic Area) Regulations 2006 was passed in 2013. Rutledge (2014a) explains that it:

> introduces a 6 month statutory presumption for Jobseeker's Allowance. The Regulations make changes with respect to the definitions of 'jobseeker' and "worker" in the 2006 Regulations to the effect that:
>
> > EEA nationals seeking to reside in the UK while looking for work must provide, from the outset, evidence that they are seeking work and have a genuine chance of being engaged;
> >
> > EEA nationals seeking to enjoy the status of 'retained worker' – i.e. a worker who is involuntarily employed – must provide, from the outset, evidence that they are seeking employment and have a genuine chance of being engaged; and
> >
> > EEA nationals may not enjoy the status of jobseeker or retained worker for longer than six months unless they provide 'compelling evidence' that they have a genuine chance of being engaged;
> >
> > There will be an absolute limit of six months for the retention of worker status for an EEA national who is a retained worker and who had worked for less than 12 months before becoming involuntarily unemployed.

In January 2014, the UK government introduced a number of measures aimed at restricting EEA migrants' access to income-based Jobseeker's Allowance (Income-Based) or JSA(IB). A key change was the introduction of a statutory presumption that entitlement to JSA(IB) would be limited to a three-month period unless the jobseeker could pass a Genuine Prospect of Work (GPoW) assessment (Rutledge, 2014b). As Rutledge (2014b) notes, the report laying out these measures:

> arose from the Committee's consideration of the Housing Benefit (Habitual Residence) Amendment Regulations 2014, SI 2014/539, which, from 1 April 2014 onwards, had the effect of removing access to Housing Benefit for EEA jobseekers who have a right to reside solely as jobseekers who are in receipt of income-based Jobseeker's Allowance.

Rutledge (2014b) concludes that 'Member States should not use the right to reside condition as a blanket rule which automatically excludes EU citizens who are not economically active at the time they apply for social assistance'. However, Rutledge (2014b) notes that:

> The Government wishes to deter EEA migrants from coming to the UK if they do not have a firm offer of or realistic chance of securing work. Those who come to the UK to look for work should ensure that they have sufficient resources to pay for their accommodation needs, as well as other support that they or their family may need while here. The best option for those EEA migrants who are unable to find work, who lack savings or support networks and who are at real risk of ending up destitute is to return home.

According to the research findings, claimants did not give up that easily and tried to find their way between changes and restrictions.

Complexities of welfare applications are twofold: (1) getting benefits is confusing in the first place and (2) overlapping benefits makes it even harder to become elegible for any UK state support. Yet, these challenges are also breeding ground of changes, expectations, misunderstandings and creativity in many application cases. Because of this system, immigrants who normally are not trying to "take advantage" of the system end up "abusing" these provisions because that is what complex benefit claim process "teaches" them. In other words, the UK has built a neomanagerial digitalised welfare system that essentially forces migrants to engage in behaviours they are trying to prevent in the first place.

Although ideas about conformity and harmonisation form interrelated links between different benefits, the complexity of the benefit system teaches clients how to increase their income depending on their registered circumstances. As described in Chapters 7 and 8, clients try to learn the preconditions of different entitlements and assessment strategies of their claims. When there is an error in their application process, they are able to trace the mistakes and weaknesses of particular structures. In addition to interrelationships between claims, clients learn the rules of complex benefits (like JSA or Income Support) and others that consist of several benefits bundled together. The real challenge starts with the interaction of multiple overlapping benefits.

In his article titled *Five Types of Complexity*, Spicker (2005) describes a lack of balance between agencies, constantly changing guidelines and rules developed for benefits. Some rules are intrinsic, like those based on a points-based scheme that help establish who meets certain criteria. There are also two main classes of additional imposed rules: conditional and administrative. There are various sorts of conditional rules: 'some benefits are conditioned morally: rules about voluntary employment and availability for work are illustrative' (Spicker, 2005, p. 3). Administrative rules are concerned with operations like complexities caused by management procedures, because 'the landscape of the benefits system changes like the sands of the desert' (Spicker, 2005, p. 3). The restructuring of local offices, agencification, computerisation, the new public sector management, and radical changes in the division of labour between different agencies are leading to a loss of expertise in the delivery of specific benefits.

Spicker (2005) distinguishes between three changes in administrative procedure that contribute to the loss of expertise. The first is computerisation; an obsessive pursuit of comprehensive technological solutions has failed since these programmes cannot cope with the complexity of the operations required. The second is file management; because these programmes cannot store paper copies, there always have to be two files and files also migrate between different offices (Spicker, 2005, p. 4). In addition, the files are not accessible to everyone. The third is the growing division of labour between the offices (e.g. a local office, a regional office and the national agency), leading to misunderstandings about responsibilities for particular parts of processing a case.

Processing time and changes to individual circumstances are the biggest challenges, since clients move, age and divorce and the benefits system rests on the assumption that people know their situation and will report it. This is where clients are able to abuse or be victimised by the interaction with different service providers (or lack thereof) and can potentially be subject to sanctions. The growth of short-term contracts, casual and intermittent patterns of work, changing physical conditions and dependency like disability has increased uncertainty and has made survey estimates unreliable. Because child care is so often "shared", people are not sure when they are responsible for it. Income and marital status fluctuates; consequently, the benefits offices have to recalculate and attribute it to different time periods. Overpayments are actively tracked without regard to claimants' ability to pay, which increase fear and anger in clients who are accused of fraud. Long-term payments are the most efficient when they are independent from other benefits and based on stable circumstances, like State Pension and Child Benefit. However, disputes about priority for claims and the Revenue's excessive caution about the possibility of duplicate claims are still causing problems and increasing distrust on both sides (Spicker, 2005, pp. 3–5).

As suggested in the previous paragraphs, newcomers have to prove that they are able to cope with their own circumstances to become entitled to a welfare provision in the UK. If migrants can provide compelling evidence that they have prospect of legal work, a short extension to income-based JSA might be considered. If not, their income-based JSA claim will stop and they will automatically lose the rights for housing benefits. It is unclear exactly how many EEA jobseekers are affected by these new guidelines, as the UK's benefit payment systems do not systematically record the nationality of benefit claimants (ibid.).

So there is a contradiction: the only people who might become entitled and supported are those who are almost self-sustaining and probably will not need structural support. In addition, the percentage of newcomers who want to claim JSA compared to the percentage of UK citizens is unknown but, according to these preconditions, no foreign EU citizen should rely on benefits in the UK in the first place. Even if migrants try to claim support, the Nationality Immigration and Asylum Act 2002 limits their support provided under section 17 of the Children Act. As local authorities are increasingly overloaded with time-consuming assessments and complex matters that take up their staff and resources, there is less time and fewer human resources to provide legal aid for foreign claimants

(Rutledge, 2015). What is left for newcomers wishing to complete a claim is an informal exchange of knowledge, NGOs or trial and error.

In short, recent legal approaches and their impacts increase the dangers of unfair treatment through methods of social sorting. This top-down pressure makes central authorities control practitioners by shaping the discretionary power of civil servants to achieve better outcomes. As Diller (2000) warns us:

> This channelling takes place through a variety of means, including performance-based evaluation systems and efforts to redefine the institutional culture of welfare offices. These techniques are part of a broad trend in public administration that seeks to make government agencies function like entrepreneurial organizations. This new model raises serious questions of public accountability. In the new system of welfare administration, critical policy chokes are reflected in incentive and evaluation systems rather titan formal rules. As policy decisions are made in ways that are less visible, there are fewer opportunities for public input. Moreover, in the new regime the efficacy of administrative hearings as a means of holding agencies accountable to recipients is diminished.
>
> (p. 1121)

Due to a lack of public accountability, benefit claimants become suspects of crimes and become moral hazards to the welfare industry – hunted down like figures on the chessboard. There are generally two ways public institutions implement these absolutist values: by sanctioning and monitoring.

4.6 Criminalised by welfare – perceptions of welfare fraud

As part of this target-oriented bureau-professionalism, hostility toward recipients is intensified during efforts to shrink welfare rolls through fraud persecutions (Kohler-Hausmann, 2007, p. 333). This suspicion-based service system extends monitoring strategies that might harm the privacy of clients. Consequently, it has a major impact as a punitive state policy in directing public antagonism toward specific target groups such as benefit claimants.

Over the past 20 to 30 years, a preoccupation with benefit fraud has become a distinctive characteristic of governments in Britain (Dean, 1998; de Parle, 2004). Cruikshank (1999) argues that it is important to understand the development of welfare fraud administration over this period as a system established to discipline the welfare system rather than the recipients per se (Kohler-Hausmann, 2007).

Fraud investigations and sanctions have always been a part of welfare administration. From the 1970s, the penal and welfare systems intertwined to create new political, legal and technological means of shrivelling and disciplining welfare recipients. Anti-fraud initiatives are embedded in the long history of welfare bureaucracies' struggles to limit costs while policing racial, gender and class hierarchies (Kohler-Hausmann, 2007, p. 332). Law enforcement agencies have taken on new responsibilities for identifying and penalising welfare fraud. The increased monitoring of welfare recipients hardened claimants' marginalised position in society due to its unintended side effects, such as homelessness.

> Relentless media attention about welfare fraud convictions and indictments tangibly linked criminality to what had been a more elusive, moral stigma against [the] poor. The spectacle of the actual indictments framed welfare recipients as dishonest criminals, eclipsing their status as mothers and citizens.
> (Kohler-Hausmann, 2007, p. 331)

Particularly ethnic minorities have been objects of suspicion and intense scrutiny of their financial and moral worthiness.

Recently, sanctions applied by Job Centre Plus on benefit claimants raised new dilemmas about the real function of these measures and the extent of harm they might cause, as they might cause serious financial problems for claimants. The most problematic issue is the restriction on JSA, because it might affect other benefit payments to clients, causing a domino effect in different benefits. The problematic aspect is the application of sanctions by case managers. Many sanctions are based on administrative errors, like sending letters to the wrong address.

For instance, JSA claim cases in which clients were immediately sanctioned for not having the right ink to fill in an application, or for missing appointments due to sickness. They experienced this as condemnation instead of support. The *Guardian* (2015)[6] also listed several cases of sanctions for "trivial reasons" or due to DWP's "administrative errors". They gave examples of hospitalised clients who were unable to appear at the JCP office due to their own sickness or caring for a sick partner, or clients who missed their job centre appointments because of an actual job interview. In one case, a diabetic client was found dead because he was not able to afford to keep his insulin properly refrigerated. This case led to a parliamentary select committee investigation of sanctions (Wintour, 2014).

Oakley's (2014) independent review of the operation of JSA sanctions touched upon several barriers defined by respondents in this study, notably the increase in ESA sanctioning since 2013 and the lack of appropriate, fair and proportionate sanctions. The increase since 2013 in the number and proportion of ESA claimants who were sanctioned, is related to "claimants" failure to participate in work-related activity – i.e. predominantly non-attendance at mandatory Work Programme appointments. As several media reports suggested, this increase partly resulted from the pressure case managers dealt with regarding their targets, and also because of increasing errors due to fast changes in policies and restrictions of specific groups. Transparency in sanctioning clients was one of the major problems (Oakley, 2014).

6 https://www.theguardian.com/society/2015/mar/24/benefit-sanctions-trivial-breaches-and-administrative-errors

The government rejected the recommendations, although there was a staggering amount of evidence concerning approaches of some individual Job Centres, especially about whether targets for sanctions exist (Oakley, 2014). As Dame Anne Begg MP, Chair of the Work and Pensions Committee, said:

> Benefit sanctions are controversial because they withhold subsistence-level benefits from people who may have little or no other income. We agree that benefit conditionality is necessary, but it is essential that policy is based on clear evidence of what works in terms of encouraging people to take up the support which is available to help them get back into work. The policy must then be applied fairly and proportionately. The system must also be capable of identifying and protecting vulnerable people, including those with mental health problems and learning disabilities. And it should avoid causing severe financial hardship. The system as currently applied does not always achieve this.
>
> (Oakley, 2014, p. 9)

As the following chapter illustrates, the hardships of social sorting have their questionable advantages too. Claimants learn to control these agencies, include their expectations into their performance and use those systematic dysfunctions that enable additional claims for benefits. They also pit different agencies against each other and employ experiences of others with particular case managers. However, problems also arise because clients are often unaware of the application process or about additional possibilities like hardship payment. Clients then tend to hide information that can be essential for new claims or changing circumstances, or they are put off from applying at all because of the difficulty in understanding the system (Commons Select Committee, 2015). Due to technical developments, there is a growing awareness about the strategies of clients who are successfully navigating the system but who are defined as underserving EEA claimants. Therefore, new inspections are introduced that harden the social division of welfare-dependent groups along the lines of gender, ethnicity and citizenship.

4.7 Conclusion – differential surveillance treatment or the digital poorhouse

As it has been argued in this chapter, with the securitisation of intra-European migration, control measures are extended into the field of social service provisions and with the growing privatisation of public sector activities new values and mechanisms are introduced through welfare services. On the one hand security has become defined in terms of financial dependency, and on the other hand governmental services turned into a poverty-management industry, adapting efficiency-oriented strategies and competitive values of the business sector.

These values define foreign welfare claimants as social economic threat that should be eliminated. Consequently, welfare-dependent newcomers become targeted by extra control measures and welfare restrictions as geopolitical technologies in order to make the financially dependent outsiders move on.

By including privatised services providers into the management of the poor and enabling new technologies for monitoring and profiling applicants, social benefit provisions turned into new mechanisms of population control and provided a new platform for social sorting. According to the Deleuzian surveillance assemblage we can trace the dynamics of the interrelation between migration policies implemented through financial screening of a business like public sector and adaptive applicants. By focusing on the "viewer society" which explicates the dialectical interaction of panoptical (top down) and synoptical (bottom up) processes transmitted largely through the media and professionals, it can be demonstrated 'how a complete understanding of contemporary surveillance systems must take seriously the social and cultural forces which give rise to, and sustain, assemblages' (Hier, 2002, p. 400).

However, this process is more complex then it seems. As Hier argues,

> when surveillance technologies began to facilitate the monitoring of a wider population base this has been interpreted as a shift in the cultural character of surveillance with its concomitant leveling of hierarchies. In an effort to account for the more fundamental forces and desires which give rise to, and sustain, surveillant assemblages, the functioning of a dialectic embedded in many surveillance practices is revealed in the present analysis to contribute to a polarisation effect involving the simultaneous levelling and solidification of hierarchies. The impetus, however, is not located in powerful social actors or elite bodies. Rather, it is purported that considerable foundational support derives from popular social grievances, various antagonisms directed at a variety of socially constituted risk groups from below, which come to secondarily culminate in the intensification of top-down regimes of surveillance.
>
> (2002, p. 401)

Shortly, in such a dialectic process different stakeholders shape the parameters of selection by leading the public discourse associating crime with financial dependence in interplay with cultural references.

'Surveillance programs were aimed at ferreting out and eliminating fraud in its welfare programs rather than ferreting out' (Gilliom, 2001, pp. 127–128) and assisting any vulnerable poor. However, recent restrictions and selections – in contradiction to welfare incentives – highlight the uneven distribution of burdens and benefits in the social division of welfare surveillance. As Henman and Marston (2008) write:

> Some contracts of benefit claimants offer forms of regulated freedom for those receiving payments, while others are administered with excessive interference. Such interference, whether it takes the form of restraint, state-sanctioned surveillance or coercion is morally questionable when it is applied to one part of the population but not another.
>
> (p. 194)

Distribution of what we call "welfare surveillance" is not new: heightened surveillance of the poor has been well documented (e.g. Fox Piven & Cloward, 1971).

Priorities in the risk society not only define the threat, but also the worth, of particular individuals, placing them into a new type of social division based on surveillance practices that measure economic values. Ramage (2008) notes:

> Statistical surveys are analysed to provide an outline of people with an above average risk of incorrect payment, with other words, risk of fraud. The computer selects clients with these characteristics and regional office staff is asked to review these. All results are recorded in the computer system, so the Department of social security can increase its knowledge of the characteristics of clients receiving incorrect payments.
>
> (p. 213)

This means that there is regular improvement in the targeting of clients who are most likely to be incorrectly paid (DSS, 1987, p. 24). Note that such risk-based surveillance targets people on the basis of predicted – not actual – behaviour. It is expected that with the increasing levels of computer power, data capture and data mining practices, such differentiated surveillance will continue to intensify (Gandy, 1993).

While considerable attention has been paid to the questions of privacy rights and data protection, it should be clear from the presentation of these social sorting mechanisms that adopting such a framework as the sole public policy response to surveillance is limited because it fails to engage with relations of power and authority that pervade the social relations of welfare. Indeed, the privacy paradigm overlooks the capacity of various sectors of society to repel practices of surveillance or configure them to their own benefit, while the personal realities of other sectors of society are investigated in ever-greater intensity.

Henman and Marston (2008) note that a social policy perspective on welfare surveillance 'interrogates the ways in which surveillance mechanisms operate to construct and categorise populations, to inequitably scrutinise citizens in the seemingly routine and mundane processes of distributing services and resources' (p. 187). In doing so, we can draw attention to the unequal distribution of benefits by following claimants in application and control processes.

This chapter gave a detailed overview of how welfare provisions are changing in values and practices and the extent to which local social services are included in the selection and control of newcomers in the UK. It discussed how different restrictions have been implemented for accessing benefits, and how managerialism has changed the tools and methods of service providers in their interactions with their claimants. Of course, these measures are manifested in interactions with claimants who are learning the values and tools of these services and who anticipate the changing incentives of local authorities.

Roma newcomers are subjected to suspicion, control and sanctions for several reasons. Newcomers who are unable to prove their labour history, who are stigmatised culturally as non-productive and who are framed in the political discourse as welfare dependent, poor and uneducated, are representing the parameters of the financially threatening population defined in profiling mechanisms of social security restrictions. Although Roma are not associated with benefit fraud, but with opportunism, by targeted sorting mechanisms, they get excluded from basic service provisions. Although these profiling mechanisms are not constructed in cultural or ethnic terms, Roma applicants compare these exclusionary mechanisms with their previous experiences of institutional racism and justify several coping strategies that eliminate such social sorting measures.

In the following chapter it will be discussed how parameters of such profiles are constructed and how different stakeholders contribute to the transmission of ethnic frames in a transnational context.

5 Mediators, protectors and pathfinders – invisible players in mobility approaches

When Roma mobility and the use of social services are discussed, it is often framed as a direct interaction between migrants and local bureaucrats. However, there is growing criticism of the role of actors directly or indirectly bridging these interactions and reinforcing particular stereotypes, as well as changing local perceptions of ethnic migrants. Although these cultural transmissions are mostly well meant, many emphasise prejudices that might have legal implications for local bureaucratic practices and authomatised application systems. Although the Roma themselves are generally blamed for their marginal position, it has hardly ever considered how stigmatising assumptions have lined the mobility path of Roma migrants. In recent decades, several reports have been discussed the failure of Roma inclusion in Europe. Although there have been successes (Simandi, 2015), the focus is mainly on the poor results of human rights campaigns, EU integration projects and NGO activities, e.g. the national integration strategies, the Roma Decade programme or academic publications that have contributed to the criminalisation and evacuation of many Roma migrants (Sobotka & Vermeersch, 2012; Spidla, 2009; Themelis, 2009).

With the Europeanisation of Roma integration politics, millions of euros have been invested in local, regional, national and transnational Roma projects at various bureaucratic levels. The results not only signify the structural inefficiency of these interventions, they also emphasise the counterproductive, self-supporting projects that benefit from the marginal position of the targeted group, while sustaining their marginal position and negative image. Based on my fieldwork findings and previous literature studies, I analyse the role and impact of intermediaries involved with, working for or writing about Roma migrants. There are two major levels of interaction, with bridging actors actively involved in the relations between of Roma migrants' and local authorities. Advocacy workers, NGOs, interpreters, community representatives and legal advisors personally act on behalf of migrants in their daily lives. At a more abstract level, there are those who indirectly shape welfare policies and frame general ideas about Roma ethnicity. They can be differentiated here by their roles as policymakers at the EU level, academics and international activists. These bridging actors geographically transmit structural connotations about the Roma as a cultural, economic and political construct defined by ethnicised features. This chapter demonstrates how these actors shape our ideas about the Roma minority and shows the recent implications of these narratives in the host society. I first discuss the role of those who indirectly frame the interaction and recognition of the Roma in the network of welfare provision and then go on to the role of academics and professionals. I reflect on the challenging position of Roma activists and how they impact the discussion of Roma exclusion. This chapter closes with the role of language interpreters, which is analysed regarding ethnic framing in welfare bureaucracies.

5.1 Constructing belonging – framing the Roma with margins

To understand the relationships between welfare policies and the attitudes of service providers and bridging actors, we need to see how the framing of Roma ethnicity developed in the last few years and led to special attention and targeted support for ethnic Roma in the EU member states. Most social science studies that use the concept of framing drive their definition from the writings of Erving Goffman (Goffman, 1974). He uses the term "primary framework" to refer to what he calls a 'conceptual structure that organises interpretation, or a "mental set" to enable people to understand and construct social events' (p. 22).

Goffman's concept provides an important source of inspiration for scholars who study social movements (McAdam et al., 1996). 'Frames not only serve an interpretative function, they are often promoted with a specific intention, as in the case of Roma ethnicity. Activists use these frames to mobilise potential adherents and constituents, to gathner bystander support, and to demobilise antagonists' (Vermeersch, 2003, p. 885).

As is noted in the following section, the promotion of their type of framing had a major impact on recent assumptions regarding Roma migrants moving to the West. Social movement scholars have been more interested in framing, as the way stakeholders 'disseminate their understanding of social reality in order to appeal to a constituency' (ibid., p. 42). However, these frames are not always beneficial for the group in question. Several studies have been carried out on individual control over framing processes that analyse the role of the actors like civil society, and how they assign meaning to social reality and promote a certain understanding of reality. 'These actors mobilise specific narratives as conscious strategic efforts by groups of people to fashion a shared understanding of the world and of themselves that legitimate and motivate collective action' (McAdam et al., 1996, p. 6). In the case of the Roma, and their vast diversity and fragmentation, these narratives are not appreciated if people cannot identify with these realities. In addition, these framings do not take place in a vacuum, but 'in negotiation with complex, multi-organizational, multi-institutional arenas in which they take place' (Vermeersch, 2003, p. 885). Considering these processes of conscious framing of the Roma in the European context, we need to understand how recent Roma ethnic categories have been formed and implemented by representatives in the political arena.

The problem starts with the politicised and racialised academic definition of Roma ethnicity emphasised in victimising narratives. These static notions are frequently employed by activists and civil societies, stressing the marginal socio-economic position of the people seen as the Roma. Although it is important to acknowledge that these problems are real and definitely relevant to greater recognition of discrimination issues in Europe, it is counter-effective in integrative processes due to its emphasis on the otherness of Roma migrants. As I note in the previous chapter, when decisions about the eligibility and distribution of welfare are defined, access to governmental support is based on the social construction of groups in need, not only in the host state but also in the sending countries. When these definitions include ethnic connotations linked to economic deprivation, the references are now included in the welfare construction of deserving citizens in the geopolitical control strategies. In short, policymaking uses connotations produced by academics and non-governmental actors who are mapping the situation of marginal groups and their cultural, social and economic characteristics.

In the case of Roma mobility, these narratives now interrelate with top-down narratives, stressing the excluded and marginalised position of Roma in the European Union. As is noted earlier, in a process of liberalisation and democratisation after the fall of communism, the Roma were granted the right to participate in public and political life as an ethnic minority. 'Responding to economic insufficiency and aware of the danger of being scapegoated by the majority population, new political Romani elites and non-governmental organisations emerged. They raised the Romani issue and put forward cultural, social and political demands and attempted to mobilise Romani communities' (Novoselsky, 2015, Chapter 2). In short, a new European Roma Policy developed. Although the risks and negative side effects of ethnicisation are regularly debated in the literature, recent political voices keep emphasising the marginalised situation of the Roma, reproducing existing narratives on a lack of self-sustainment that lead to direct implications in welfare measures. It is thus unavoidable to include a discussion on the political framing of Roma identity to understand how it shapes interactions between Roma migrants and welfare service providers in London (Nacu, 2012).

Roma political advocacy and self-representation become controversial in the last decennia. Roma advocacy tries to claim more attention for the structural exclusion of the Roma by political representatives who are mostly not Roma, but at the same time, many Roma distance themselves from Roma politics because they think these ethnic frames contribute to their daily exclusion. Hemelsoet and Van Pelt have recently criticised how the "ethnicisation" of Roma identity in policy measures influences the way mediators like academics and activists contribute to the construction of Roma identity and how the use of these connotations (Hemelsoet & Van Pelt, 2015, p. 148) reinforces stigmatisation schemes. As my respondents have also confirmed, Roma identity is always in the foreground throughout their contacts with public institutions and determines their daily interactions. The Roma are subjected to these notions and try to use them in their own narratives to turn the situation to their advantage. This process, of course, is thus not unidirectional. Beyond the question of how a constructed ethnic identity shapes the politics of Roma migration, there is the issue of how

Roma self-definitions the may in turn be meaningful for a different conception of policy. In order to see how the Roma define their own attribution of their identity and how it is defined by other professionals, we need to understand the fringes between them and challenge the recent socially constructed framework (Hemelsoet & Van Pelt, 2015 p. 150). This process starts in the European discourse about the Roma. As an illustration, we can see how in European parliamentary presentations, marginalised and victimised aspects are stressed in references to the Roma in their home countries:

> I've seen mothers who come to me crying asking me to help them because they have not been issued a health insurance card, which is why they had to give birth outdoors which resulted in their newborn child dying.
>
> - I've seen mothers leaving their children crying because there was no work or social aid and they had to leave and go begging in other countries to get food for their children.
> - I've seen families where the father and grandchild were shot dead by neo-Nazis.
> - I've seen Roma houses burned down by extremists.
> - I've seen youngsters who have been beaten by their fellow citizens just because they were "gypsies".
> - I've seen teenagers living in urban sewage systems because they had no other place to live. (Vuolasranta, 2015).

A common denominator in these political narratives is the conviction that the Roma face a set of problems that differ considerably from those faced by the majority population (i.e. spatial segregation, discrimination, low educational level and inter-generational poverty) (Sigona & Vermeersch, 2012). As Kostka explains, 'it is this understanding that is most pronounced in policy literature, stubbornly isolating questions concerning characteristic features of contemporary European society from questions pertaining to the living conditions of Roma communities' (2015, p. 81).

These deprivation aspects have been theorised and conceptualised in recent policy guidelines by an essentialist, one-sided picture of the Roma underpinned by normative contentions about the causes of poverty and marginalisation.

> While policy-makers rely on empirical assessments to formulate the definitions of Roma exclusion, these assessments tend to be mediated by the existing cognitive and moral maps that orient their actions and routines. In turn these politically accepted definitions legitimise a specific course of action, even if it is not needed or demanded by the final beneficiaries.
>
> (ibid., p. 87)

For example, the EU Framework for National Roma Integration Strategies (2011) and the European Roma Institute (ERI) (2014) mark a significant step in the politicisation of Roma identity by ensuring a further increase in the initiatives, projects and programmes explicitly targeting the Roma. However, both initiatives are harshly criticised by academics and activists, claiming that they represent particular interests of small groups. For instance, the leader of the MIGROM project, Prof. Matras argues that "ERI is a Roma elite oligarchy, dedicated, ostensibly to the fight against Anti-Gypsyism, though in fact its main purpose was to showcase the self-proclaimed 'Roma elite' that has recently acquired political recognition" (Romani Studies Network, 2015).

The political collation of disparate Roma groups into a national political community is a historical process that 'scrutinizes different strands of identification practices that have contributed to the longue durée development of today's Roma as an epistemic object and policy target: police profiling of particular communities; administrative surveys; Romani activism; Roma targeted policies; quantitative scientific research' (Surdu & Kovats, 2015, p. 2). Historically, Roma have been externally identified by police-led censuses, expert estimates and policy-related initiatives based on physical appearance and social context rather than self-identification. However, recent economic and political conditions have turned this identity-framing process into a self-sustaining cycle where Roma knowledge identifies Roma problems requiring a policy response, producing more Roma knowledge, more needs and more policy responses. This results in an expert framing of Roma groupness in an essentialist narrative that differentiates them from any majority. This has affected social solidarity by disconnecting and distancing the Roma from their fellow citizens. Political tendencies of this kind make it possible to differentiate Roma mobility from other intra-European movements and justify specific measures in host countries.

People who identify themselves as Roma experience a separation from (institutionalised) majority society since they attribute a far more limited meaning to an ethnic concept than in the public debate (i.e. as an ethnic group versus an international movement). According to the research respondents, there are also inter-generational identification differences (youngsters have much more out-group communication and identify less strictly with the Roma than older adults) as a result of migration experiences. In short, there is a distance between the specific community (i.e. one's own network that predominantly consists of the extended family) and mainstream society, but there is no desire to identify with the broader Roma community. As Hemelsoet and Van Pelt confirm, these communities claim 'no support whatsoever for a targeted approach towards "the Roma" as such. Moreover, the affirmation of a present gap with the rest of society further strengthens the argument against particularisation. Listening to the insider narratives of Roma might imply recognising them as persons, rather than as Roma' (Hemelsoet & Van Pelt, 2015, p. 158). This ethnic focus as a reference is noted by many respondents who feel they would prefer not to be labelled this way but by other social characteristics. As later examples show, there is a structural disagreement between Roma political representatives and academics and civil society in the role of ethnic framing and how it is adapted in local integration policies. Nonetheless, deconstructing identity also fails to result in structural solutions to the problems the Roma and the majority around them.

Most Roma-specific policies result in *Roma projects* that contribute to the ethnicisation of the problem, because they prevent a systemic transformation, since the targeted Roma groups only experience short-term benefits from subsidised activities. As an example of the counterproductive effects of Roma policies, Kostka (2015) discusses the use of Slovak Social Funding and how this programming frames social exclusion in terms of individual or group adaptability with very little attention devoted to general institutional inequalities.

> This neglect enforced channelling of funding towards measures that aimed to change the behaviour of target groups – Roma communities. The adopted targeted approach was supposed to offset the pervasive practice of re-directing funding from the most marginalised communities, instead leading to the isolation of Roma measures from regional and local development strategies. This de facto only reinforced the re-direction of funding to other priorities.
> (Kostka, 2015, p. 6)

These findings challenge the perceived positive influence of the targeting approach championed by the EU and numerous international Roma advocacy organisations, since the example shows they might lead to the ethnicisation of the problem and its separation from mainstream policies. This often leads to disenchantment and the de-legitimisation of the entire Structural Fund programming. In the case of Kostka it was also confirmed that an increase in the allocation of funds for Roma integration priorities generated greater contestation of their usefulness in facilitating inclusion (Kostka, 2015, p. 8).

Brubaker (2004) defines several aspects to be considered in framing ethnic groups, and stresses the importance of sensitivity to framing dynamics of 'the generalised coding bias in favour of ethnicity' (2004, p. 176). Similar to Matras, he warns against a reductionist view of politicised ethnicity (i.e. elite manipulation), the performative nature of ethnopolitical, groupist rhetoric and the personal interests of key actors, who live off politics. He also stresses the differences between the interests of leaders and those of their alleged constituents, as well as the contingent nature of groupness and he advocates a disaggregating approach focussed on intra-ethnic mechanisms (Brubaker, 2004, pp. 176–177). Although these aspects seem to be simple, Roma identity framing has nevertheless proved that the political construction of Roma ethnic minorities is an extremely complicated and sensitive issue, and most of the stakeholders have conflicting interests with long-term implications for Roma policymaking.

5.2 Ethnic framing of Roma from academic perspectives

To develop a political strategy, European institutions needed a bureaucratic apparatus with specific objectives to problematise the different aspects associated with the Roma. They generally rely on expert narratives which, according to Surdu (2015), serve in turn to strengthen the ideology that guides institutional policy. However, the lack of a theoretical perspective in studies about the Roma "renders

Romani studies a marginal position in academia" (Surdu & Kovats, 2015, p. 14). Academics and the activist elite identify the "classifiers" that make up the social construction of the target population of these policies. While political scientists concentrate more on the role of international organisations and Romani activism, the role of academic scholarship emerged in the construction of public Romani identity. In turn, quantitative researchers most often use a-theoretical and a-historical perspectives when explaining the Roma they are discussing (ibid., p. 16). There are many striking epistemological issues in different disciplines working on Roma-related topics. There are not only distinctions between academics based on different epistemological backgrounds but also based on affiliation. Some scholars are linked with universities, while the work of others is published and disseminated by policy bodies such as the OSCE, ERRC, OSI, the World Bank or the Council of Europe. The latter enjoy wider dissemination, but the distinction becomes blurred when academics assume the role of advocate consultants paid by NGOs.

This fragmented academic field represents not only the disconnections of disciplines, but also the fragmented nature of Roma activism, advocacy and policymaking, which are built on the same narratives as Roma studies. The fragmentation results in more studies on Roma health care, gender, labour and education issues financed by local or EU funds. Most of these studies aim to prevent Roma children from leaving school early, change health conditions, decrease school segregation, widen access to non-formal and informal learning validation systems among the Roma, provide legal labour and better housing conditions, improve political participation, and change the negative attitude to the Roma. Still, these studies employ common ethnic frames, subjecting the Roma to structural inequality and social economic dependency. Some also use the cultural framing of ethnicity and Roma ethnicity is associated with cultural traits that conflict with the majority's expectations. Recent critical studies stress the theoretical and methodological limitations, but more importantly they challenge academics who avoid sensitive topics and fail to analyse illicit behaviour (Tremlett & McGarry, 2013; Stewart, 2013; Stewart & Rovid, 2011).

In the following analysis I provide a brief overview on why these isolated narratives of academics might influence inefficient policies and how they can lead to further stigmatisation. First, I discuss the general issues of ethnic framing in academia. Particular aspects provided by anthropologists, criminologists and human rights studies are presented along with the limitations of these academic frames in studies on Roma migrants. Then the roles of activists and NGOs are discussed and how their practices – in conflict with, but also interdependently with academics – shape ethnic frames in Roma policymaking. Finally, the direct impact of interpreters is presented and how their ideas of Roma ethnicity are transmitted in their interactions with Roma migrants in bureaucratic processes.

When the Word Bank describes the Roma as having an aversion to education and health care, and holds Roma culture responsible for their precarious situation, we need to critically evaluate the role of the academic framing of ethnicity in this kind of policymaking. This description of the Roma was suggested in a World Bank publication written by Jean Pierre Liégeois, a consultant of the Council of Europe's ROMED programme. This programme promotes the need for mediation and, according to Surdu (2015), implicitly promotes the view that 'their culture leads Roma to disengage from public institutions' (Matras, 2015, p. 168). This essentialist statement in Liégeois's work is just one example, such as "a Traveller is someone who remains detached from his surroundings" or "the Gypsy worldview emphasises the present moment" (Liégeois, 1998), that made his name one of the links between policymaking and academic misconceptions.

Institutions adopt expert statements and impose a narrative, which is then perpetuated via repetition across a sector of institutions, becoming a dominant policy narrative. But how can Roma ethnic identity be defined in the face of such diversity? It is generally claimed that a pragmatic construct is needed to develop efficient policymaking on the Roma. Even without territorial claims and popular depictions of nomadism, there is one key classifier, a historical narrative on their Indian origin and the validity of the Romani language that might serve as a classifier for the Roma. These aspects divide academics based on ethical arguments. Those who disagree state that this approach constructs a non-European Roma ethnic group, just like Roma cultural practices, and thus reinforces the opposition between Roma and non-Roma. A similar argument claims that 'describing Romani practices in itself already amounts to "essentialising" and creates boundaries' (Matras, 2015, p. 168). Can we speak of any Roma ethnic classifiers that can be constructive in policymaking?

Although often used as such, academic constructions of Romani ethnicity are not objective concepts. Disciplines have contradicting definitions, which then become products of political institutions. For instance, *Roma*, which is generally a politically correct synonym for *gypsy*, now denotes a much wider and more vaguely defined group in the EU consisting of diverse populations (Matras, 2015). The term Roma was introduced as a programmatic overarching label to eclipse the terms burdened with negative or overly romantic connotations (Gypsies or Tsiganes). The use of the term Roma is closely connected with the "political project of representing, defending and speaking in the name of all those groups with myriad self-designations that were previously widely associated with other but mostly pejorative overarching labels" (Vermeersch, 2011, p. 93).

There are two types of studies on the Roma: those that contain Roma ethnic framing, and do not mention any illicit phenomenon, and those that focus on deviant behaviour, but avoid using any ethnic framing of the Roma. Although later ones are based on good will to prevent stigmatisation, they also have side effects. Criminologists have long been interested in correlations between deviant behaviour, ethnicity and migration experiences (Aas & Bosworth, 2013). Although academic discussions often focus on the "race and crime" debate, and there have been many attempts to explain why ethnic minorities are overrepresented in the prison population, exactly what the role is of the formulation of minority perspectives in criminology was never questioned. When we discuss elevated rates of offences or discriminatory treatment in the criminal justice system, police discrimination, harder sanctions or ethnic bias in crime statistics, a conceptualisation of ethnicity seems to be a given variable. The attitudes to migrants in the law enforcement system, selective crime registration or law enforcement, when government officials exercise enforcement discretion based on racial prejudice, have hardly been researched topics in the case of the Roma. Although there are many assumptions about the targeted policing of the Roma in Europe and the cultural explanations of deviant Roma behaviour, or illicit trade across borders, it remains an eluded correlation in academic studies.

In his latest book, Bovenkerk (2014) includes various theoretical approaches to explain the link between crime, ethnicity and migration. One of them is the Import Model that explains these interrelations based on the migration process of newcomers (Shaw & Mckay, 1942) on the assumption that deviant behaviour is taken with them from their home country. However, since Roma come from several countries and have no shared homeland, it would be a mistake to apply this notion.

Other academics use explanations such as the lack of social control due to changes in gender roles and family structures or a culture conflict. The latter occurs when the rules and norms of an individual's culture conflict with those of conventional society. This can be quite common when Roma move to Western countries. Sellin (1938) believes that in any culture, the behaviour of individuals that does not conform to the social norms is seen as a violation of these norms. It has also been stated that an ecological fallacy can explain the high percentage of delinquency in particular minority groups but no correlation has been proven. Empirical research is needed to challenge these theories and the ethnic frames they employ.

Whereas some academics fear that collecting data on ethnicity may reinforce stereotypes, others argue that data are needed to get a complete and rigorous picture of the population, including forms of discrimination and inequality. Consequently, recent studies that focus on ethnicity (independent from nationality) in relation to crime tend to remain largely qualitative, providing a micro but in-depth picture of criminality, while studies on immigration and links to crime tend to rely on quantitative methods, showing a broader but less nuanced view of crime. In addition, crime data show the nationality of offenders but not their ethnicity nor, in the case of foreigners, their migration status. This results in great obstacles to statistical research by official state institutions and academics. The failure to collect particular kinds of social data effectively results in the silencing of certain social evidence, which is counterproductive in efforts to address problems and inequalities that thus remain concealed. As is noted in the following chapters, my research reveals that stereotypes, and prejudice exists, but it is perceived by migrants as ethnic discrimination, even when the objective living conditions of these ethnic groups are shaped by other types of exclusion practices.

Although Bovenkerk et al. (2003), warned against the essentialist use of ethnicity, these notions are still common in criminological analyses, which are often transmitted into new control policies. Connotations about the Roma and crime have historical roots, especially in institutional discrimination cases and with the recent transnational movement in Europe. In fact, attention is increasingly devoted to interrelationships between mobility and ethnic groups and criminal networks (Siegel, 2014).

Cultural explanations based on Sutherland's differential association theory are still popular in explaining the differences in crime rates and the causes of deviance between different groups in society. However, the strategic use of culture requires critical attention because 'culture is not a given, it is not a *thing* that shapes human conduct outside the individuals themselves' (Baumann, 1996, p. 11). Culture should be considered the outcome of the process in which people give meaning to their world, and the formation of ethnic groups is a process that develops by collective identification (Kinket & Verkuyten, 1997). Yet interpreters, activists and civil servants often rely on static cultural differentiations allocated to particular groups, based on their names, nationality, skin colour or dress code. These stereotypes exclude the Roma who do not fit these assumptions from ethnic framing and add to existing stereotypes of the traditional Roma image.

> The formation of ethnic groups is frequently accompanied by drawing ethnic borders and cultivating or even inventing traditions. Conceived in this way, culture and ethnicity are in themselves qualities that require an explanation, and not fixed givens of traditions that provide an explanation for whatever phenomena are under examination such as special forms of crime.
>
> (Ferrell et al., 2004, p. 86)

Police officers and even some social workers state that the Roma "sell their daughters", "prostitute their wives" and "exploit others, who are not their relatives". "Cultural offences" or "culturally motivated crimes" (Van Broeck, 2001) constitute an intriguing variation of the ethnicity and crime nexus. In keeping with the reasoning of Thorsten Sellin in 1938, crime may result from ethnic minorities following their own conduct norms and violating the law of their new homeland. 'Many of these customs are not viewed as being against the law, in fact if they did not adhere to them they would endanger their position in their own community and perhaps even run the risk of being ostracized' (Bovenkerk & Yesilgöz, 2004, p. 4).

Crime is always defined as undesirable deviant behaviour, but cultural crimes evoke a great deal of approval in certain communities and the individuals we might view as the victims do not necessarily define themselves as such. As Bovenkerk and Yesilgöz (2004) argue, 'in culture-related crime the offences are committed by individuals who prevent deviance from happening or getting worse' (p. 87). In fact, offenders are not lured into crime due to *differential association* but that is what they are expected to do according to their community values. Their social status might become diminished if they do not respond to these exactions even if it means committing a crime. In many cases crime is a tool to restore harm. This geopolitical fringe about socially accepted deviance and the cultural fluidity of ethnic codes defining these restorative tools is critically analysed in the next chapter.

Although there are cases of cultural crimes among Roma migrants, it is more the cultural misinterpretation of local bureaucrats that leads to their criminalisation in the host countries. Due to mutual distrust among the Roma and service providers, there is a selection in the information they exchange that leads to further misunderstandings and expectations. The implication is that ethnically specific crime emerges within a certain social context and in interaction with the environment. Clients use their *culture* creatively and manipulate it to get what they want, for example by convincing civil servants that they are in a threatened situation or strategically using a reference to a specific image of their families to get the upper hand. Van Poeck and Vandenabeele (2012) also state that in contrast to previous explanations, cultural aspects can not be seen as independent from socio-economic factors, like solutions developed in subcultures. Hebberecht and Baillergeau (2012) add that comparative research is unavoidable to understand these cultural determinants considering their socio-economic circumstances in relation with law enforcement, and the political structure as determinants of decision making. Baumgartner et al. (2009) note that cultural and ethnic factors have no effect on the risk of delinquency, but social deprivation can play an important role in socio-economic factors. Multifarious studies have been conducted on issues of immigrant and ethnic minority crime, particularly among the second generation (Tonry, 1997; Marshall, 1997) but there is still little consensus on how to define the problem and why some migrants are highly politicised in security discourses as has recently been the case with the mobility of the Roma.

Ethnic connotations are taboo, as is manifested in a polarised discourse, where law enforcement ignores the facts in favour of romanticised approaches. As Petintseva (2014) explains, academic voices presented in the discourse might end in dividing practices, which specify who or which viewpoints are acceptable, and which are useless or naive. The discourse is not just the interpretation of academic voice, it also shapes the conditions that are created by these representations and that gain importance. In particular, it defines the dominant discourses, and which groups are dismissed or stigmatised (Petintseva, 2014, p. 214). As Petintseva argues, ethnic taboos are still avoided since criminologists are demonised by other scholars and are described as a danger to the Roma empowerment movement.

This process is most obvious in analyses of the interactions of the European Academic Network on Romani Studies (Romani Studies Network, 2015). This online network has about 400 members and intends to support efforts towards the social inclusion of Romani citizens in Europe.

> The project facilitates intercultural dialogue and increases the visibility of research outside the academic community to foster cooperation with policy-makers and other stake-holders. By creating an interface between academic researchers and political decision-makers while promoting and improving resources on the European Roma communities, the project hopes to ultimately make it possible to implement better conceived policy initiatives based on reliable evidence.
>
> (ibid.)

I have been following the network discussions for more than three years and have offline contacts with several members. Although the network covers many disciplines and has well-known academic members, only a few are regularly active. In the last three years 'the essence of the "cultural identity" of the Roma' (Romani Studies Network, 2015) has been extensively discussed, which might illustrate how different conflicts feed the Roma framing with controversial images and definitions of the Roma. The network members have several conflicting affiliations with the EU, the Open Society Institute or each other's NGOs, Roma programmes or journals.

Topics have been discussed online related to Roma identity, ethical and methodological issues and the political affiliations of academics. These discussion points provide a detailed overview of the conflicting Roma frameworks created by Romani scholars. In the fragmented field of Romani studie, academics represent stratified objectives and conflicted affiliations. Discussions about the situation of the Roma often illustrate the conflicting interests and epistemological differences between stakeholders of Roma research projects. This was clear after the Radio interview on Channel 4 about the Roma migration project of Salford University.[1] After a radio interview with the project leader, the UK news was inundated with the notion that this study states there are more than 200,000 Roma migrants in the country.

The relevant numbers are one of the major topics attracting conflicting views among academics, but in this case the critique was started by the ethical implications of the radio interview as a source of moral panic about the Roma influx. Many felt the Salford report harmed the Roma and fed extreme right-wing populist narratives with unverifiable data by presenting research findings in the popular media.[2]

Since this study did not include empirical data, one of the network members tried to emphasise in his critique the importance of ethnographic methods, using data on exploited Slovak Roma in the UK as an illustration. He was stressing the importance of data collection methods and in the end, he was criticised for not reporting the crime cases he mentioned to the police and accused of being racist and unprofessional.[3] Topics and accusations continuously shift in the debate in where crime issues related to Roma are a hypersensitive topic, provoking furious reactions and offensive remarks. Similar discussions occurred when the European Romani Institute was developed with support from Gyorgy Soros to promote Romani culture and protect Romani grassroots. Several members presented their concerns about this initiative, though it was not the top-down political interest that bothered them but the interrelation with Roma representatives selected by the stakeholders.

1 https://romamatrix.eu/about-us
2 http://romanistudies.eu/documents/email-list-archive/
3 See discussion 'Compiling data on Roma. Discussions on Roma migrants in the UK and the number games' ed. Durst, J. (2014) Download from: http://romanistudies.eu/documents/email-list-archive/

It was claimed that the ERI portrayed the Roma as the object of Soros' educational enterprise and not as subjects. These Roma frames differentiate between the elite Roma who are not raised with their kin and poor authentic Roma who are suffering and need political advocacy. The normative differentiation between Roma categories is also transmitted into Roma research projects where successful or middle-class Roma are hardly included. The policy implications of these academic frames are often discussed, but network members hardly take any responsibility for the failures.

5.3 Interrelations between activism and civil society

Although Roma activism is frequently seen as a political construct, its controversial relation with securitisation policies is often disregarded. Roma activism started in the 1920s and 1930s when Romani organisations in Bulgaria, Yugoslavia, Romania and Greece started to promote education for Gypsy youths and published periodicals about local minority issues (Marushiakova & Popov, 2004; Klímová, 2002). However, the First World Romani Congress in London in 1971 is seen as the real beginning of the international Romani movement. In the Visegrad countries, post-transitional conditions became a breeding ground for Romani activism and emerging Romani political elites, who advocated a shared Romani ethnicity (Puxon, 2000, p. 94). After the Communist regime collapsed, 'ethnopolitical mobilization was increasing in the region as well as racial intolerance and violence against the Roma, triggering a new wave of activism that united a new generation of Roma intellectuals' (Puxon, 2000, p. 94). EU membership has been the main motivation for CEE countries to live up to the Copenhagen Criteria and support NGOs that prepare well researched and focused documents on the situation of the Roma for the European Commission. In the end these reports are turned into verbatim passages regarding the improvement of the situation of the Roma in the Commission's explicitly formulated criteria for joining the EU (Kóczé & Rövid, 2012, p. 12).

Member states defined "Roma strategies" as a sign of political commitment, but in the daily lives of the Roma, not much changed. These processes increased the critical voices among Roma activists and conflicts emerged between Roma activists with EU affiliation and those who were sceptical about these top-down international initiatives.

In addition to these tensions, 'some Romani activists are hesitant about bringing the Roma into the discourse of national minority rights, because they fear that national minority rights do not primarily reflect Romani interests, but rather the interests of the authorities' (Vermeersch, 2003, p. 890). Thus, instead of inadequate minority protection being seen as an obstacle to EU membership, many activists fear that the Roma themselves would be perceived as the obstacle. That this fear is not unfounded is illustrated by the way far right domestic movements responded to the problem of Romani migration and asylum seekers (Bárány, 2002). In fact, international pressure on Central Europe exerted by individual EU states responding to Romani asylum seekers even seemed to exacerbate this problem (Kóczé & Rövid, 2012, p. 13) as is noted in Chapter 3. To put it briefly, local Roma activists are sandwiched between local political interests and political pressure from the EU.

The framing of ethnic identity by activists is contrary to the above-mentioned narratives of academics and politicians. Activists' narratives are founded on critical power relations in which the Roma are defined as a suppressed national enemy, constructed by political entities to disrupt the majority's attention for real social economic problems. Roma as an ethnic group are defined in terms of critical reflections on governmental rhetoric in which the definition of the Roma serves as a political tool. These critiques claim that the political framing of the Roma denies the structural and historical development that forced most Roma into geographic segregation and welfare dependency. The activists advocate multiculturalism and turn Roma cultural identity into the central focus of a political struggle for recognition by relying on culturally constructed elements of Romani identity. They tend to construct a minority identity that fails to give full expression to individual identities and is "stigmatised" in the sense that it is associated with stereotypical images of Roma culture, and moral and economic deprivation. While these minority rights claims resonate well in international forums, they run the risk of reifying cultural boundaries, stimulating thinking in ethnic collectives, reinforcing stereotypes, and hampering collective action. Following the ideas of Kóczé and Rövid (2012), this section reflects the ambiguity in contemporary Roma projects of minority rights advocacy represented by Roma activists.

Roma framing focuses on the urge for ethnic minority mobilisation as community commitment among a wider audience.

> An ethnic minority is not simply a group of people that differs from the rest of society in terms of language, tradition and so forth, but rather the result of a process in which such differences are made socially and politically meaningful and are acted upon. By employing the concept of framing to the subject of ethnic mobilization, an opportunity is created to examine the element of choice in the construction of an ethnic identity (the use of intentional frames) as well as the element of designation (the presence of counter-mobilizing frames or the (in)ability of a particular frame to resonate in a given context).
>
> (Vermeersch, 2003, p. 882)

Vermeesch draws a distinction between activists based on political affiliations, using the terms "opportunists" for those who have clear local relationships with the governmental parties, and "radicals" for those who distance themselves from the local political forces. Roma activists have increasingly separate agendas. There are more small grassroots groups and a growing network of professionals, who play a central role in establishing political bodies affiliated with the CoE and OSCE and other advocacy groups like ERRC, which is an international public interest law group. Several online Roma radio stations have been set up and a handbook for Roma activists has even been published by the ERIO with guidelines on how to advocate for Roma inclusion at the local, national and European level. As a symbol of the professionalisation of Roma activism, the handbook has been developed with the view that Roma community-based advocacy needs to be better promoted, especially at the level of grassroots groups, networks and organisations with the necessary information and advocacy skills to demand that Roma community needs and priorities are addressed.[4]

These developments increase awareness of structural problems and are entrenched in an essentialist ethnic framing of contextually diverse socio-economic issues. In addition, these processes increase the tension between local political representatives and radical activists like Mirga, who are accused of becoming, in effect, diplomats who no longer understand their own communities. Others, like Florian Farkas, are accused by international Roma leaders of distancing themselves from the reality of everyday Romani experience. In general, the Romani movement has its Malcolm Xs and Martin Luther Kings too, who reveal that their socio-economic marginality is clashing with scholarly activism (Bárány, 2002, p. 263).

Although there is ample progress in the professionalisation of Roma activism, there is also a growing division between the real needs of the Roma and the needs the activists represent, and a growing disconnection between the international and local needs of Romani communities. These discrepancies developed with the framing of the Roma as a "non-territorial nation" based on its "Indian origin" and "transborder cooperation". These are academic notions and fail to bolster domestic mobilisation. As Kóczé and Rövid (2012) suggest, the "ordinary" Roma are not interested in being regarded as a nation, they do not want Romani schools, they want to be equal national citizens without any differentiation. Promoting the Roma as a nation was primarily in the interest of individual states, since it shifted the focus away from the states' responsibility (ibid.). Many Romani activists perceive the IRU strategy as potentially undermining the position of the Roma as a national minority in the domestic context.

Other activists who present Romani identity via a "national minority" frame also distinguish between the Roma and the ethnic majority but do not demand a special European status for the Roma. They maintain that nation states are the "homelands" of the Roma where they should be conceptualised as a national minority and find support from other national minorities and non-Romani supporters of minority rights (Vermeersch, 2003, p. 890). This framing is also debated, since the Roma, who never demanded political autonomy, experience their situation as a minority that is different from other national minorities. This has been confirmed by interest groups from other national minorities who distance themselves from the Romani perspective, like the Hungarian minority in Slovakia.

Since most of the local projects were developed along the guidelines of national strategies initiated by non-Roma, Romani activists involved in these macropolitical

4 www.erionet.eu/doc-handbook-roma-activists_en

structures have been criticised by the very people they mean to represent. They are accused of earning money on the backs of their brothers living in deprivation and betraying their own people for their own individual interests. These tensions emerged in many internal fringes of the Roma activist networks (Kóczé and Rövid, 2012, pp. 117–119). The tensions should be linked back to the way the Roma and their problems have been ethnicised by Roma activists. Discrimination issues are undeniably a serious problem in many countries, but ethnic framing in reference to other problems can be counterproductive, e.g. as regards migration.

Many activists claim that structural and institutional discrimination is the root cause of Romani migration. Others use migration to put pressure on the local government, e.g. in the case of RIS supporting activists, who stated that even more Roma will leave the country if no efforts are made to improve their situation. Some activists argue that refugees moving to Canada in recent decades had negative effects on Roma activism, especially after their public speculations about deliberate efforts by Romani political parties to organise the migration. There have also been concerns about the responses of host countries to the position of the Roma in their home country, as in the case of British visa restrictions as a result of Roma asylum claims. Some governmental narratives use the case of these Roma refugees against activists by saying Romani migration was deliberately organised to discredit the Hungarian government and the Hungarian Roma. Romani activists do not want to see the Roma blamed for blocking Hungary's entrance into the EU, as the president of the National Gypsy Self-Government, Flórián Farkas stated (ibid., p. 27). The activists who cooperate with government institutions openly disagree with the argument that Roma are really fleeing persecution and undermine the legitimacy of the claim of those who want to put pressure on the government by referring to the waves of migration. Other Roma activists are convinced that host countries have been discriminatory to Roma asylum seekers by seeing them as economic refugees (Vermeersch, 2006). This framing is detrimental to the people involved and makes them even more eager to hide their identity in the host environment. Several problems caused by the ethnic framing of Roma in a transnational context have made Roma activists even more divided in their positions. These tensions were also fuelled by financial conflicts that increased with the European funding for Roma integration projects. These conflicts are easy to trace via the interrelations between Roma activists and NGOs.

In recent decades, Roma rights activism has been accused of being counterproductive and even backfiringandt reinforcing anti-Roma prejudices and worsening local conflicts between the Roma and the majority (Van Baar, 2015). Many of these arguments are built on the financial dependency of activists and their loyalty to organisations such as the OSI. Others state that EU Roma civil society also slips into discriminatory framing by differentiating the Roma from other minorities and remaining vague about the minority protection criterion of the Roma. As a consequence labelled in the media as "ethno-business", controversial practices have been developed under the Roma flag, and political entrepreneurs started to use the legal framework for the protection of national minorities to obtain material, financial or political gains, as are also assigned to activists propagating Roma human rights claims (Cârstocea, 2012).

The conflict started with the expanding European funds resulting in local ethnic competition, since this support is seen and actively portrayed as solely focused on helping an ethnically defined segment of the population (the Roma) and not the entire local community. The NGOs that receive these funds have become key players in the field, merging with the competition and cooperating with local activist groups.

Traditional social movements have been absorbed by the "culture of projects" (Sampson, 2002), in which NGOs generate new, unprecedented forms of Roma activism. In the case of the Central European Roma migrant, one cannot help but see how these ethnicity-based activist narratives are included in the project definitions and how many tensions and contradictions activist alliances and collaborations have produced in specific settings. These narratives should be read as representations of emotions, qualities of transpersonal ties, bonds, or relations and 'collective emotional processes that shape social constructions of ethnicity and mobility' (Nagel, 1994, p. 155). By emphasising a victimisation narrative with essentialist concepts, Roma activist movements extend the emotional dimension of policymaking. By intensifying local tensions and formulating political arguments, Roma activism has a increasing role in the securitisation of Roma migrants and in ethnic connotations that shape the dynamics between law enforcement and collective emotions of security, crime and punishment. This process is strongly intertwined with Roma NGO developments and their support in European politics.

At first glance NGOs seem to be disconnected from recent Roma activism, and activists seems to publicly distance themselves from NGOs, but the boundaries between formal NGOs and informal groups of activists are more complex, affiliations are blurred and there are several forms of crossover and collaboration between the two. These interrelations have the direct implication of Roma framing in civil societies and many images are transferred from one network to the other. Roma activist and NGO links can be defined as a mutually beneficial *surreptitious symbiosis that enables sustained activism to improve social exclusion without becoming a part of the civil society industry*. As a result of their individual ties, activists rely on NGOs for contacts with funders and formal institutions and for technical support to avoid direct reliance on funders or for legal aid. Some activists also work for NGOs and NGO workers can escape the constraints imposed by managerialist NGOs in activist networks. This is a cyclical logic, however. Some activists institutionalise and scale up, bringing their constructed ideas about the Roma into an institutionalised field. And vice versa, challenging the cosy relations some NGOs have with donors and the state, NGOs are also reconnected with grassroots activism in cases where they re-radicalise from within. In some cases, the opposition between NGOs and activists can grow into conflicts or lead to hybrid organisations such as social businesses.

> For NGOs, given the growing competition for funding and pressure from both governments and donors in which NGOs are required to demonstrate

> their professionalism and efficiency, being too close to movements that are radically critical of governments could be seen as endangering NGO contracting relationships or grant-based support.
>
> (Glasius, Ishkanian 2014, p. 34)

Although some Roma activists steadfastly reject and criticise the "managerialism" of NGOs, many activists recognise their advantages and, via the cooperation noted earlier, they create alternative spaces as well as new practices and forms of organising that preserve the ideational and emancipatory logic of activism. Still, activists continue to denounce and oppose NGOs that have embraced the material and coercive logics of the market and state respectively. The main difference between the two is their individual interest in daily practices that structurally shape the representation of the Roma. Considering these conflicting frames constructed by different expert, let me explain the situational selection of ethnic frames applied by NGO workers and how their managerial practices shape interactions between Roma migrants and local services.

5.4 Living for or living off the Roma? – the role of funding in civil society

> They make a living off our backs', she said. 'I am sorry Veronika, but I am not going to go there', she said when I invited her to the office of the local NGO I had contacts with. 'These people are making money off our problems. Maybe they mean well, but in the end, look at us. Nothing is changing. We have to solve them all. This is a new business. We are the new cash cows.
>
> (HF73)

As the preceding quote shows, there is scepticism among many Roma migrants about the role of NGOs that supposedly support them. Some avoid them because they feel exploited and refer to NGOs as part of the bureaucratic system that raises funds for the Roma, keeping ethnic minorities in a dependent relationship to justify their existence and gain more financial support for their own organisations. Others use small NGOs to exploit their connections with local services for their own benefit and accept only practical when they want to claim benefits. Some feel they are fully supported and even become NGO workers, partners or trustees while some Roma activists publicly accuse NGOs of taking money from those in need. Shadowing several small NGO practices enabled me to understand the underlying relationships and their structural effects on the everyday practices of Roma.

There are several conflict angles that increase the tensions between different groups and NGOs, in particular because of the competition for resources. In general Romani civil society is driven by distrust and rumours reinforced by conflicting connotations of Romani identity. Due to the majority of non-Roma activists in the Roma movements, it is often suggested in the public discourse that the Roma are not willing to engage in their own political representation.

Many young highly educated Roma who try to play these roles often give up. Facing conflicting interests, they say they are pulled apart by different stakeholders without making any progress. Then they prefer to assimilate into the majority and avoid the expectations of being a representative to prevent the negative connotations surrounding their Roma identity in their daily lives. 'One has better opportunities on the labour market and a better chance of protecting the children from bullying if the Roma identity remains concealed, especially abroad where we are less often recognised as Roma and able to stay as "Eastern Europeans" by referring to our national identity'. These patterns have different explanations.

Due to the influence of the Open Society Foundation, the Roma Decade and the National Framework of Roma Integration project, there is a strong hegemony of the Hungarian NGO perspective on Roma issues that marginalises others in civil society. Their narratives are transmitted to other organisations that use the same narratives in their fund-raising to compete for financial support for their projects. This has led to a structurally adapted framing of the Roma as the poor, homeless minority of Europe like an image of an avant-garde non-territorial stateless nation. As a consequence, an ethnic conceptualisation of this international "pro-Roma" civil society focuses more attention on the socio-economic status of these minorities in Western countries where Roma NGOs keep re-emphasising Roma exclusion. In addition, the organisations create a blueprint as a political organisation for the Roma representing Roma issues that is more suited to the global world than to the nation states.

In conclusion, compared to the classical concept of NGOs as a progressive response to neoliberal globalisation, Roma civil society is now seen as the opposite, injected with international funds in the service of a neoliberal agenda and European migration policies. In this section I define my findings about the role of neoliberal businesslike civil societies and how their managerialist structures shape Roma civil society and the political framing of Roma.

The commodification of humanitarianism

Non-governmental organisations have a difficult position in the field of Roma empowerment. They are regularly accused of being involved in scams to maintain their legitimacy, and that their activities sustain the Roma dependency. NGOs are often portrayed in idealistic tones as "entities set to do good" unattained by either politics or the market, and as agents of democratisation, development and empowerment of weak or marginalised groups. For neoliberals, the significance of NGOs lies in the socio-economic realm. They view NGOs as 'part of the private sector, delivering services to the poor cheaply, equitably and efficiently' (Payes, 2005, p. 19).

Shadowing NGO workers and spending time with them gave rise to two controversial issues about loyalty to the Roma, which might have counterproductive and ethical implications concerning engagement with NGOs. One NGO worker, who was working full-time in a state-funded rehabilitation project, said she felt uncomfortable at her NGO and in her spare time because of loyalty problems. 'A good liberal member of the civil society does not work for the government'. She raised this issue when she was complaining about the fact that the other members of her NGO saw her as a spy of the government or someone who cannot be fully trusted.

Interviewed NGO workers often defined civil servants and local authorities as enemies of NGOs, bureaucrats who have no social sensitivity, no critical view and are partly responsible for the problems of their clients. Although it is often claimed that their role is to challenge the hegemonic social order, these organisations also serve as a venue for the dominant group to consolidate this hegemony, by providing information about their clients (ibid., p. 38). In every city where I visited the Roma, I was usually given access to the NGOs that supported local Roma families, organised activities and promoted their bureaucratic issues, in particular concerning housing problems the Roma face in their neighbourhoods. Most of these organisations are small and are run by local social workers engaged in Roma advocacy. They see Roma as vulnerable underdogs who undergo social and physical exclusion and have financial difficulties. These NGOs mostly have an office in a Roma neighbourhood and a staff specialised in educational, financial or legal support. These employers are critical and very protective of their clients. Most of them are tired of seeing researchers and ignore new requests for information and interviews since they cannot see any benefit from these PhD programmes and international reports. Many researchers have offered voluntary jobs in exchange for information for PhD projects. While shadowing clients and NGOs, it was surprising that although the organisations provide so much assistance for Roma families, they also reproduce fake data and willingly or unwillingly assist in illegal activities. What is even more problematic is that organisations such as the IOM that work on Roma migration issues also adopt these data and reproduce the very images of the Roma created by the falsified data. These images are constructed during the daily interactions between NGO workers and their Roma clients, who hide additional information about the background of their cases, thus leading to modified data in their welfare applications.

In face-to-face interactions, NGO workers serve the will of their clients and remain loyal to their organisations, even if the tasks required of them might be legally debatable. I saw how NGO workers ignore the background of families they work with to fulfil the expectations and keep their trust in the organisation. In one case I was asked to appeal decisions by the HMRC on overpayments, but I realised the tax credit claims were based on false payslips. In other cases I filled in forms for NGO clients as an advocacy worker and realised the data I filled in was fake or outdated. This was problematic since the name of an assisting person is also on the forms. When I asked other NGO advocacy workers how they cope with these issues, and if they ignore these claims or assist, they said 'if the client doesn't tell us the truth, we don't know they are not completely honest'. These strategies are different in cases of Roma workers with Roma clients, since the clients seems to be more open about their cases, claiming the loyalty of the Roma workers when requesting assistance.

With non-Roma workers, clients are more selective with information and try to present the claims as real. Since many family members use the services of the same NGOs, advocacy workers know the real living conditions of the families and know the contradictions in their claims. In fact, NGO workers inform their clients about the claim procedures, the weaknesses of the system and how their claims are monitored. They appeal when the claims are refused and help legitimise issues if the clients have no proof. I never witnessed a case where a worker refused a client, since they try to keep their relationship of trust with their clients and also preserve the number of clients. When I asked the workers if their director was aware of these practices, they said it was just business as usual. 'What do you think Veronika, who is running this criminal organisation? There is too much money in this to risk it' (NGO worker, London).

Although many NGO clients really need help and are unable to solve their problems on their own, some are using the facilities for their own financial gain. Making a phone call might take a really long time at a call centre it can be quite expensive, so NGO workers are asked to call on behalf of their clients to solve their problems. In other words, NGO workers are trapped between the ethical issues of individual claims, the organisational guidelines and the neoliberal principles that do not always benefit Roma empowerment. While the clients remain dependent on NGO services, these processes also involve NGO workers in fraudulent claims.

In addition, Roma empowerment depends on the level of their commitment to local political processes. However, many NGOs profile themselves as non-political actors representing empowerment principles.

> This perception leads NGOs to shy away from political confrontation and promote technical solutions to problems with political roots. The preference for non-political solutions for political problems in turn limits their impact on processes of political, social and economic change.
>
> (Payes, 2005, p. 41)

As a volunteer and researcher working with several NGOs, I attended training sessions for NGO employees and studied several questionnaires for NGO donors with the clients. The questions were sometimes irrelevant or culturally sensitive, time-consuming and in some cases led to distrust among the clients (Srinivas, 2009). The figures on the actual success of the NGO projects are often manipulated, and sometimes aspects are defined that seem to be more representative of effective jobs offered by development agencies. Advocacy workers are often contacted to translate when phone claims are made for social benefits, so they started to register the number of cases in which they were translating to gain more funds for providing translation services for the Roma. In comparison, I saw fewer successful projects like after school homework groups and health care training programmes that modified their description or were overlooked in annual reports. I hardly ever read about projects described as inefficient or a professional failure. Especially in international EU projects, Roma NGOs are deemed a success.

These processes driven by key stakeholders lead to the conclusion that Roma NGO projects, financed and monitored by donors, do not challenge Roma governance on the local, national and international level. Instead they contribute to it by implementing the same victimising narrative under the ethnic framing of the Roma.

Critical notions on NGOs and professionals in Roma civil society

Roma are often described as an underdeveloped, uneducated tribe in Europe, victimised by the harassment of local majorities. Escobar (2011) argues that although development projects often benefit different groups, they actually maintain underdevelopment by depoliticising the issue of income and submitting the Roma to external political and technical control. Roma NGOs throughout Central Europe identify ethnic tensions as the main source of the low socio-economic status of the Roma, and concentrate on providing services and humanitarian aid for the communities. According to Stroschein (2002), this NGO targeting is often counterproductive because it relieves the government of its responsibility to provide equal services and keeps the Roma separate from other ethnic groups. Most Roma NGOs avoid open dialogue, due to concerns that the Roma, as members of the poorest and most disenfranchised minority in Central Europe, may not be able to express themselves properly. This, in turn, accentuates the existing stereotypes (Payes, 2005, p. 104).

The most important aspects in transmitting ethnic frames about Roma migrants through NGOs are defined in the goals of these networks. For NGOs to intervene and take on a more prominent role, something else is required in addition to gaining visibility, attracting funding and support from powerful institutions, and being well placed to capitalise on the opportunities created by neoliberal structural adjustment. They require a "need" for their work, a humanitarian subject, as is explained in the following quote:

> NGOs overemphasize poverty and stories of discrimination to construct a 'needy subject' – a population constructed as a 'problem' in need of a 'solution' The needs identified by NGOs may not correspond to the actual needs of the people in question, but it is nonetheless the dominant discourse by which those people come to be defined as a 'humanitarian project'. To attract funding and gain visibility by claiming that its work is *necessary*, a NGO must have 'tales that inspire pathos and encourage people to act'.
>
> (Timmer, 2010, p. 268, in Forte, 2014, p. 12)

These NGO practices are shaping a project elite via funds gained through close access to the donor community. In competition for funding, NGOs increase their professional power by employing intellectuals with good English and management skills. So 'if they are willing to "spout the civil society-free market-alternative development line" and collaborate with policies of neoliberal regimes and international financial agencies' (ibid., p. 115), together with these donors they indirectly enhance state control as their by-products. This occurs regardless of whether or not they achieve their economic and social objectives. In addition, by providing potential ideological responses from their professionals and with the use of foreign funds, Roma social projects help elevate local representatives (Ferguson, 2007, p. 34).

Consequently, these elites feed the tensions between radical activists, big international NGOs, small grassroots associations and the formal political parties who criticise their establishment. Although non-governmental organisations have made a sustainable contribution to democratisation through their active efforts to influence social meanings and challenge the terms of governmental "truths", the Roma political frames work the other way around. This "strategic reversibility" of power relations and the terms people think of Roma in are not shifted but shaped by transnational organisations such as the Open Society Institute or the ERRC (ibid., p. 119).

By restraining inequalities and the macro-sociological and economic processes of Central Europe, the NGOs oversimplify social relations, mainly blaming the local majority for discrimination. These narratives often overlook the internal conflicts among the Roma and the local aspects of inter-ethnic relationships. Similar to Roma activists, highly educated Roma describe the social effects of their NGO work, and how they have been blamed for becoming detached from their roots, refusing to help family members and earning money off their poor community members. Some of them choose migration as a way to escape these expectation clashes. On the one hand, they are expected to represent the Roma in "gadjo society" and there is pressure to participate in Romani politics, but on the other hand they experience frustration and a lack of recognition by their own minority.

During my fieldwork, I was regularly associated with these narratives by friends and colleagues who verbalised their concerns about me and my contacts with these organisations. In Hungary and Slovakia, for example, it became obvious that these NGO narratives feed the local right-wing political forces, which turn these discrimination-centred narratives inside out and blame the Roma for local crime problems and social deviance. One of the Czech experts on Roma integration stated that Roma NGO funding should be stopped because he also witnessed how the funding is shared among corrupt politicians who set up their own NGOs to benefit from local Roma integration funds. Roma activists also accused international organisations of loyalty and priority issues defined by donor priorities that conflicted with those of local Roma communities. Even radical conservatives are critical of the funds. Since several pro-Roma organisations are financed by the OSI, they are seen as the employees of Gyorgy Soros, whose name is linked to several conspiracy theories in Eastern Europe, linking the xenophobic connotations of Soros to Romaphobia. These right-wing populist voices define NGOs as being financed by the West to destroy the Hungarian culture and economy and benefit the Jewish community that exploits Hungarian society. To put it briefly, these advocacy groups are seen as the protectors of criminals in an effort to destroy the nation state. In addition, local Roma representatives criticise these organisations as being technocratic and detached from the traditional values of community service (Trehan, 2001). Roma feel patronised by these networks and complain that they have become the social customers of professional benefactors.

Roma civil society has turned into a privatised EU government project. Besides dependency issues related to donors, there are clear barriers in the Roma NGOs related to Roma participation. Due to fragmented Roma communities, rigid and inflexible organisational structures and their lack of transparency regarding their funding effectiveness and selection of board members, there are constant conflicts on a personal and organisational level. When the Roma are included, their relations remain highly hierarchical and leaders largely appoint their own relatives to their boards (Bárány, 2002, p. 292).

Ethnic governance by civil society

EU geopolitical control measures are based on incentives to define and select different groups, which have increasingly fed the workings of NGOs in global civil society. Many Roma advocacy organisations are involved in this type of governance, yet at the same time they work to expand, challenge, undermine and reorient the measures towards 'other objectives than those proposed by the apparent and visible official governmentality of society' (Foucault, 2007, p. 199). NGOs demand that these efforts remain within the framework of "good governance" characterised by the broad and meaningful participation of all the stakeholders, transparency in funding and decision making, and respect for the rule of law.

However, the ethical basis for NGO managerial actions and the social consequence of the corporate power of NGOs and governments seem to be controversial (Grey & Willmott, 2005). Martin Kovats explains this citing academics and intellectuals who often inadequately address the wider socio-economic and political context of poverty and inequality (Kovats 2001). By linking academic, activist and NGO responsibilities, the Roma have become stuck in 'ghetto economies, where they contribute to isolating disadvantaged communities by this localised [aid-based] circuit of capital, disconnected from the mainstream economy' (Amin, et al., 1998, in Mayer, 2003, p. 121). Indeed, NGOs and activists have often helped connect the marginalised Roma to the global aid and development circuits of capital, rather than include them in the economies of their region or country, a process that has produced its own forms of political and cultural disintegration. Under the current circumstances, this process leads to a fully funded self-fulfilling prophecy and the problems are reinforced rather than countered, thus undermining solidarity in foreign contexts. In short, NGOs extend governmentality by making more people and places governable and administrable.

The promotion of civil society as the realm of social action and organisation serves the neoliberal agenda of minimising the role of the state in society. Politically, civil society-based organisations lack the permanence of the state and have no capacity to address the distribution of wealth on a systematic basis (Kapoor, 2005). In addition, the political outcome of transferring development work to NGOs is 'to place the burden for poverty alleviation on the structurally poor which, in turn, leaves NGOs de facto legitimising neoliberal structural adjustment programmes because they fill the welfare delivery gap' (Mohan, 2002, p. 149). Development volunteers and aid industry "professionals" alike are key social mediators of neoliberalism and new managerialism in developing states (Georgeou, 2011). In short, strategies toward European governance have explicitly encouraged building on the extensive participation of non-governmental and other non-state agencies to more effectively facilitate the EU's politics of integration throughout the Union's member states.

In conclusion, Romani activists and NGOs need to be highly critical with neoliberal discourses, entrepreneurship and human and social capital formation in civil society. Ethnic discourses have often contributed to isolating target groups from the wider socio-economic and political circumstances. Not only activists and NGOs, but international donors as well have often encouraged these ethnic connotations to encourage the sustainability of projects to justify their political objectives. It has been convincingly and repeatedly argued that by concentrating on the marginalised as agents of their own improvement, theories of self-help and human and social capital-building obscure 'the structural sources of inequality produced by the present political-economic conjuncture' (Rankin, 2002, p. 10). This critique does not imply that all NGO projects are essentially problematic, but that when mobilised in isolation, they may actually lead to defending or reinforcing existing hierarchies along the lines of class, ethnicity or gender (Van Baar, 2009).

5.5 Transmitted stigmas, bureaucratic guides, migrant interpreters working with Roma

NGOs and activists are indirectly shaping ethnic connotations of Roma while they echo the neoliberal professionalism of governmental bureaucratic structures. These private-public partnerships with their managerialist values appear in other services as well, in particular with service providers who have face-to-face contact with Roma in formal interactions. The following fragment of my conversation with a police interpreter focuses on the role of interpreters:

> *– Can you help me Veronika? Actually, I want to make the police understand who the Olah Gypsies are, and what typical Olah last names are. Because last week they (the police) spoke of the name of Kolompár, as if it would mean something, but I think it means no more than the Orsós, right? Just because someone has Kolompár as a surname, does not mean they are more dangerous than Orsós, right? Or any of the Vlach Roma names . . . how can you get to know them . . .*
>
> *– Such a conclusion would be utterly dangerous.*
>
> *– Or to which areas they belong to in Hungary?*
>
> *– You cannot classify any behaviour based on their relation to a subgroup. The territorial distribution is even less relevant.*
>
> *– Because, as far as I understand, most organized crime is linked to the Olah Gypsies. Here we are extremely interested from a criminonology point of view,*

like we should draw something so you can see what these connections are (SEE drawing). . . . *We'll talk about this later, only because crime is related to culture.*
– Please don't conclude anything (for the police). It is pure discrimination.
(IN9)

The interpreter quoted above sent a handwritten overview of an outline of Roma classifications to ask for confirmation (see Figure 5.1). The table on her draft contained two main groups based on language use: 'czigany natives' and 'non-czigany natives' referring to Romani and non-Romani speaker ethnic groups. Among the so called non-czigany speakers she separated Hungarian speakers (musicians as well as established social groups and labourers, the poor groups among Roma) and Romanian speakers.The latter group is specified in terms of Roman czigany, and 'tekenővájó' – also called as Beash – who are associated with surnames as 'Dunás','Füstös' and 'Tiszaháti'. The czigány native speakers were mapped in two main groups: 'Kárpátaljai' and 'Oláh', who were associated with geographic locations and specific surnames. In an additional note it was stated: 'primitive volks, they do not respect women, they make a living from criminal activities, prostitution and exploitation of others'.

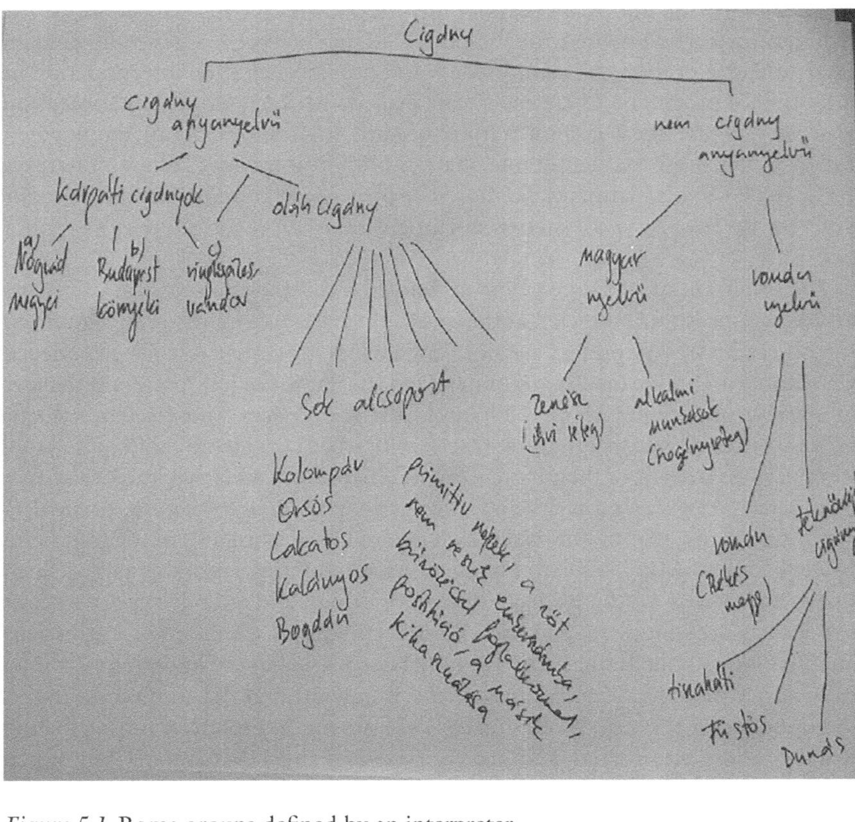

Figure 5.1 Roma groups defined by an interpreter.

As she explained in the call after this message, her intention was to support the police with information and according to her narrative she clearly identifies herself with police forces working with Roma suspects where she provides information about Roma like an expert.

This legal interpreter used to be a police officer in her home country and was clearly willing to transmit her "cultural knowledge" to support the police forces working with Roma migrants. These narratives on Roma illustrate different connotations on ethnic subgroups with reference to crime used by the police in the sending country, without a real understanding of the correlations between crime and ethnicity. To understand the long-term impact of these practices, we have to analyse the role of interpreters in the construction of Roma ethnicity in a host country.

Interpreters who play a central role in bridging bureaucratic service providers and Roma newcomers are often described in studies on bureaucratic practices. As of their arrival, migrants need formal and informal support in becoming part of the local system and bridge language barriers. There are self-employed interpreters who help newcomers for a small amount of money and there are also professionals who are paid by the service provider to translate applications or in specific cases at the police department or court. Those who work more informally and provide information about local administrative rules are more trusted than interpreters who work for the police. Many interpreters generally give initiqal guidance in the settlement process and provide a cultural interpretation for local service providers. These mediators provide background information about processes in the local administration system, suggestions about employment agencies and most frequently information on housing issues. These "interpreters" can be friends, flatmates, landlords or professional interpreters who provide different types of services, such as document translation and support in application calls.

The implications of suggestions on guidance and the transmission of cultural notions about Roma ethnicity, as the quote illustrates, are increasingly significant. In this research, interpreters are not only included because of their experiences with Roma migrants, but also to understand the impact of interpreters at the level of cultural understanding in local administrative services. Interpreters not only witness the challenges migrants are faced with, they also identify different coping strategies. As a result of their involvement in advocacy cases, they might use their own personal view of ethnicity and unwillingly provide information, particularly about the Roma, that might result in changes in legal assistance in the long term.

Depending on local legislative regulations, interpreting is contextually defined. I have interpreted for the Roma in different settings, and attended court sessions, Job Centre appointments and school interventions to see different institutional interactions with the Roma. I tried to understand whether the interpreters' knowledge about the ethnic background of the Roma affected the communication or the outcome of the cases. I also interviewed several interpreters, most of whom work as court interpreters and are registered in the UK National Register of Public Service Interpreters. Many interpreters are concerned about the legislation on qualified interpreting, claiming that unqualified migrants are taking their jobs because they offer cheaper services and destroy the reputation of trained interpreters. However, working with diverse ethnicities is not only a training issue. Sensitising issues seem to be generally underestimated in the basic training of interpreters on the topic of Roma ethnicity. A lack of cultural awareness enables interpreters to use their personal views about the Roma that might echo narratives of the sending countries' majority, referring to the Roma as a backward and uneducated criminal group. In the following section, three major implications are presented related to cultural assumptions when interpreting the practices of local service provisions. The first addresses the cultural mediation of interpreters and how they import ethnic stigma into the host country. The second has to do with the practical involvement of interpreters in interactions with the Roma and how advocacy, mediation and administrative interpreting overlap. The third is about how emotions are transmitted as a result of the identity construction of interpreters working for Roma migrants abroad. Finally, the key implications are summarised as the change in legal policies and the local understanding of Roma ethnicity by civil servants in the host country.

Interaction through interpreters not only means practical support for migrants, it is also a way to transfer ethnic connotations about clients to local service providers. The notions of interpreters, who are often from the same country as their clients, need to be classified in order to differentiate and categorise ethnic newcomers in host countries, such as the Roma in the UK. Professional interpreters are often seen as bilingual entrepreneurs who translate documents in a live interaction. According to the experience of Roma migrants in London, that is a much less important task of interpreters who transmit the cultural connotations from their home countries. The term "cultural mediation" is often used as a blanket term to cover translating and interpreting. However, an interpreter and a cultural mediator are complementary and distinct. The ability to speak two languages does not make one an interpreter, just as familiarity with two cultures does not make one a cultural mediator. There are several definitions of cultural mediation, regarding the role, training, codes of interpreter practice and how the core principles resemble or differ from those of interpreters (Phelan & Martín, 2010). Transmitting the ethnic connotations of the Roma as part of a cultural mediation plays a central role in defining the suspected attributes of welfare claiments that contributes to the digital sorting process.

Since cultural mediation goes in two directions, interpreters might fulfil several roles in interactions between the host society and the newcomer. Interpreters can pass information on to the Roma about local legal procedures, application forms, eligibility rules and the possible outcomes of different claims. So they are able to clarify bureaucratic processes for newcomers, such as how to fill in a claim form to qualify for something as soon as possible. Some interpreters openly admit they feel morally obliged to help families with their applications to increase their chance of being eligible and inform them about the preconditions for benefit entitlements. They tell them about counter-indications and what personal data have to be hidden or emphasised to pass the screening process. Some interpreters feel uncomfortable with demands of this kind since they see them as in conflict with their code of conduct, so they also avoid the Roma who request their support to "give the right answers on application forms". Some interpreters are also scared to talk to me because their income is based on this kind of advocacy work. Many interpreters work for several families, go to their houses and "fix their claims and appeals" or "help them" as they call it for a fixed sum of money. Their clients know how much they ask for which type of forms or what their hourly fee is. I was also confronted with similar expectations when doing fieldwork: phone calls, invitations, letters, emails, Facebook messages. The more my involvement was known to the migrant Roma networks, the more requests I received. Respondents shared their concerns and I was mostly asked to advise on applications based on their calculations. I would call different agencies on behalf of my respondents, writing appeals to HMRC against its decisions, and requesting forms for them. I tried to explain the possible consequences of different decisions regarding the personal data they shared. These tasks were ethically debatable, but helped me get in-depth knowledge on the real conditions of migrant families and how they represent themselves in digitalised bureaucratic procedures. It also gave me a better understanding of institutional dysfunction and the lack of professionality.

The Roma I helped were regularly ignored by service providers, or their claims were not taken seriously. When I emphasised my role in these conversations, I got a different response, which often led to clarifications about the mistakes made by client managers. Due to loopholes in the technocratic social service provision and the rapidly changing eligibility rules, there are many misunderstandings and controversial decisions about benefit claims in the current procedure. This fluid process of "helping applicants" raises dilemmas around the limits of responsible "cultural mediation" since they might trigger the clients of interpreters to submit fraudulent benefit applications. The question is, where are the borders for interpreting and providing mediation between cultures?

Interpreters regularly refer to the complexity of their role in certain situations, such as court or police interpreting, and the communication problems involved. Some emphasised their role purely as "verbatim" – as a reproducer of messages in another language – and one is therefore expected to remain "neutral", "invisible", a "non-person" (Berk-Seligson, 1990). Others mentioned their presence as a guarantee for fair hearings, where they felt like a bystander, which guaranteed that the Roma would not be discriminated against. However, there is also an expectation that the interpreter is 'acting as a cultural mediator, rendering services of "conciliation"' (Merlini & Favaron, 2003, p. 212). This involvement is highly problematic in the case of cultural mediation for the Roma and how they express themselves in the perception of interpreters.

Many interpreters say they recognise Roma by their vocabulary, language use and surnames. If they have the impression that pure verbatim translations of messages produce tension due to structural misunderstandings between the Roma and civil servants, they say that they try to clarify this by cultural framing. For instance, family relations are defined in different terms for many Roma families, who call their cousins brother or sister or refer to their nieces and nephews as their own children. According to legal interpreters, they often define household situations like multiple occupation differently than non-Roma. These aspects become relevant when interpreters try to clarify the behaviour or living conditions of their clients in different interactions. Based on situational aspects, four forms of interpreting are differentiated: dialogue, liaison, court and ad hoc interpreting (Jiang, 2007).

The first refers to a dialogic setting (in hospitals, public service, business or diplomatic situations) with professional encounters such as 'police, immigration and welfare service interviews, doctor-patient interviews, business negotiations, [. . .] and so on' (Mason, 1999, p. 147). During the period of my fieldwork I translated these dialogues and collected data on these interactions. Research respondents were cautious in these conversations and consciously selected the information they shared with the authorities. These selections of information are symptoms of distrust, result in confusion since incomplete data provokes more suspicion on the part of service providers. This can lead to further accusations of fraud and dishonesty in cases where administrative bodies are confronted with mismatching or missing data about the families.

Liaison interpreting verbalises the link or contact between speakers who do not speak the same language. In the literature, the term is used synonymously with 'delegate interpreting' (Kade, 1967, p. 9). These practices were most common in church ceremonies or conferences with attendees from different Roma ethnic groups with different nationalities. This is fairly common practice at the European policymaking level, but has only limited implications for local interactions with Roma migrants.

Two important fields of interpreting that contribute to images of Roma ethnicity are court interpreting and public service interpreting. They reflect a specific legal situation-related (institutional) aspect of interpreter-mediated communication (Mikkelson, 2008). Community interpreting in a legal context involves the main legal domains where interpreters work (police interviews and interrogations, tribunal hearings, courtroom hearings and trials) in the English-speaking world, highlighting the importance of qualified interpreters for accuracy (Mikkelson, 2008). As all the interpreters say, neoliberal market principles have also infiltrated the field of interpreting, resulting in unprofessional practices due to financial decisions to hire agencies that employ uncertified interpreters. Due to high competition and low job security, there is strong rivalry among the interpreters working in the same field. One of the respondents complained about the unintended consequences:

> Like one of the barista came to me in one of her cases. And she said I don't want to work with this interpreter . . . because this interpreter thinks that Roma are just drinking, spending money on food and my client doesn't trust her. So, if you are unable to establish a relationship as a professional person, if they don't feel they can trust you, they are not going to talk to you and if

> they are not going to talk to you they are not talking to a solicitor, so they cannot be appropriately defended. Because the link in between is impeding the communication. And they change what they say, because they might be ashamed of it.
>
> (IN2)

Clarification efforts in the conversation just create more confusion. Untrained interpreters might not fully understand the discourse strategies of the courtroom and the role of the interpreter and have inadequate linguistic and interpreting expertise. Hale also studied court cases where a misunderstanding of the interpreter's role is common among non-professionals hired as interpreters. Instead of seeing their role as that of an impartial interpreter, they see themselves as advocates or gatekeepers. These attitudes can be manifested overtly in their comments or advice to their "client" or to the legal practitioner, or covertly (Hale, 2004). Some of the untrained legal interpreters I worked with shared several cases with me and provided a follow up on the legal issues where Roma migrants were involved. Once we had a discussion about how to maintain a neutral position as an interpreter most of the non-professionals stated that it is impossible to stay neutral. Others said they 'support justice'. When I asked what justice is, an interpreter explained her partial position by supporting 'those who are right', referring to taking sides in the conversation on behalf of those they feel deserve it morally. Untrained interpreters often see themselves as local experts who support newcomers. They provide translations for individuals as a part-time job, and help in ad hoc interpreting, such as calls with landlords or other service providers when the services are rendered by whoever is immediately available, such as medical hospital staff, even family members (Jiang, 2007).

These interactions are valuable in understanding cultural transmissions since they are spontaneous and occur in a face-to-face situation (as distinguished from note taking in consecutive interpreting) without contextualising (Jiang, 2007). When following court cases, I interviewed court and police interpreters, police officers and former police officers and teachers who are now interpreters. Some also refused to give an interview because they didn't want to break the code of conduct. In some cases, we were in contact with the same person who had been involved in legal cases. I followed a Crown Court case on human trafficking for sexual exploitation involving Roma migrants, but ethnic background had no relevance in the court case. Ethnicity was never mentioned by the court interpreters. At the police hearing, interpreters were more frequently willing to tell the police they were translating for the Roma, assuming it would help to understand the suspect's situation from a cultural point of view.

In general, two contradictory narratives are distinguished regarding ethnic connotations about clients from the same country. One sees the Roma in court as victims of circumstances who have a lack of contextual knowledge, in particular about child care norms in the UK. Others stress the well-informed and skilled characteristics of the Roma who are shy and know how to take advantage of the contextual aspects, such as the lack of knowledge about Roma stereotypes. These narratives refer to Roma migrants as innovative newcomers who cooperate and support each other and benefit from their hidden identity in a foreign country where they are spared daily discrimination. I have met interpreters who quit due to frustrations about the discriminatory attitude of police officers. In short, stigmatising ethnic connotations in the legal context and stereotyping cultural transmissions have several explanations. A key argument involves the limitations of interpreting in the legal service world due to managerialist autocratic measures, as well as financial cuts of contracted governmental services. These all shape the profiling mechanisms of service providers and the suspicion towards culturally differentiated applicants.

According to these interpreters, many professionals don't really understand what the role of the interpreter is. It is common for lawyers to resort to the third person (e.g. 'can you ask him') when they lose control or want to reprimand the witness. Service providers, police officers and lawyers often expect the interpreter to rectify the situation or reprimand the witness, rather than do it themselves. This mutual complicity was highlighted by one of the Czech interpreters: 'It is their [the interpreters'] job to explain the cultural differences, but it should not be up to them. But as you know yourself, it is expected (by the institutions)'.

Inter-cultural commentaries regarding Roma differences and what they call "the situation" in Central Eastern Europe lay the foundations for future interest in getting to know the "culture" of the Roma/Gypsy by many state employees working with migrants. During my fieldwork, cultural assumptions about Roma were being spread throughout police and social service networks, causing confusion about the reasons for specific forms of behaviour, such as domestic violence. As an advocacy worker, I was approached by the social services to confirm the cultural acceptance of violence within Roma families and the child exploitation issues. Interestingly, "class" or Eastern European cultural notions are not included in the explanations of civil servants, nor is the post-industrial, rundown neighbourhood in East London where most of them live. The dominant classification is in terms of culture and community. Regardless of their actual sympathetic or negative attitudes toward the Roma/Gypsies, most dominant white Slovaks openly avoided interaction as well as any symbolic association with the Roma.

With cultural mediation, ideas and expectations are transmitted by interpreters, as are negative emotions with direct implications for the interaction and long-term policies developed in local bureaucracies such as social sorting practices. The Roma are often described as vulnerable, underdeveloped, welfare-dependent people who often live outside the law and society. These connotations emphasise the otherness and a lack of compatibility with the rest of society.

These notions are also stressed by Roma activists and NGOs, which leads to suspicion and fear in the host society. In addition, interpreters stress the vulnerability of Roma to victimisation and organised crime or the opposite, their involvement in human trafficking. The ideas about the dangerous "other" might have implications for crime control measures and the definition of a threat in host communities. Some interpreters suggested that as a result of ethnic notions, recent human trafficking laws could be applied as a migration control technique to exclude suspicious groups. Others said that on a micro level, social workers seem to apply the rules more strictly to the unwanted Roma to make them move on to another borough. Several references to situations described by interpreters have been defined in emotional expressions that clarified their role in the logic of the "civilization survival" that is increasingly part of the public sphere. These discourses 'which (re)produce fear among the public at large are routinely mobilised by state officials to justify practices such as the increase in covert policing' (Pasquetti, 2013). Interpreters not only transmit stigmatising notions about Roma, they even report them to the police when they view them as suspicious, which increases the association between the Roma and the risk of crime. As most CEE interpreters link the Roma with human trafficking, one interpreter describes these as ethnic strategies:

> There was one case where I went to a church ceremony and two Roma ladies and a big Nigerian family were present. It was the first time in my case and I did not know how to react, so I informed the church minister and she said it happens everywhere in the UK. And she didn't even talk to me about it anymore. I didn't know what to do so I didn't report it, but if I would find myself in that situation again I would go to the bathroom, make a call and say this is what is happening right now. You have to be very quick, so I have to say what is happening right now and I cannot delay the case. . . . The women don't report it because they don't speak the language, they are forced into these marriages. They are not there of their own free will, they just want to get out, so they would agree with anything to get out of this country. They would normally be reported by the registrars or the police would have some kind of informant who would report it.
>
> (IN2)

Although research respondents who used to work with interpreters never complained about them, some interpreters complained about people they worked with being prejudiced and transmitting to authorities "what Roma means". Along these lines institutional actors like interpreters have a direct impact on state responses to these types of "external threats" (Pasquetti, 2013). The incorporation of state practices of security and discourses of suspiciousness into everyday life – which includes everyday practices such as spotting "suspicious" people on buses and driving circuitously around "dangerous" neighbourhoods – has important emotional components that justifies semantic differentiation of migrants.

5.6 Conclusion

Today's Roma are the contemporary inheritors of the gypsy legacy, an identity historically fabricated by scholars, experts and bureaucrats. To be clear, the claim that I make is not that the Roma group does not exist, quite the opposite. It can be stated that "the group is being formed and that the driving force behind this process is competitive social and political interest" (Surdu & Kovats, 2015, p. 7). Academics, activists and interpreters, just as any policing and security agency, play a role in the (re)production of emotions in which law-enforcement practices interact with a key ethno-national cleavage within the citizenry between Roma and non-Roma citizens (Pap, 2014; Brubaker, 2004).The question is, how current law-enforcement practices can affect those people – mainly, but not exclusively, minorities or incorporated non-citizens – who are constructed in such policies and public debates as dangerous and unworthy outsiders.

Roma narratives offer insights that are not found anywhere else, and as such, they "inform" policymaking. They break through existing prejudices, affirm existing conceptions, clarify underlying motivations or causes and bring in new elements. They add to the discussion on the proper understanding of social surveillance practices and the securitisation of suspected migrants. Ethnic migrants are not static realities though, social practices change over time and the process of understanding is never-ending. The selected case studies not only inform us, they contribute to the constitution of that reality and form part of it in a creative way. This study aims to opens up space for participation in an ongoing conversation and in discussions on what is in the best interest of the Roma and how they anticipate these socially constructed control practices.

6 Accessing benefits abroad

After the EU expansion, old welfare state bureaucracies began changing their priorities toward business structures and increasingly including private organisations in social service practices. These organisations are characterised by efficiency-oriented practices, targets and reduced the workers discretionary power. These changes in social service practices have altered the role of bureaucracies in the surveillance society. Welfarism has turned into targeted policing of the unemployed. Currently, the digitalisation of population control has resulted in new strategies with selection parameters that are independent of nationality and ethnicity but profile tracable economic status. Service users are encouraged to adapt to the demands of the neoliberal market and become self-sustaining assertive applicants with verifiable financial history. As a result, social service clients try to exhibit the desired citizen dispositions consistent with shifts in this bureaucratic field (Woolford & Nelund, 2013, p. 23). These strategies to prove their reliability and willingness to work should prevent suspicion of service providers online and offline. Since these applicants are not passive actors in these control processes, the monitoring practices of local social services has to be constantly updated. Various generations of newcomers develop suitable strategies to find their way in these procedures by manipulating, bypassing or hiding from these techniques of governance.

Dialogues between service providers and newcomers constantly shape the preconditions of benefit entitlements. Profiling methods retarget suspicious claimants, who are identified based on updated information registered in digital databases. In response, applicants look for new loopholes in the system to avoid the selection mechanisms. Bureaucratic application systems have been developed to include several screening moments that push benefit applicants toward participation in the labour market and restrict their eligibility (see Figure 5.1).

The last part of this book addresses migrants' coping strategies. Each chapter focuses on one particular form of interaction with welfare bureaucracies. The first addresses the provision of basic conditions in the host country and the challenges of digital job seeking. The second analyses the struggles the Roma face with online tax credit applications and algorithmic financial surveillance. The third summarise the impact of the dividual identities on the mobilites of migrants in the financial surveillance context.

6.1 The first stage – preconditions for settling

Simply qualifying to apply for benefits can be difficult for newcomers in the UK. They need to prove their address to apply for a National Insurance (NI) number. Bank accounts are required for every benefit application, but it is difficult to get one without proof of income. While a newcomer has to pay rent from the start, housing benefits are only available to those who have a job or who are entitled to Jobseeker's Allowance. However, Jobseeker's Allowances are only available to people who have passed the National Habitual Residence test. This test requires proof of residence in the UK, so even EU migrants are unable to claim anything in their first three months. The complex interdependencies are not only interpreted as obstacles but also as a bureaucratic fringe space where well-informed newcomers are able to circumvent restrictions and become entitled to these social benefits. Although these practices are not different for Roma migrants, profiling mechanisms in the control procedures are associated with ethnic profiling Roma have experienced in their sending countries. In a detailed analysis of ethnographic data on Roma mobility, I would like to show how changing bureaucratic practices in London shape the knowledge of Roma newcomers about financial profiling, monitoring and selection practices. Extensive case studies can chronologically illuminate the changes in mobility patterns and coping strategies Roma use when coming into contact with social services. This chapter then analyses the different stages of settling in the UK, in particular interactions with Job Centre Plus offices.

First the stages of interaction between local bureaucratic structures and migrants will be clarified from the moment of their arrival. The stages are differentiated by using three central questions. What are applicants supposed to do according to social policies? How are they supposed to manage their claims and what are they expected to do to achieve that? How do they actually react to these social sorting mechanisms?

I first describe how brokers are the key actors in these interactions. I then address difficulties with basic registrations, such as access to NI applications. Lastly, I present interactions at Job Centre Plus, as well as the recent managerial implications of welfare provisions like financial sanctions.

The central argument in this chapter is that "deservingness" is constantly defined in the interplay of interaction between service providers and clients in the UK bureaucracy.

To be able to stay in a foreign country, a person virtually needs to know someone familiar with the foreign bureaucracies. These actors can be paid interpreters who provide extra information about local procedures, landlords who benefit from the applicants' success, family members who try to make their relatives self-sustaining to prevent extra costs, or professional brokers who make a living from the commodification of information. As is illustrated below, these agents combine a wide range of tasks, such as providing accommodations and selling information to job applications, bank account registrations or national security numbers. However, there is a blurred line between consensual or predatory relationships with these middlemen.

One of the Roma brokers (BR5) I interviewed, a Hungarian in his mid-thirties, had lived in London for five years. He explained how he stepped out of the grey market and started his own letting agency. Like many other settled entrepreneurs, he rents houses from other ethnic minorities and sublets them to his countrymen. He contracted a friend in Hungary to help him recruit migrants and assists them after their arrival. He started as a recruiter for another agency and after he made enough money, he rented spacious premises and started subletting. Nowadays, he has several houses and lives in one of them.

In addition to acting as a landlord, he offers a "complete package" to continue assisting the migrants recruited from Hungary with practical arrangements to help them find a job. He complains that everything he does for the new arrivals makes him look bad because people do not realise how much easier he makes their lives for a £200 fee. For that fee, he provides newcomers with information and a corrupt job interview at a local hotel. This essentially means he pays an intern HR manager to sell the job interview questions and tells him the names of the applicants, so they are hired by the hotel. He helps newcomers apply for a bank account and NI number. Without an NI number and proof of an address, it is difficult to open a bank account, which is a precondition for job applications and social benefits. He claims that he pays £150 of the £200 administration fee to the hotel recruiter and about £20 to cover his transport. So in the end, he barely earns £30 a person.

> When I asked why he went to so much trouble for such a small payment, he was stressed and irritated. 'Why? Because you will live in my house and you will pay the rent for me. So it is good for everyone, you see?'
>
> (BR5)

In short, information, complex applications and "favours" like interpreting provided by a middleman can cost a newcomer up to £200, which is a serious financial investment. Newcomers also pay their rent, housing deposit and travel costs, all of which are organised by the broker. Since legal aid is no longer available to these claimants, they depend on the agencies and often acquire debts. Although NGOs also assist migrants with application forms and appeals, newcomers are usually not aware of their existence and outreach services are quite uncommon. These restrictions increase the role of middlemen with local connections who help newcomers pass through the welfare sorting machine, although these dependency relations with a stranger do increase the risk of data abuse.

Although many Roma middlemen are highly exploitative toward their tenants, some of whom live and work for them as modern-day slaves, the middlemen are also viewed as role models by people who are inspired by their lifestyle. One of the research respondents (BR3) who was in London for the first time, working as a cleaner at a hotel, followed the same strategy as her recruiters. First, she was unable to keep her job due to her disability and moved back to her home country.

While preparing her return, she invested in online friendships on social media and made arrangements from her hometown to move back. When she returned to London, she was more prepared than the first time and had invested her back-dated PIP payments in a property she was subletting, as did the brokers. She used the same techniques but reduced the preconditions for clients to one week's rent plus one week's deposit. She advertised her rooms on social media and invested in personal relationships with her tenants, who also supported her by providing babysitting and translation services.

Agents participating in this study have their own specific target groups (e.g. recruits for hotel work, factory jobs or just tenancies), but surprisingly none of them were willing to rent to Roma migrants, which raised the question of ethnic solidarity. A respondent who sublet houses and was raised in a traditional Roma family asked for my help with a room she wanted to rent out. Interestingly, she was willing to have a relationship with a Roma, but unwilling to have Roma as tenants, as she explained: 'I don't want Roma, they don't work' (BR2). Other respondents regularly mentioned these discriminatory practices, stressing that they made it hard to find accommodations or jobs. This leads to repetitive social and economic exclusion. As a result, the Roma have no trust in "professional recruiters" and prefer to rely on their own social networks.

A few respondents, who already returned to their home countries, assisted by these middlemen, described them as exploitative brokers who often abused their clients' naiveté or trust. Some not only sold their know-how about benefit applications, they recruited newcomers to use their documents for credit contracts or tenancy agreements. Some described the recruiters as traffickers who make the Roma sign benefit claims or open bank accounts in their name and then send them back to their home countries. Predatory relationships of this kind have resulted in a growing awareness among migrants and service providers alike.

Via social media, newcomers are now better informed about the brokerage options and can verify the agencies they pay for their services. More newcomers are able to make their arrangements alone and fewer are victimised by exploiters who increase the distrust that damages the businesses of fair trade middlemen:

> They are no longer easy to rip off, or fewer are now coming. It was messed up at that time when 90% were cheated, and now they do not trust the agencies anymore. . . . But some who are told they will get £20 an hour are still tricked. . . . A few years ago, many more people were coming, but now you have these social media and other websites, so they are more careful. And yet many competitors discredit each other too. I am also tired of constantly being compared to others [his business is discussed on several websites]. I used to do stupid stuff, I admit it.
>
> (BR5)

Thanks to the experiences during previous waves of migration to London, many Roma have enough social and symbolic capital to act quickly within the interstitial spaces of the various systems that opened up after the EU expansion. These pathways were often temporary and quickly closed off. As Grill (2015) notes, Roma migrants 'were aware of the limited duration of these efforts, and knew that the key to success was not only to understand certain techniques or mechanisms but also to explore these at a particular moment' (p. 101).

Within the continuous dynamic of control and proof, monitoring authorities have discovered several manipulation techniques. They made their screening mechanisms more restrictive and introduced high sanctions for any misuse or abuse of personal data. This led to new types of dependency relations, innovative data abuse and the increasing visibility of exploited migrants. Later it will be highlighted how marginal newcomers find the most inventive solutions.

6.2 Documented traces abroad

Every EU member state has basic administrative procedures enabling foreign EU citizens to live and work there. Migrants are expected to pay their own travel expenses and find their own accommodations. Although newcomers are often first housed by relatives, their address can usually not be used to apply for an NI number, because the application might affect the main tenant's tax credit payment. And if a room is sublet illegally, landlords are unable to provide tenancy agreements. To put it succinctly, newcomers need to find an address to use for proof of residence.

Unlike some other EU countries, the UK has no central database that records tenancies, so there are other requirements to prove UK residency. If a tenant rents a room from a registered local agency, the agency provides a formal document. However, these agencies have many preconditions and usually require several months' deposit, long-term contracts and higher rents than the informally sublett rooms described earlier. Many Roma cannot afford such a high rent for a room, and even more documents are needed for a free property. The preconditions for a tenancy contract are not problematic for the tenant who is subletting the room, but they are for the landlord who is not paying taxes and has not registered the property, especially if he claims Housing Benefit or other benefits for the property.

If landlords are unwilling to provide a tenancy agreement, migrants are forced to use a different strategy. In interviews, most respondents said they used a temporary address when applying for an NI number. But there are also tenancy agreements for sale that are registered at "polluted addresses", which brokers sell for a small payment. Other respondents falsified their own tenancy contract and sold it or gave it to their friends. There were hardly any respondents who lived at their registered address for the first few months, which pollutes the service providers' data analyses. After a lot of applications, these *commodified addresses* are checked, but due to the high fluctuation in the London housing market, this is not considered a priority for law enforcement agencies. The real problems start when benefit applications have to be registered with such a data.

The most important part of the registration process is the "NINO", the National Insurance Number. After newcomers get a tenancy agreement, they need to make an appointment to apply for an NI number on the phone in English, which often requires an interpreter. And if newcomers are able to book an appointment with their local Job Centre Plus office, they are invited in an English letter for an interview. The offices are often unwilling to provide interpreters (the conditions for the provision of interpreters are not defined), which makes the applicant dependent on others who are willing to translate for them. Many newcomers prefer to attend the appointment with someone who can clarify the questions and indicate which the "right answer" is. However, these informal interpreters can cause misunderstandings, delays in the application process and even rejected claims.

The questionnaire for the NI number is long and complicated and has questions that migrants need to learn "to answer properly" to be entitled to an NI number. One respondent mentioned a general example about the "will to work" as a precondition. Many families try to register their parents via stipulations on family reunion. Although the parents are often retired in their home country, to receive an NI number and health care, they have to *confirm that they are coming to work*, since they are not entitled to a pension in the UK. In short, people who don't come for the purpose of work or study have almost no chance of being included in the national registration system. In short, potential benefit claimants are sometimes forced to lie about their real intentions to get access to social provisions since otherwise they would be unable to get a National Insurance number. Some respondents said that during interviews, even the officer processing their claim suggested lying to make the applicant eligible for registration.

As an interpreter and advocacy worker at different NGOs, I made several appointments for newcomers from different countries and attended their interviews. Almost everyone was aware of the importance of this process, and some respondents even changed their names and ID to be able to apply for a "second" NI number especially for credit checks. One of the respondents told me he 'had a lot of trouble' when he was living in London. He committed fraud, took day pay loans and thus had a bad credit history. He went back to his home country, changed his name and applied for identity documents to claim a new National Insurance Number. By claiming a new 'NI' he could create a new debt free identity. Central European Roma who have been in contact with local NGOs in London have a strong overview of the bureaucratic system and are aware of how the different eligibility regulations are related. Still, many were unable to apply this knowledge due to language issues or registration defaults online. In addition to limited access to interpreting, another barrier erected in the fieldwork period is the restriction on bank account applications. Without an account in the UK, there is hardly any way to be employed or claim a benefit.

Although there is free mobility in Europe, migrants are expected to have a British bank account in the United Kingdom. To open an account, foreign citizens are asked to provide evidence of their identity and confirmation of their address. For those who have been living abroad and are planning to move or return to the UK, this is problematic because they have no credit history in the UK.

Various general preconditions make it difficult for the respondents to produce the required documents. They need original passports, NI cards or birth certificates, and their travel documents have to be current (i.e. unexpired). Letters about utility bills need to have a recent date and, for students, the dates of courses in the letter of acceptance have to reasonably correspond with the date of the account application to the bank.

Most banks are unwilling to offer domestic banking services to people without an address in the UK because of concerns about fraud prevention and extra administrative costs. Migrants with no income and no proper address regularly have problems opening a bank account. Even those with proof of an address can be stopped by a suspicious bank employee. One of the respondents I assisted, an older lady who had just moved to East London to stay with her family, was wearing traditional clothing and had an old-fashioned hairstyle when she tried to open a bank account to be able to claim JSA. She tried all the banks on High Street with her daughter, but she was refused at every single one. Her daughter was upset and told a bank employee she had opened an account at the same branch under the same conditions as her mother. The employee replied that 'the preconditions were modified two weeks ago'. After several failures, she managed to open a Santander debit card account online (BR3).

Due to extreme cuts in legal aid by the local councils, access to assistance is restricted. Solicitors are often so overloaded they are unable to take on new cases. An experienced advocacy worker at a local NGO stated that this is worrying since the cuts also stop people from building legal cases against the government. Any irregular situation of bureaucratic exclusion thus needs to be channelled to NGOs with the capacity to build a case.

Fear of fraud causes banks to make opening accounts more difficult. As one branch manager in Ilford clarified, after a few fraud cases involving Eastern European migrants, a central decision was made to have banks only provide accounts to foreign EU nationals who can provide written documents such as bills to show they are actually residing at the address on the application form. The general impression is that these restrictions are due to money-laundering regulations introduced in 1993. In short, even banks have introduced extra checks and place limitations on new clients based on their bureaucratic track records.

As a solution to being denied a bank account, many respondents use a relative's card or only use debit cards that are easily accessible but less secure. Respondents explained to rely on information provided by family networks or online social media forums. They ask for suggestions and ideas about how to create a credit history and try to follow online instructions. Although there are many paper tracks of their mobility, it is still not enough to settle in a new society.

One respondent who had been living in Canada and Ireland explained his tactics concerning these restrictions. He informed me that a few years ago, before the restrictions took effect, he was able to open several accounts when his family had debts or short-term loans linked to his accounts. He said there are similar practices in Canada and Ireland (HM36). This family regularly sold bank cards, credit cards or even bank accounts with a PIN code and documents. After the transaction, they would tell their local branch that the card had been lost or stolen. These practices are still common, but according to many respondents involved in similar commodification practices, recent restrictions make newcomers even more vulnerable for these practices. However, it is even more profitable for those involved in such fraud cases for a longer period of time.

After arrivals manage to arrange a tenancy agreement, an NI number and a bank account, they need to generate a source of income. On the British labour market, job applications are mainly processed by employment agencies. The agencies play an important role in the financial stability of newcomers, especially those looking for unskilled work. As many respondents note, it is a stressful and unpredictable way of life. Jobs provided by these agencies are short-term, irregular and poorly paid, and applicants are usually only informed a day in advance that they will be going to work. Many Roma are recruited though these agencies to work for the local council, warehouses and factories. Most of the respondents without an extensive network in the host country had to face the bitter reality of the British dream; before their debts increased, many applied for social benefits to be eligible for housing benefits.

Since rents are extremely high in London, the most important benefit is the housing benefit. However, the route to become entitled is quite complicated (Appendix F). In the following section, I present the basic tactics of respondents who apply for basic social provisions. This stage of their contact with bureaucratic processes increasingly includes the digital welfare system, which requires specific skills and knowledge of the application processes to ensure their elegiblity.

One of the targeted groups of benefit claimants monitored are newcomers who are unable to work. As one of the most interesting bureaucratic processes, Personal Independence Payment (PIP) applications were followed in the fieldwork period. PIP was introduced in 2013 as a new form of disability benefit to replace the Disability Living Allowance (DLA). It was a major change in the disability benefits available to claimants aged 16 to 64. After the new legislation was introduced, almost every DLA claimant had to be screeed for the risk of abusing their entitlement. The forms became long, and applicants had to provide many medical documents to prove their disabilities. There were believed to be over 3,000,000 claimants for DLA in 2013, but the aim was by 2018 to reduce it with 600,000 claimants for the new PIP. Many DLA claimants lost their payments in 2013, not because they moved away or recovered, but because they were not eligible for PIP according to the new screening tests. This new selection measure was introduced in addition to restrictions about the habitual residency of claimants. To apply for PIP, the applicant had to have been a resident of Great Britain for two of the last three years, should not be subject to immigration control and must have a long-term disability that presents problems related to mobility and daily living.

This new PIP programme means disabled people arriving to the UK are unable to claim PIP in the first two years but are also unable to work. This effectively closes the border to chronically ill migrants or forces them to lie about the length of their residency, which increases the production of false paperwork.

As the latest statistics confirm, the UK government appears unwilling to support people with health care problems and is trying to force everyone back on the labour market (O'Hara, 2015). The latest DWP report concludes that almost two out of three people who apply for PIP get nothing at all unless they are terminally ill. The statistics also expose the massive backlog created by the combined failures of Atos, Capita and the DWP. Fewer than one in six claims have been decided so far. Many claimants do not receive a decision and only 37% of those who do are awarded some amount of PIP. To put this in perspective, it means only 12,654 of the 220,300 people who requested PIP in the nine months after April 2013 were awarded PIP. This contrasts with the report on the success of new DLA claims, which showed a 43% award rate in the year ending March 2011 (DWP, 2014).

It would appear that the government is on track to successfully reduce spending on welfare benefits by delaying awards and payments for many months, and also by finding a higher percentage of claimant's ineligible for benefits. Most claims are not properly investigated and applicants who are not eager or devastated enough to appeal a negative decision are left to accept this decision and apply for jobs they have no chance of getting. A respondent told me that when he appealed, he was asked at the court hearing to tie his shoelaces. When he managed to do so, his claim was refused. Many respondents were told that their documents had been lost at the welfare offices or, when they phoned, they were told they were not in the computer system. That is impossible since the phone application for benefits registers everything in the computer. Such restrictions and re-selection of unproductive citizens also represent the parameters of selection in social sorting procedures.

Government organisations do not send letters of decision on time and claimants are unable to appeal if they receive the decision too late. When I called on behalf of some of them, I could hardly get any information. Employees promised to call me back, but it almost never happened. Civil servants are not cooperative, instead they try to refuse new claims or discourage claimants. NGO workers are aware of these tendencies and have learned to express or even exaggerate applicants' complaints.

One respondent was almost blind, but she had to apply three times before her claim was accepted. I her case forms were regularly lost or the NHR test was not sent out. She asked someone to attend the meeting with her to make it clear that she is really disabled. She regularly had to pay an interpreter to help with the forms and had to manage phone calls on her own. Her disability made her unable to work, but the test asked how she was supporting herself while she waited for approval. This was quite a quandary, since her income could be used as an excuse to refuse her claim. She patiently kept trying until her claim was finally accepted after five and a half months. However, the delay meant she had no formal income for the first half year of her stay in the UK. In short, only well-trained and persistent migrants are able to make an honest claim if they are able to financially support themselves till the decision is made. As the respondent said, 'we are forced to lie to survive' (HW61).

PIP applicants often felt it was not enough that they had to wait for years, they had to make their situations appear much worse than they were to be taken seriously by the PIP office. Some argued that they had to prove they were in debt.

Dependence on external funds such as study loans or other credits made respondents felt controlled by their debts.

These shifts in the financial support of newcomers have been recognised as a strategy to force unproductive migrants out of the country. However, not enough attention is devoted to the individual tactics that challenge these restrictive control measures every day. As the peceding cases illustrate, newcomers combine local facilities from third parties to effectively overcome those barriers designed to keep them out of the welfare system or even out of the country. Neoliberal values not only trigger those who are willing to find work, they also trigger those who are willing to be supported.

6.3 The ivory tower of Job Centre Plus

Job Centre Plus offices are primarily responsible for NI number interviews and the provision of benefits and control of everyone claiming Jobseeker's Allowance, Income Support, an Incapacity Benefit or Employment and Support Allowance. Different claims have different implications. All of them are managed in the uncomfortable environment of JCP offices protected by security guards and reminiscent of a police station. Here, claimants regularly report their activities and efforts to find jobs or minimise their costs.

The application process is full of minor obstacles to discourage people from becoming benefit claimants. Most claims for financial support depend on the first application, which has to be submitted online. Then claimants receive a form for an NHR test. If they pass the test, they are invited to an interview with a client manager to discuss the preconditions for their payments. Being rejected for a claim can have a domino effect, since rejection for one claim can make the applicant automatically ineligible for several other benefits. These processes serve the social sorting processes by selecting and excluding people unable to prove their deservingness.

Time is a strategic tool, not only for service providers but also for applicants. Since these procedures take a long time, some migrants employ other strategies until they are approved. Many end up with debts like unpaid rent and facilities bills, and migrants are regularly evicted. In that case, they are forced to submit a new application under their new address, so they are constantly on the move. According to advocacy workers at local NGOs, landlords and agencies run a thriving business exploiting tenants and workers in a marginal position. In the following section, I provide a brief overview of how respondents manage to get through these bureaucratic stages to access basic benefits.

There are several tests to confirm ones geogrpaphic and economic belonging to the host country. After applicants apply online for any benefit claim in the UK, the National Habitual Residence test (NHR) is sent to them to verify their term of residence and financial background based on their labour history in the host country.

When my fieldwork period started in 2013, almost all the applicants who managed their tenancy agreement, NI number and JSA application passed the test, even though the questionnaire was long and many needed some translation assistance. The test changed on 1 January 2014. After that date, everyone who came to the UK and applied for benefits during the first weeks was denied, since the new test required a minimum fixed period of three months' residence for claims for income-based benefits such as JSA. In addition, the maximum term for JSA was reduced to six months, so claimants have to be employed after that period. These requirements caused one of the most controversial situations for many people who realise, after a month, that they are unable to support themselves after such a short period in the host country (Rutledge, 2014c). As one respondent explained:

> The system forces you to lie. Because when you go to the Job Centre, you have to lie and say that you have already been here for three months, and then with the bank account you have to lie that you have been here for six months because there are preconditions even there. Then you try to turn to those who can help (with receiving short-term loans) like Money Shop and Speaking Cash (short-term loan shops) and then you slide into a situation where you are better off if you forget your account and open another one that you can keep clean. The interest rates are really high and maybe they cancel your account after a while, but at least they register you for two, three, four years.
>
> (HF37)

In summary, those who are willing to apply have two choices, either lie about their length of stay and apply for their NI number or return to their home country to generate some income and apply for JSA three months later to pass the NHR test. If they come back with an NI number of three month and they can manage a tenancy agreement, they have a chance to pass the test. So, the main strategy of newcomers is to wait.

As a bureaucratic encounter, *waiting* implies an expectation if someone is oriented toward the future (Trehan & Sigona, 2009, p. 30). There is a clear distinction between an individual waiting for someone or something and an individual who expects something to be done at a certain time. The difference between waiting and expecting can be defined as the degree of control over the situation.

Respondents constantly calculate the costs in relation to the time for payments. Although there is a common assumption that the Roma live day to day (Szuhay, 2011, p. 116), I witnessed the opposite. Many potential newcomers approached me on Skype or Facebook to ask about the terms of payment and the minimum term for eligibility. As one respondent explained, many families were coming up with a plan for processing the different stages of their application:

> *If you submit a claim, maybe you will be eligible after three months for the benefits. If you can manage for three months with your family, you can get that small amount of money to fix your situation or you apply to be self-employed . . . so he (another Roma) fixes his self-employment registration 'that they call work', but*

> *he doesn't work in the meantime. He just receives tax credits and as a result of this fake employment, his family might receive housing benefits. For three months even if he doesn't receive it, but generally they come for the big nothing because they live for free.*
>
> (HM49)

As this statement suggests, the three-month waiting period is supposed to end in monthly payments in the future. According to Lefebvre, 'waiting is an inevitable product of the bureaucratic appropriation of everyday life – the development of large-scale economic systems, the increasing segmentation of time, the rigid separation of public and private spheres' (quoted in Moran, 2004, p. 219). As Hoag (2011) notes, 'for many people, *bureaucracy* signifies slowness and delays, unnecessary paperwork, complicated protocols, and other measures or conditions that generally constrain the individual' (p. 82). Claimants searching for confirmation, compare their supplication and calculate their chance of success. With the digitalisation of data exchange, Hoag (2011) writes:

> *These organisations' rules and hierarchies are often clearly spelled out, and yet bureaucracies are always at some level opaque, inscrutable and illogical to both 'insider' and 'outsider' alike. This opacity empowers bureaucracies and bureaucrats – they become gatekeepers, with control over the flow of information and resources.*
>
> (p. 82)

Once the data is registered in the system, these gatekeepers have more knowledge than the applicants themselves.

> In times of budget cuts and increasing workloads, this flow of information is put under increasing pressure with waiting becoming a growing feature. In short, waiting in certain situations can therefore also be examined as a form of exchange and power between actors, where the individual who has more power succeeds in avoiding waiting since he or she has forced the others to wait.
>
> (Gasparini, 1995, p. 35)

A key theme in negotiating these controls, as Humphris (2013) states, is the role of waiting and the temporal aspect of bureaucratic practice in granting access to rights (Hoag, 2011). Waiting can be seen as a strategy that gives bureaucrats and clients room to manoeuvre (Sigona, 2009) and waiting for the end of transition controls in 2014 adds to the concept of the "hope-generating machine" (Nuijten, 2004).

In the following interaction with service providers, we can trace how information and relationships are brokered in the waiting process. This leads to an examination of what information is not given, what questions are not asked and how "public secrets" develop. The Roma and bureaucrats can create an environment of confusion, scepticism and resentment on both sides, leading to increasingly partial positions. Bureaucracy's capacity to act as a "hope-generating machine" and waiting for a future change shape decision making in the present.

When waiting tactics failed to discourage more newcomers from applying for benefits, additional restrictions were introduced as a response. Although JSA and Income Support give recipients very small amounts of money, without the eligibility and the NHR tests, newcomers were unable to apply for housing benefits, which used to cover most of their rent when they had to rent their own flat. So their access to JSA and housing benefits was restricted. The previous regulation 10(3B)(k) was abolished, so receiving JSA is no longer sufficient in itself to gain access to HB. Consequently, only EEA jobseekers who have retained their worker status can access housing benefits while receiving JSA (Rutledge, 2014d). HB A6/2014, quoted in Rutledge (2014d) says:

> *A person who approaches DWP to claim JSA after a period in employment will be treated as a jobseeker and not a retained worker where the employment they were previously engaged in did not meet the MET and fails the enhanced scrutiny of whether it was genuine and effective. So long as that claimant has been in the UK for three months, they will be immediately eligible to claim JSA(IB), but as an EEA jobseeker will not be eligible for HB.*

In short, there is one way left to go: back to work! Golynker, quoted in Poptcheva (2014) argues that:

> *The special treatment of jobseekers in comparison to economically inactive European Union citizens such as students has no justification in the Directive. . . . It is therefore argued that the Directive makes no distinction between the three categories of EU migrants – short-term visitors, students and newly arrived jobseekers – as regards access to social solidarity within the host society. The Directive is thus seen as excluding such migrant EU citizens from national welfare systems, as they are neither contributors nor integrated into the host society through long residence.*
>
> (p. 15)

Broeders and Engbersen (2013) describe the constant struggle between the state and migrants in terms of foggy social structures:

> *The state diverts funds, technology and manpower to surveillance and detection (their weapons of mass detection) and the immigrant tries to circumvent these policies and innovations, sometimes by simple, yet effective means. Policy on irregular immigrants resembles an arms race: action provokes reaction. Illegal aliens will attempt to frustrate government policies that aim to identify and control them using strategies that can be captured under the notion of 'foggy social structures': social structures that emerge from efforts by individuals and organizations to avoid the production of knowledge about their activities by*

> *making them either unobservable or indeterminable or, put another way, the practical production of fog (FOGSOC 2002, p. 5 of 133). Caplan and Torpey (2001, p. 7) noted that states and their subjects/citizens routinely play cat-and-mouse with individual identification requirements.*
>
> (pp. 2–3)

As a reaction to increasing restrictions on benefits, newcomers changed strategies and tried to "make themselves employed". Many respondents registered as self-employed and those who were honestly willing to work and stay felt forced to cheat on their documents, for example by buying payslips and fake employment contracts so they could claim tax credits and keep their housing benefits. Migrants with strong transnational networks slide int the grey market economy or into irregular labour. Slowly, as a consequence of restrictions on benefits, job seeking claimants turned into tax credit claimants. While many respondents were changing their strategy to keep their income, those with children under 5 years of age were still eligible for housing benefita if their Income Support claim was accepted.

Income support – a single mother from one day to another

After passing the NHR test, Income Support is meant to be one of the most stable sources of income for many families. Not because it is so generous, but because it is for the long-term and might ensure that families receive their housing benefits. To qualify for Income Support, applicants have to be pregnant, a carer or a single parent with a child under the age of 5 or, in some cases, unable to work due to illness or disability. Claimants need to be older than 16, live in the UK and have no income or a low income (working less than 16 hours a week). Income Support is paid until the youngest child turns 5, so newcomers willing to settle with their family in London have a structural coping device that is also regularly utilised by the British majority.

One respondent, a singer living with three children in a council flat in East London, stressed her problematic image as a Roma migrant. I once visited her at her perfectly decorated flat, which felt like a little palace. She sipped her coffee from a Chanel coffee cup and was dressed in elegant clothes while restlessly pacing in her tiny living room, smoking and explaining, 'You know Veronika, we can choose to be the filthy Roma at home or the filthy welfare scum here' (PF26). She also described how stigmatised she felt by living on welfare and explained how she would like to get a job when her children were older. Still there was no good option for her in this situation other than living on benefits.

Many parents with small children choose to claim Income Support by falsifying data about their marital status or hiding their partner's income. First, the applicant registers as a single mother and signs the tenancy contract in her own name. Fathers register at a different address where the real tenants do not claim any benefits, so the fathers can earn money with a regular job. The mother then applies for housing benefits, child tax credits and child benefits, so together they generate a full income for the family. Although these practices are common in

London and the local authorities are aware of them, it was not checked at any of the single households I worked with, whether the mother was really living without a husband or not. The real challenge starts when the children grow older and the mother is forced to find a job.

Jobseeker's allowance – policing by tick boxing

Jobseeker's Allowance is the least favoured benefit among newcomers but is often the only legal way for CEE migrants to become eligible for housing benefits. JSA is meant for adults under the state pension age, not in full-time education and available for work, actively seeking work or working less than 16 hours a week. The intensity of controls is relatively high compared to other benefits and claimants need to explain, on a weekly basis, their job search progress. The government website (UK Government, 2016) gives a vague description of the requirements, but one sentence is striking in the middle of the page: 'Your JSA payments will be stopped if you don't keep to your agreement to look for work and can't give a good reason'.

Those who obtain access to JSA are expected to work on improving their employment options in a transparent and active way and sign a contract with their case manager. The UK labour market is mostly open via employment agencies or government Universal JobMatch applications, which means internet literacy is necessary. For anyone with have limited skills, online applications can be extremely complicated, even if they are obligatory for JSA. Since JCP offices have targets, case managers control and sanction anyone who does not meet with these requirements, which has direct implications for additional benefits such as free school meals, housing benefits or council housing.

JSA pays a really small amount of money and if a claimant leaves the country, the payments are cut. To generate enough money for a household, many Roma men claim JSA and work in the grey market (e.g. selling cars or cigarettes) while their wives apply as single mothers for Income Support and housing benefits. These families earn a normal income, but they live under a constant threat regarding their circumstances. As the following respondent explains, some claimants are more often controlled or need to do more for the same payment, which creates a paranoid relationship:

> *Like a month ago, I had to prove on a weekly basis that I had sent 20 job applications to get the JSA. Others need to do this every two or three weeks. So I asked how it works. I even had to click on to jobs I had nothing to do with. But I have to, because if they cannot see I am active they immediately pick on me. Honestly, they just check why you didn't get the job. Like they have this job search site and many jobs ask why you are unable to take the job so there are two options you can choose from. There is nothing like how would you be able to take the job! When you apply for a job, you cannot add that it is too complicated for my educational background or it is too far from home. It is total nonsense.*
>
> (HM50)

Benefit applicants are constantly monitored by service providers trying to force them into self-sustaining economic conditions. Claimants are defined by calculating distinctions based on notions of "risk" to welfare dependency that have been measured by data collected on the government job search webpage. Those people are determined by complex statistical methods that calculate who poses a greater risk (e.g. of fraud or long-term unemployment). They encounter greater surveillance and, in many cases, higher expectations when proving their eligibility.

Benefit recipients are subject to various forms of technological surveillance in combination with face-to-face interviews carried out by JCP. Public housing tenants first undergo a rigorous application process to prove their eligibility. Then there are inspections of their tenancy agreements and regular income reporting to set the rent levels. There are extra control measures targeting those suspected of fraudulent practices, such as tax credit claimants who work very few daily hours as self-employed cleaners.

In addition, transactional websites force users to engage in specific dealings with the agency online as they actively look for employment. Users need to authenticate themselves to the agency and register their identities. They can then complete the transaction with the agency online and check the agency's databases at various levels of security to try to track the progress of an application. Although many of the transactional websites have been taken over by semi-governmental organisations, case officers are not fully aware of the limitations of these and how they can be manipulated. As is analysed in the following section, transactional websites increase suspicion among the case officers and fear among the claimants. These attitudes shape their face-to-face interaction, in which they both try to bypass the rules and use the tactic of rhetoric to reach their targets.

Online and offline interfaces – interaction with CEE Roma newcomers

In the first bureaucratic procedures, Job Centre staff are practically the only people who make face-to-face contact with applicants. Migrants view Job Centre case managers and digital application systems as policing instead of support, since it includes the constant screening of personal conditions, activities and income. Financial sanctions are the greatest fear for migrants who do not always keep up with the payment conditions. Case managers are also under pressure from this target system. They are aware that they sanction people who need government aid, but they have to reduce the claims as much as possible. Bypassing the rules is thus a dialectic process in which case workers and clients alike develop coping strategies to circumvent the rules.

For example, one respondent was struggling to help his mother move to London. She had no right to health care without an NI number. She was already retirement age, but not yet eligible for UK pension payments, so her son was hopelessly trying to find a way to get her medication. He says a JCP officer helped by telling him what to say:

> *So when she [his mother] was asked about why she was coming [to the United Kingdom], I told them, to work! The officer put this into my mouth; I said she*

> *is old, so it is obvious she is living on a pension and her family is here. So she [the officer] said she does not have to give her number if she says she is working less than four hours. I said fine, let's make it four hours. That's how she got her NI, otherwise she would have been unable to get her medicine.*
>
> (HM36)

As this example shows, some officers are willing to support applicants, especially in cases involving children, but still take a moralistic approach to clients for several reasons. The support, ranging from informal to more or less formal arrangements, enables professionals to act according to the law and simultaneously ensure that inhumane and threatening situations do not occur. Officers are also forced to get their clients onto the employment market as soon as possible and, due to their individual targets, are more willing to help the more promising clients. However, that means they are often more restrictive to clients with fewer skills and opportunities. who often receive sanctions and more restrictions. Witnessing several interviews at Job Centre Plus offices, I saw case officers approach claimants disrespectfully, presuming they were unwilling to work or lazy, or describing their husbands as reckless about taking care of their families.

For example, a young respondent with three children living in East London was divorced and her youngest son was almost 5 years old when she had to show up at the local Job Centre. The purpose of her interview was unclear, but the benefit officer explained the situation to her as follows:

> *Your payments (Income Support) will be cut when your son turns 5. It will be difficult for you. This country wants people coming here who want to work. Who would support you in your country if you lived there? The father of your children is responsible for taking care of them, not the UK. Do you expect the state to take care of your child? You have to learn English! Now it is too late to attend job search training. You have to find a job and submit 20 searches every two weeks to receive a Jobseeker's Allowance. . . . Your housing benefits will be cut and you will not be eligible for tax credits.*
>
> (JCO2)

These narratives are often offensive, demoralising and in some cases, threatening. Advocacy workers also postpone and hold back their clients' data: 'they deliberately fail to send the decision, so clients are unable to appeal' (JD).

Respondents regularly complain about decision-making processes and stress that '"equality before the law" more or less loses its meaning' (Dowling et al., 2006, p. 152). Impressions about decision-making processes are constantly evaluated by applicants and they say they need to "invest" in a good bureaucratic relationship.

Lipsky (2010) describes these dialectic processes as being associated with street-level bureaucracies where civil servants elect people for certain government services or social support by applying their discretionary authority to the general rules of law with regard to their clients. If they believe a client deserves a certain kind of service, they can bend the rules, conduct extra research to find a solution tailored to the client's needs or ignore minor infringements or omissions in the application. In line with Lipsky, these strategies involve cherry-picking. Frontline officers select the most promising clients with good prognoses or those they can use well-acknowledged or prestigious treatment technologies for. Or they choose clients with the promise of a rapid and inexpensive process and not those most in need or first in line.

In conversations where newcomers' lack of language skills prevent a sophisticated interaction with officers, claimants employ manipulation techniques to avoid future payment cuts. The Roma also invent coping strategies to prevent additional stigma and motivate officers to provide assistance with their benefits.

6.4 Narrative management technics self-censorship and self-profiling

In response to the businesslike attitude of officers, Roma claimants use specific techniques in face-to-face encounters. They use self-censorship to protect themselves from the risk of sharing sensitive personal information with officers. Many JCP claimants try to profile themselves as good neoliberal job-seeking citizens unable to work due to temporary conditions. This image is meant to fit the deserving claimant parameters of benefit users and reduce the pressure on officers to activate their clients. If the Roma feel their ethnicity is visible, they may try to rectify the ethnic stigma, assign it to others or stress their positive attitude to work. In the following overview, I briefly clarify these practices and the extent to which they change claimants' ability to succeed in their interaction with officers.

Controlling and selecting information shared with case managers is a common strategy for benefit-dependent migrants. At meetings at Job Centres where the conditions for benefits were discussed, I heard clients constantly amend their living conditions to present their needs according to the prevailing requirements. The rapidly changing legislation creates a foggy structure about the actual conditions, even for case managers (Broeders & Engbersen, 2013). These circumstances make claimants suspicious and sometimes even paranoid, so they try to influence how they shape these relationships.

Many Roma live in constant fear of scrutiny. Some worry that scrutiny may result in a loss of welfare assistance for not reporting income, having partners stay overnight or being reported for child abuse and losing their children (Falkiner v Ontario, 2002, p. 515). As a result, they engage in continual self-censorship (Little, 1998, p. 180). Even when officers make erroneous assumptions about the data relatrfto their clients, the Roma regularly remain quiet, avoiding arguments or corrections.

Some welfare-dependent newcomers see themselves as deserving welfare recipients who take part in workfare programmes or language training and feel like contributing members of the host society (Chunn & Gavigan, 2004). Some also feel resentful and more deserving than others on welfare, whom they feel are 'faring better in the distribution of scarce resources' (Swift & Birmingham, 2000, pp. 94–95). These arguments are increasingly used by migrants from Roma subgroups who describe each other as criminals or free riders.

Other respondents living on JSA strongly reject the neoliberal tone of current welfare legislation and policy, characterising workfare programmes and their rationales as government propaganda. They do not stress their disadvantages due to ethnic stigmatisation or family relations, but emphasise the temporary aspects of their unemployment. Although self-censorship is mainly about selective data sharing, there are also coping mechanisms that refer to data production and "deservingness" to justify entitlement to welfare payments.

Service-dependent minorities employ identity-making and self-characterisation as conscious coping strategies online and offline. The Roma reconfigure certain aspects of their identity to meet with the neoliberal ideal that entitles them to certain benefits (Engbersen & Broeders, 2011; Woolford & Nelund, 2013, p. 292). Although Roma ethnicity is racialised and romanticised wherever the Roma live, stereotypes and criminalising assumptions are increasingly contested by identity-making in bureaucratic processes at several levels. Historically persistent ethnic connotations are challenged by situationally variable representations of their putative identities and challenge essentialist assumptions by a counter-identity.

Creating a formal labour history is a regular type of self-profiling, sometimes with assistance from NGO workers who make suggestions about the types of jobs clients could create as evidence of their work ethic. The Roma emphasise their individual skills and accomplishments to overshadow the effects of their stigmatised ethnicity, particularly regarding the notion of being "work shy" that makes them unattractive to case managers.

Respondents also transform or amend ethnic boundaries in specific de-stigmatising discourses and regularly capitalise on ethnic resources in managing their everyday problems. For instance, by jettisoning the Pakistani and other ethnic Roma subgroups, claimants transfer the stigma to them and position themselves more advantageously in Britain's ethnic hierarchy. In response to stigmatisation efforts by others, they dissociate themselves from the stigmatised group by blaming other Roma. This contributes to redrawing ethnic boundaries.

Diverting the stigma to other minorities in bureaucratic relations increases ethnicity's everyday relevance in face-to-face interactions. Some Roma erect a boundary between themselves and other minorities by "educating" others about their ethnic deference, their roots and the consequences. By diverting stigma to the economically less deserving, they also emphasise their own dependency position. When they suggest that the Olah or Vlach Roma are less deserving, Romungro respondents overestimate the stigmatising effects this has, since many bureaucrats are unable to draw a distinction between the different subgroups. Although strategies such as conflating stereotypes to redress status might reinforce the salience of ethnicity (Moroşanu & Fox, 2013, p. 447), it is often compensated by a switching to personal skills and recalibrating in positive terms. As Moroşanu and Fox (2013) write:

> *These narratives invoke achieved qualities to dismiss the effects of a stigmatised ethnicity, blurring boundaries in the process. However, respondents cannot be easily divided between those who favoured ethicised discourses and repertoires, and those who adopted non-ethicised perspectives. Indeed, the very same migrants often embraced both strategies depending on the social situation or referent involved, drawing thus on multiple tools to build status.*
>
> (p. 447)

In these interplays of shifting coping strategies, the Roma ethnic lens is in a state of constant fluctuation (Glick-Schiller et al., 2006).

In addition, colour-based and innate moral character differences and work ethics supposedly linked to skin colour help to valorise differences. By discursively invoking differences to describe both "the self" and "the other", differences between Roma become even more salient.

The valorisation of differences leads to certain social-psychological benefits expressing the migrants' anxieties and frustrations and helping them restore the "reversals in status" that are part of the migration process. Roma migrants invoke and assert their own putative whiteness and Europeanness to darken "less white" Jamaican and Asian segments of the labour market. In short, "race" is often a culturally mediated interpretation, representation and reproduction of social differences (Brubaker et al., 2004, pp. 41–44).

When the Roma refer to Pakistani minorities in the UK as "dirty" and "illiterate", it draws on home-grown and local contextual referents to construct a meaningful framework for arranging the sorts of differences the Roma encounter in comparison with other minorities in the UK.

In referring to the labour market, the efficacy of racism is vividly illustrated by the production and reproduction of racial differences, even when migrants and natives supposedly share the same category. Racism is not a static disposition that resides in the individual, but a dynamic discursive strategy (Brubaker et al., 2004) used for specific purposes.

Ranking differences into racialised hierarchies clearly has the potential to deliver certain material advantages. A fuller account of self and citizenship performances by the Roma requires a broader constraint of these performances. As Woolford and Nelund (2013) suggest, we also need to focus on the immediate normative context, as well as the variety and complexities of human interaction and interpretation. Economic productivity and the social practice of racism are thus interrelated in recent welfare provisions.

The significance of Roma identity to social service employees is meant to ensure the continuity of basic benefits and retain access to housing benefits, which are often the main income of families who rent their own flats. Housing issues are strongly interrelated with many other family conditions, and it is the only payment provided by local councils. In the final section of this chapter, I describe three elements used as a coping strategy to access local service provisions.

6.5 Housing as a capital

After spending almost a year in London, staying with families, helping with interpreting contracts and acting as an advocacy worker, I realised that housing benefits are the major source of income for welfare-dependent families in the UK.

There are generally four housing strategies for newcomers: subletting rooms, renting rooms from agencies, renting a house or applying for council accommodations. All of them can provide eligibility for housing benefits, since the conditions are mainly interrelated with entitlement to other welfare payments and income. In the following analysis, I describe three tactics the Roma use, such as forcing the local authority to provide social housing, renting a property registered in another person's name or selling documents for a credit history that enables others to rent a house.

In the first case, a council house, I followed a respondent for two years. She was an unemployed mother who had a council flat in her home country before she moved to London. After a few months in a small rented flat in London, she decided to divorce her husband. All the benefit payments and the tenancy contract were in her husband's name and he left. The mother was living on JSA and the children were registered for child tax credit in the father's name at the HMRC. She tried to apply for a council flat with a homeless application to force the council to help her find a new flat. She was not yet eligible for a council house, since she had only been registered in the UK for seven months, so she was forced to move back to her home country to avoid the risk of the children being taken into state care. She went home after she learned about the requirements for a council flat, but she did not inform the authorities in the UK.

Almost a year later, she was back in London with the children. She forced the children's father to rent a house for them but registered it in her name. When she received the first eviction notice due to a conflict with her neighbours, she again applied to the local council and without any temporary placement, she managed to get a council flat in three months. This occurred so quickly because she remained registered in the UK the entire time she was back in her home country.

Others are less fortunate, though they think if they make a homeless application they can automatically get a council flat. Well-informed Roma in London know which boroughs are easiest to convince, but most families are unwilling to leave their social network. Many respondents were forced to move on a regular basis, for example, one family had moved eight times in 2013. So, the question is: How do some succeed?

Benefits are often suspended due to changes in claimants's circumstances. The decisions are often unpredictable, and most welfare payments are interrelated. In short, reporting a new address means a new application for JSA, causing delays in the housing benefits that are often the main resource. Documents are often lost, and incomplete applications might result in a rejection which, after a few months, leads to a new eviction notice. As a result of this vicious circle, many applicants lie about their address to prevent the repeated suspension of their payments.

People who can rent an entire building have another major source of income. They can turn it into an investment by subletting while claiming housing benefits for the same property. Subletting is a common strategy that newcomers learn from other local minorities. Most private accommodations are rented from Pakistani landlords, who help tenants apply for housing benefits. It is to the landlords' advantage to have poor tenants, because their benefits ensure payment directly from the local councils and they are dependent on others, making clientalist relationships possible. Many Roma who are unable to stabilise their income rent housing, apply for housing benefits and then sublet the rooms for extra income.

Inter-ethnic relations are often underestimated in these coping mechanisms. Similar to the cases described by Greenfields et al., the enforced settlement of newcomers puts them in close proximity with other deprived and socially excluded populations increasingly concentrated in areas of social housing, such as the Pakistani in East London. It has been argued that 'social relations between different social and ethnic groups are often non-existent, and that a deficit of civic identity or polarisation of shared values along racial, social class and cultural lines is the reason for social and community segregation' (2010, p. 8). However, bonding social capital, while creating strong in-group loyalty, 'may simultaneously result in strong out-group antagonism. (. . .) The unintended consequence of such "clustering" may be that the development of "bridging" (or inclusive) ties to the wider community is inhibited and pre-existing social and economic exclusions are compounded leading to the creation of closed "parallel communities"' (2010, p. 4). These suggestions rely on a static construction of group and inter-group relations while interpersonal relationships between inter-ethnic groups are in a constantly changing process. Contact between the Roma and Pakistani residents in the same neighbourhood can be described as a clientalistic dependency relation, in which the older ethnic community supports and exploits the newcomers in a situationally changing context. Inter-ethnic relationships might change from personal to labour or business contacts that operate outside the legal bureaucratic procedure, or might serve as a bridg with the rest of the community. However, over-reliance on localised forms of bonding social capital (Putnam, 2000) may also intensify existing forms of social and economic exclusion through hindering the development of wider "bridging" ties to other sections of the community' (Greenfields et al., 2010, 4).

The commodification of informal relationships with landlords (Palomera, 2014, p. 107) and the formation of a rental submarket allow some newcomers to rent more than one flat and to become entrepreneurs within their own social networks. Thus, several respondents accumulated their property capital by subletting to others who were in more precarious positions. In the flat where I lived with a respondents' household, rent payments became integrated into a wider circle of mutual moral obligations predicated on a sense of friendship. Rent payments were absorbed as one form of support and a dynamic hierarchy emerged among the series of tenants or "protégés" (Gellner & Waterbury, 1977). Some landlords who were aware of these practices offered a lower rent if the housing benefits were paid directly to them. Furthermore, in boroughs where landlords are aware of discretionary housing payments, it makes it even more attractive for them to accommodate poor families with several children. In conclusion, the Roma often anticipate the exploitative relationships of Pakistani entrepreneurs who gain their income from housing benefits payed by the their borough.

The last mechanism is strongly interrelated with the activities of brokers aware of the requirements for renting who sell documents to give newcomers access to a property for subletting. In brief, if a family arrives with no money, a broker gives them a loan to use for the two months' rent deposit and one month's rent in advance. If a family finds a property, they have to prove their income by providing payslips, their own tenancy agreement and a bank statement. One of the respondents asked her flatmate subletting a room from her to sign the tenancy agreement. Some tenants earn a low wage and cannot prove their income to apply for housing benefits. They might purchase a bank statement and payslips for £125 each from a broker. In cases when however, ethnicity becomes a hidden issue as regards the new tenants. The commodification of these informal relationships helps the Roma sublet their rooms and gain access to housing benefits.

Based on the central research objective regarding the Funnel of Expulsion, I argue that although Roma newcomers are targeted for abuse, discrimination and marginalisation, they can hardly be defined as passive and resigned actors overpowered by bureaucratic structures. In fact, the Roma continuously demonstrate their resilience in a shifting surveillance field.

6.6 Conclusion

This study started with the hypothesis that the Roma are one of the least attractive groups of newcomers in transnational mobile populations because they are associated with unemployment, benefit tourism and a cultural threat. Unattractive populations are supposedly targeted by selective surveillance measures that make Roma newcomers distrustful. The main intention of targeted approaches is that when productivity is screened by internal migration control, such as welfare elegibility, those who fail to pass the control are forced to move on. Although this study has confirmed the selective aspects of digitalised welfare practices, it also shows how innovative responses might challenge existing social sorting practices and contribute to new monitoring mechanisms.

This chapter presents several tactics used by Roma newcomers adapted to demonstrate the key role of cutbacks in welfare services in contemporary migration flows. Since several control measures are reactions to the strategies of benefit users, they constantly change, so even civil servants are unaware of them and treat them inconsequently. Therefore, migrants regularly receive conflicting information, and this makes them suspicious, which becomes a major factor in their decision making and information sharing practices. Recent welfare barriers trigger migrants to adopt a range of tactics cross-cut by divisions of gender, ethnicity, nationality, class and length of time in the UK. In turn, this chapter analysed how Roma newcomers create a range of innovative responses in their interaction with social service providers to ensure their short-term survival and consolidate their long-term ambitions for the future.

The monitoring of applications and the selection of benefit recipients as political social sorting technologies are thus implemented at several levels. It is not just an audit of recipients or a surveillance of eligibility criteria, there is an extensive consolidated verification procedure based on joint databases and, in some cases, enforced with computer assistance. As the examples illustrate, these notions are constructed as governmental incentives for profiling the bad foreign opportunists versus the good citizens who deserve state support and protection. These disincentives for foreign benefit claimants can also be traced in other screening instruments. The ongoing transformations in modern penal practice such as benefit sanctions reflect the capitalistic need to carve a docile and hardworking workforce out of the unruly, undisciplined and sometimes riotous "dangerous classes" (Schumpeter, 1942).

Although Her Majesty's Revenue and Customs (HMRC) applications are less complicated than the claims mentioned above, there are limitations to face-to-face contact and most of the applications and appeals need to be managed from a distance. In the following analysis, I reflect on the surveillance development of HMRC and how it forces tax credit applicants to adopt riskier coping strategies.

7 Commodification online – social security claims in virtual bureaucracies

Several dystopic movies and literature use the character of a hero who innovates and employs various strategies in a futuristic virtual hegemony. This symbolic role used in *Matrix Revolutions*, in *Blade Runner*, or in several romans of Kaffka or Orwell illustrate the contemporary tactics used by welfare claimants in digitalised state bureaucracy systems, such as the UK's social security system. Businesslike structures are increasingly adopted by state service providers, such as Her Majesty's Revenue and Customs (HMRC), which employ technological tools to select and monitor welfare claimants. Although Job Centre Plus (JCP) clients still have face-to-face contact with the service provider, HMRC is moving towards entirely online applications and data exchange. An analysis of the strategies and "innovations" used by newly arrived migrants to cope with the digitalised bureaucracies constitutes the second part of my core argument. This chapter describes the technocratic surveillance strategies of HMRC (including spider diagrams), how digitalisation is changing the social sorting process, and the tactics claimants use in online communication with HMRC.

The digitalisation of the service system creates a gap between the data on individuals and the actual people this data is meant to identify. The gap affects the attitude of service users. As the hypotheses suggests, claimants in a virtual application system are less likely to represent themselves accurately in the data they provide than to try to come as close as possible to an "ideal type" based on the requirements for benefit entitlement. In short, claimants learn how to differentiate between real personal data and data that meets the required parameters in eligibility screening. Via these data selection practices, welfare applicants modify screening algorithms. In this digital dialogue, screening methods and welfare applicants continuously change the parameters of screening requirements, and this in turn triggers more restrictive application procedures. The question is how these coping mechanisms are developed considering the limited technological skills of foreign welfare claimants in the UK.

This chapter analyses the digital field of welfare application within a broader financial context. As eligibility for a Jobseeker's Allowance and housing benefits in the UK is increasingly restricted, a shift has occurred in applications. Applicants increasingly seek to profit from tax credit claims and apply for loans to generate income while keeping their housing benefit payments. This chapter examines the tactics used by applicants to obtain working tax credit and child tax credit.

According to the formal requirements in 2013, I demonstrate how some of the respondents obtain benefits via transgressive technics, such as a commodifying identity, avoiding updates or submitting fake documents. In addition, two types of credit claims are analysed, student loans and short-term loans. I describe how digitalised financial platforms sometimes replace welfare payments and can force potential newcomer claimants into debt. This is illustrated by an overview of the interactions with HMRC, followed by a description of how newcomer claimants operate, and the kind of sorting mechanisms applied to claimants who are considered suspicious.

7.1 Tax credit procedures and HMRC's electronic monitoring mechanisms

When restrictions on the Jobseeker's Allowance were introduced, the respondents stated to become more dependent on HMRC benefits, like tax credit claims, designed to assist low-income taxpayers. Therefore, several documents are required by HMRC as proof of income, including payslips with the applicant's PAYE number and employment contracts. HMRC is a non-ministerial British department responsible for collecting taxes and paying some forms of state support. HMRC is responsible for working tax credit and child tax credit. It is an efficiency-oriented tax control office that has adopted security approaches from the commercial sector. The following cases illustrate how private sector and e-commerce surveillance methods prove dysfunctional when adapted to e-governance. The problem lies in their objectives: public administration focuses on the well-being of society, while e-business strives to maximise profit and increase the market share (Lau, 2006, p. 39). As to privacy issues, information manipulated in an e-government process should be treated with a higher level of sensitivity than in a commercial business and there is no need for the same level of standardisation and optimisation of processes as in a commercial business (ibid., p. 39). In addition, state processes involve more parties, which may have conflicting interests. Although HMRC employs strict sanctions and control measures, surprisingly many respondents prefer claiming through HMRC rather than Job Centre Plus because of the impersonal interactions. Although both systems serve the social sorting of the British Welfare Banopticon, HMRC tools are far less transparent than those of the Job Centre. It is a British non-ministerial department responsible for collecting taxes and paying some form of state support.

The obstacles that respondents encounter when claiming tax credits are similar to the administrative procedures noted earlier. The first barrier for applicants is the lack of personal contact with advisors. There are several inquiry centres where clients can make free phone calls about applications, but this often requires an interpreter. The phone centres are vast office halls staffed with an officer who distributes a list of phone numbers for different types of applications. Arranged at a proper distance, all the desks face the same direction, resembling a classroom or shared office space. Each phone call starts with a control question. If the client is unable to answer the question, the officer will terminate the conversation. The process is stressful and time-consuming. Clients know they will be asked to provide their name and National Insurance number, but get confused when suddenly confronted with extra control questions. Although respondents are usually aware that these questions are designed to protect them from fraud and exploitation, they are perceived as a barrier because understanding and answering them requires the assistance of an interpreter. Some of the respondents in the study are convinced this whole process was set up to render filing claims more complicated and prolong the process to discourage applicants from following through.

Clients can also apply for tax credit online, which requires filling in a form, signing it and submiting it to the data centre of HMRC. The forms are filled in with the assistance of brokers who can supply the applicant with the right answers to satisfy the entitlement screening parameters. In comparison to Jobseeker's Allowance applications, these processes do not deal with claimants as individuals, but rely on the data they share. The absence of face-to-face interaction makes it more attractive for applicants seeking to hide information or submit false information. Unlike JCP claimants who are aware that their applications are checked by case managers, some respondents claim they are not aware of any control by HMRC. The HMRC collects and analyses impressive amounts of data, but the method of data collection and analysis is invisible. As the core argument of this book it is argued that the surveillance software and selection methods of HMRC determine how a gap can arise between a client's digitalised and real identity and how tax credit applicants can use this to their advantage.

HMRC uses Connect, a business software system for that collects data from 28 data sources and cross-matches a billion internal and third-party data items in uncover hidden relationships between organisations, customers and their associated data links. This software transforms the data into a spider diagram or "spidergram", a visualisation tool representing individuals and their associated data links for investigation by mapping addresses, phone numbers, bank accounts and employers, which are linked as graphic symbols representing a maze of connections that ripple across the screen to detect concealment patterns. If someone is operating in a hidden economy, the spidergram has a different shape. IT service company Detica is responsible for fraud investigations for HMRC and assesses a subset of tax data, cross-referencing information from several data sources to select cases for investigation, target resources and identify potential compliance and fraud risks (Hainey, 2011). HMRC statisticians produce target profiles and risk and intelligence investigators generate campaigns and cases for investigation. Automated feeds into HMRC's case management system allocate the work to the correct case workers, and their feedback further refines the intelligence in Connect.

Access to such comprehensive data allows investigators to spot anomalies and simplifies HMRC's procedure for checking information contained in individual tax returns, such as inheritance tax. HMRC receives about 300,000 paper returns for every year. HMRC can sift through information on property transactions, company ownership, loans, bank accounts, employment history and self-assessment records to spot where estates might be under-declaring. "Mystery shopping" checks, the observation of businesses by inspectors, tip offs from informers, the identification of fake PAYE numbers, third-party information, and information from businesses or government agencies are some of the tools used by HMRC to check the veracity of claims. In 2008, HMRC honed in on the medical profession, acquiring information from the National Health Service trusts, private hospitals and medical insurance companies to test its suspicion that practitioners fail to declare fees for consultations, medical examinations and other services.

The Land Registry and Driver and Vehicle Licensing Agency (DVLA) records contain data on how much people spend on their homes and vehicles registered to each address, which can be used to check whether their spending patterns correspond with theit financial situations according to HMRC. The real estate they own can be matched against any rental income declared, with any discrepancy indicating potential fraud.

By controlling the "data doubles" of personal (legal) identities in the registries and databanks of government agencies and private companies, HMRC is able to generate more knowledge on individuals' data. This "virtualization of citizenship" (Schinkel, 2010) is a crucial technique in the neoliberal communitarian strategy, making it possible to identify, differentiate, monitor and intervene when populations and individuals deviate from cultural values and individual responsibility.

> *Individual cases are reduced to a series of parameters that are accessed and interpreted by the digital system, which renders an individual's profile more accessible for bureaucratic purposes as it is stripped of the diversity and dynamism of a living, breathing individual. By reducing the individual to a series of discrete, but associated, parameters for assessment and evaluation, the bureaucracy transposes the plurality of individualism with the predictability and manageability of the digital profile.*
>
> (Jarvis, 2010, p. 13)

Furthermore, the profile represents a sufficiently docile subject for the application of power. This reduction facilitates the governing and disciplining of the individuals themselves. As Jarvis explains:

> *The surveillance/dataveillance profile works to counteract the phenomenon of de-spatialized and deterritorialised social relations by rendering the information pertinent for bureaucratic-subject relations in a medium that transcends spatial constraints and facilitates the kind of stable and depersonalised relations necessary for the continued viability of the bureaucratic model. If, then, this phenomenon is accurately described in this regard, we can conclude that claims about the demise of the bureaucratic model in the face of these de-spatializing technologies (independent from the geographical context) have been greatly exaggerated.*
>
> (2010, p. 14)

Two forms of tax credit are frequently claimed by the respondents in my study, i.e. working tax credit and child tax credit. Both require the same documents but use different screening mechanisms. The next section addresses working tax credit claims and innovative responses used by participants when making claims to ensure eligibility.

7.2 Working tax credit online – "dividuals" in the web of spidergrams

When Jobseeker's Allowance and housing benefit restrictions were introduced, many welfare-dependent newcomers sought alternative solutions to enable them to keep paying their rent. Restricting state support for newcomers from the new EU member states increased the debt level of many Roma families. Yet, loopholes in the procedures of the welfare bureaucracies created by contemporary dataveillance technology have provided welfare claimants with new opportunities to construct and invent profiles of the "deserving citizen" entitled to state benefits. Not actually having to be present in face-to-face selection encounters allows for the manipulation of identity to approximate the neoliberal ideal type of the tax-paying citizen.

Although the Roma are often described as passive victims of their economic circumstances, many respondents in the study were in fact actively trying to find solutions and, faced with discriminatory bureaucratic demands, responded flexibly to changing circumstances in order to remain eligible for benefits. Welfare-dependent respondents learned to manipulate the surveillance systems and found ways to manage their identities vis-a-vis the authorities. By trial-and-error, applicants learned the requirements for various welfare provisions and how to present themselves accordingly. Families managed and manipulated their employment histories and number of working hours to remain eligible for maximum benefits, while often enjoying significantly higher incomes in the grey economy.

In April 2014, at the end of the tax year, several families who participated in the study reported receiving a letter from HMRC notifying them of an overpayment. Most of them promptly appealed the decision, ready to prove their case, even if their claims were based on fictitious employment contracts. Many welfare-dependent families had contracts with fictitious firms that sell employment contracts and provide payslips for tax credit applications. Roma families who were notified of overpayments often made claims based on these documents provided by their landlords without the firms paying National Insurance contributions for their "employees". Many of the firms engaged in these practices provided fake payslips for cleaning jobs (of one or two hours a day), so all the cleaners were subjected to increased screening for potential tax credit fraud. Families had to pay back tax credits for more than GBP 5,000 annually. Suspicious claimants had to provide written proof of their employment. The repercussions people faced were based on their 'profile in the simulation and computer-generated projections' (2002, p. 33), not on how they actually behaved. These processes went on continuously without any personal contact (Graham & Wood, 2003).

One respondent who was assisted for a year was notified by HMRC of an overpayment in 2013. She was already paying back a 2012 overpayment of more than GBP 9,000. She received no housing benefit, because she was living in a new flat and there was no decision yet on the amount of council tax to be paid, so she had to wait for the council decision before claiming tax credit. On paper, she was a self-employed cleaner and had applied for working tax credit as single mother, child benefits and child tax credit. Once she told me that she submitted the same documents to HMRC for her tax credit claim and to JCP for income support, which meant she had somehow two identical employment contracts. Another time when I assisted her she had to look up the name of her employer's company during a conversation about her overpayment. Her advocacy worker suspiciously pointed out that "Everyone knows the name of their employer". Later this participant admitted to paying for the payslips, but was apologetic and vowed she would never do it again. Instead, she changed her status to self-employed and is hoping to avoid another overpayment next year.

Another respondent described similar practices, only the payslips were not provided by a fictitious firm, but were sold by employees of real companies:

INTERVIEWER: *Is it a copy they make for you?*
RESPONDENT: *No, it is based on a registered contract they provide payslips with. It is fake employment, but it is like a real one. It is the same with bank statements.*
INTERVIEWER: *Ok, but is it really a registered company?*
RESPONDENT: *No, it is a payslip from the Grange Hotel. I can fix payslips with the manager.* (BR5)

This interview suggests there is an extended network of actors enabling claimants to provide fictitious data about themselves and their labour history. Brokers and recruitment agents commodify documents and help use them in digitalised welfare services. Surveillance in "control societies" like the UK can be characterised as "powered by simulation" rather than representation (Best, 2010). On the surface, the data represent existing citizens transformed into a quantifiable and manageable form. However, what actually occurs is the creation of selves or "dividuals", which are simulations of the original (cf. Kilger, 1994; Poster, 1991). As Willems notes (2005), a dividual is a 'physically embodied human subject that is endlessly divisible and reducible to data representations via the modern technologies of control, like computer-based systems'. A dividual is a digital simulation of itself, an avatar, constantly 'modulating or responding to differing expectations for productivity, consumption and political conduct' (Packer, 2006, p. 390).

As theorised by Deleuze, these simulations are multiple assemblages and take on a life of their own (Nayar, 2015).

> *Unlike the previous discriminatory apparatuses, the categories of differentiation are multiply cross-referenced so that one can hardly define the factors that*

> *result in credit being denied, much less change desirability. The repercussions people face are based on their 'profile in the simulation and computer-generated projections', not on how they actually behave.*
>
> (Wise, 2002, p. 33)

> *In essence, the original self is superfluous to the processes that follow on from the gathering of information, processes that distribute impacts and effects based on these multiple simulated data-generated selves, without regard to the original referent.*
>
> (Best, 2010, p. 11)

Personal activities and documented characters are divided and the need for representation for the real slowly disappears. Data systems know more about the dividuals' parameters than the original people, and there is an overestimation of the all-seeing eye of the technocratic instruments. The vast amount of data collected about individuals often remains unconnected. For example, one of the respondents in the study was unable to complete her application for working tax credit because she didn't know where to submit her documents. The claim was closed. As she had lost her job, she was no longer eligible for working tax credit and had to apply for Jobseeker's Allowance at Job Centre Plus instead. When JCP required proof that she no longer received working tax credit, she showed the letter at the office, but her case manager failed to add it to her file. Consequently, her Jobseeker's Allowance was terminated as well, which in turn led to cuts in her housing benefit. She kept attending Job Centre Plus appointments without receiving Jobseeker's Allowance because they were paying her pension and National Insurance contribution. To receive Jobseeker's Allowance payments again, she was advised to provide proof that she had no additional income. Her case illustrates the communication gaps between the two major benefit distributors (JCP and HMRC). People often apply for working tax credit using false payslips, false contracts, registration at false addresses or self-employment registration. These gaps between real individuals and dividuals and the lack of interaction between the service providers enables tax credit claimants to manipulate data according to the changing requirements. In the next sub-section, I discuss two strategies used by claimants to obtain child tax credits. However, first I briefly summarise the credit requirements.

7.3 Child tax credit claims – identity management online

Formally, child tax credit is a weekly payment to a low- income family for the care of children. The amount is defined by HMRC based on the situation of the household. In practice, children are verified by their identity documents, which are submitted to HMRC by their school or general practitioner and using their address. Many aspects of the claim are interrelated like a spider web, and if one condition changes, all the others are impacted. Claimants try to avoid communicating any changes in their circumstances. If their circumstances do change, they use four main strategies: avoiding communication about the change, in particular about the children's residence, sending claims for children who are not related, or selling documents of children to third parties who use them for claims. Although these tactics may be considered immoral or illegal, in transnational mobile networks they are often considered a necessity to prevent future benefit cuts. The next case study illustrates the complexities of these issues.

Housing is a delicate issue for many newcomer families due to possible welfare restrictions. If a family is forced to move to another borough, it is required to inform HMRC about any change that might terminate its benefits, as the new council tax credit is based on the new address. The benefits can be suspended, leaving the family without housing benefits, which can lead to debts and anxiety. In addition, if a family moves, the children have to be re-registered in the new borough, which not only impact his school admission but also impacts child tax credit payments.

When moving to another borough, respondents report using several tactics to keep their child tax credit payments. "Buying" an address to stay registered in the old boroughmakes it possible to keep the children at the same school, which is essential to prevent the school from informing HMRC about the change. In one case, two children were registered at their grandmother's address to prevent housing benefit cuts for their aunt, who was taking care of them. They were forced to move when the landlord realised he was dealing with Roma and grew suspicious about their source of income. Now the family shares a 50 m^3 flat with nine or ten other people, including three children. The actual tenant (lease holder) of the flat sublet three rooms, which is not legal in the London area. The family was careful to conceal the arrangement at school, because Grandma was not the children's registered caretaker. These practices are common, ensure regular welfare payments, and keep children off the radar of child protection services (From fieldwork notes. London, December 2014).

Moving from one borough to another is not the only challenge Roma families face. Many report moving across borders as well. Transnational mobility entails benefit claims in more than one country and the concealment of transnational movements prevent benefit cuts. Home schooling enables respondents to move around with their children without attendance problems, so the children stay registered. If children attend school, parents may be fined if they take their children out of the school without notice. One respondent was forced to move back to her country of origin with her children but was able to keep her children registered at school by continuously updating the head teacher and postponing the date of return every month. Keeping the children enrolled at school allowed her to receive the tax credits. This, in turn, served as a proof of habitual residence, making them eligible for a council house. As she explains:

> *It is quite restricted now, but there are still some backdoors. In my case, I am registered from 2011, but I was not living here from the beginning. Actually, I was coming and going, but this country paid child tax credit from 2011, and when I claimed the housing benefit, they paid it! They pay everything as they are convinced I am a resident here. Because they are in the EU, there is free movement, no stamps nothing about my trips back home [no trace of border crossing]. So that's how I circumvent the system.*
>
> (HF73)

Circumventing the system enabled her claim child tax credit and child benefits in both countries. She first applied for welfare in the UK under the father's name. In her home country, where her children are registered for home education, she applied under her own name. So her children are entitled to benefits in two countries. Referring to the local authorities she stated, '*They would be able to check, but they don't*'. She explains that the Roma are more successful at this because they are not ashamed and not interested in the opinion of others (HF73).

The HMRC application process for child tax credit is one of the most common areas of fraud by my respondents. Network members use their foreign background to their advantage. They draw on the differences in traditions about birth surnames and the lack of central databases registering children. Many applications are accepted, even if claimants apply for child tax credits for the children of their relatives. One respondent feels exploited by her own father who claims child tax benefits for her daughters. Others file claims for their siblings, or even for deceased children. As one respondent explains:

> *So, let me say it, many people submit papers for someone else's children to receive these weekly payments. When their own kid turns 18, they already have three otjhr children under their name. It is unclear that they are not their children. I see these things because we fill out the office papers and their surname is never the same. And there are those who take the money after the child is deceased. For example, the child might have died ten years ago, but the birth certificate is still there and they use it here in the UK.*
>
> (PM21)

This quote from an interview illustrates that many local Roma know very well how to qualify for welfare provisions or increase their income without regular employment, but are also judgemental about these practices. This information circulates on Facebook, forums for newcomers, and in private messages (PM) on Facebook and also the risks one takes when a family member asks for the document of their children. Some participants involved in these strategies are known by name and easy to approach for advice online in the networks. Hence, many claimants do not see their child tax application as fraudulent, especially if relatives are raising and taking care of the children. Others fear repercussions and debts due to overpayments and therefore feel to be forced to use these administrative technics. Roma newcomers acquire this knowledge from other claimants in their networks like their Pakistani employers or landlords. Sharing information about avoiding bureaucratic barriers is seen by these landlords as support and a guarantee that the rent will be paid. The following analysis explains how disadvantaged families increasingly value their citizenship as they become aware of the loopholes in the welfare system.

7.4 The commodification of identity

The value of identity has structurally changed in digitalised societies. Technological developments in authentication, such as the use of biometric data, are hailed as the future of security and crime prevention. Assumptions like these about the prevention of data abuse presuppose a binary distinction between victims and perpetrators, the latter being involved in online data theft and the former uninformed about the risks of identity fraud and unaware of the exploitation of their personal data. The following identity fraud cases illustrate that this distinction is not that clear cut. Although these assumptions may lead to effective prevention measures, they keep the people who are taking the risks with data abuse intentionally out of sight (FPEG, 2007, pp. 30–35). Though victims and fraudsters are often defined in oppositional terms, these often overlap. However, the blurred line between the two regularly defined in normative terms by the level of involvement, investment and relative experience of benefit or loss. Without empirical data on the relative experience of victims, we cannot understand the value of identity fraud. Although the risks of future debts due to overpayments are high, it still seems situationally beneficial for victims, particularly in fraud claims in a foreign country.

Identity fraud, especially in child tax credit applications, follows the path of Central European migrants' identity fraud and usually involves the use of another person's details for gain or to avoid an obligation (Pascoe et al., 2006). This type of fraud can include a large range of methods that vary in their use of the other person's details.[1] Through online flows of information, even the most segregated societies can find out about living conditions abroad and gather information on how EU citizens access social provisions from a distance. Once EU citizenship has become a form of capital, it can easily be commodified.

Identity theft for identity fraud is defined as the misappropriation of the identity (e.g. name, date of birth, current address or previous addresses) of another person without their knowledge or consent, or when a perpetrator gives an agency false personal information (Summers et al., 2014). Individuals aware of the value of these ID data might want to profit from these activities. 'Intermediaries, who are mostly defined as fraudsters by law, are not necessarily seen as perpetrators' but as patrons (Lacey Cuganesan, 2004, p. 245). Although fraudsters are often framed as an invisible actor in the dark web, most of the fraudsters involved in benefit fraud are embedded in the social networks of the applicants, operate and live in the same community (Shover et al., 2003).

In the case of British benefit fraud cases, the intermediates' most efficient offline approach is "selling a dream". They offer something that promises profits above the average returns. As Titus argues, the lure of something absurdly cheap or lucrative is integral to many fraud "come-ons" (1999, p. 4). Fraudsters or landlords supporting their tenants target documents or data based on the verification system of financial institutions that are also subjected to some legal obligations, mostly deriving from practical requirements and from prevention of the use of the financial system.[2] Consequently, the major factors in identity fraud rely on the originality of the documents and the technical conditions of control measures that make it possible to authenticate the data.

1 For additional definition of identity theft, see www.identitytheft.org.uk/identity-crimedefinitions.asp.
2 EU Directive 2005/60/EC30.

There are many types of fraud related to identity fraud, such as fraud by false representation, fraud by failing to disclose information, or fraud by abuse of legal position. Involvement in fraud is linked to the position of the fraudster. Below I describe the major phases of identity fraud and analyse the selection phase. Ifocus in particular on the role of "victimised" individuals and the techniques applied by fraudsters to obtain their data.

Based on the first period of the transnational fieldwork three levels of involvement in identity fraud are distinguished. In the first form, guest workers who want to settle down and need to cope with bureaucratic procedures acquire knowledge on various financial resources in a receiving country and start to claim benefits using their family members' documents (illustrated by the child tax credit fraud cases).

The second form is related to the first and involves migrants who exploit their extended networks and act as intermediaries for newcomer migrants, recruiting people in their home country who are willing to provide identity documents. They do not move to the UK seeking employment, but travel there solely to sign applications and register for a social security number. Fully aware of the risks, they argue that without language skills or professional training, this is the only way for them to make a living. After the application procedure, they return to their home country and wait for the monthly payments. Some receive payments from middlemen who collect the applicants' monthly benefits. Some receive nothing, but usually do not blame the middleman, they simply assume the application was rejected. Extended knowledge on application methods develops in relatively small communities in the sending countries. In Hungary, for example, identification methods have become common knowledge in networks of marginalised young adults.

This knowledge, coupled with growing socio-economic problems, leads to the third and most interesting level of identity fraud, local households selling their children's documents like birth certificates for use in child tax credit applications abroad. These practices were considered as common in villages with extended networks in London or Manchester. One respondent explains his role:

> *My sister-in-law's husband asked me if I wanted to go to England to make some money. After Canada, I thought it might work out better. He has been living there for a long time now, making a lot of money with his brother, so he promised to get some benefits for us. He said it was easy money, we just needed to go there for a few weeks and could get 200,000 Forint a month. When I gave him my passport he gave me 5,000 Forint, but that was it. We went there by car and I lived in their house with some other guys. They gave me a job in construction, but they didn't give me any money, or only something like five poundsan hour, but the others said we were paid eight pounds anhour by the company. He helped me get a National Insurance number and apply for a bank account, so I gave them my children's birth certificates and all the other documents I was asked for. I never got my bank card and I never received any money. I haven't lost anything though. I want to go back, and now I know now how to do it. I know*

> *they were taking my benefits, but what can they do with these (the documents and his bank card)?*
>
> (HM54)

The applicants interviewd in their sending countires who are selling their documents are familiar with the UK procedures for social provisions. Interestingly, some of these claimants do not define these contracts as 'selling' their data, but as investing in future welfare benefits from abroad to avoid future debt. Even if they do not receive any benefits after selling their documents, they still consider it a good decision to commodify their data, as they have not experienced any direct loss. Their data is mostly used to apply for social benefits from foreign governments and it is not seen by the seller as a crime. After they become part of the UK system, fraudsters apply for financial services with their data. These services require information such as one's surname, first name, date of birth, address, place of residence, phone number etc.[3] To combat identity theft, the identity details used by fraudsters are sometimes checked against accessible databases containing personal data. The components of this initial legal identity data are the most relevant for state institutions. They are also supplemented by biographical elements, which build up over time to support this authentication method (FPEG, 2007, p. 11).

Legal proof of identity is usually the responsibility of the state and several vulnerabilities are defined at an institutional level to check these authentication measures (Van Der Meulen 2006, p. 21). However, the type and quality of state identity documents varies internationally. This is becoming more problematic with the introduction of biometric data, which entails a risk of falsification (Grijpink & Prins, 2003, p. 251). Regarding authentication issues and depending on the benefits sought, several techniques have been invented by fraudsters to obtain the data needed. Most of the techniques are online strategies (such as scams) and offline strategies (such as procurement fraud, lending fraud, payment card fraud or procurement fraud) (Levi, 2008).

In benefit fraud cases, the fraud is designed to be legally ambiguous and beneficial for all the actors. However, fraudsters who are often the previously mentioned brokers take the least risks and get the most out of it. In combination with benefit claims, they sometimes take over the accounts of legitimate customers and use their credit facilities. New accounts can be created by using the personal details of the victim and then applying for credit. In other cases, a fraudster permanently takes on the identity of a person (Newman & McNally, 2005). Identity fraud is even more sophisticated if information is used to secure "breeder" documents such as birth certificates. They are used for multiple applications for credit cards, loans and benefits, securing credit that is never going to be paid back (Gordon & Willox, 2003, p. 19).

The respondents report being aware of the risks they take selling their documents, but they are also aware of the limitations of international law and

3 See more details at http://ec.europa.eu/internal_market/fpeg/index_en.htm

cooperation. They often do not intend to stay in the UK, so they do not care if their actions have consequences in the UK. Still, these commodification methods illustrate several recent problems in identity fraud legislation. According to Muller, in Western societies citizenship is being decomposed into "identity management". This is exemplified by a change in focus from questions of entitlement and rights and the attendant cultural and ethnic attributes of citizenship, to questions of 'verifying/authenticating identity for the purpose of access to rights, bodies, spaces and so forth' (Muller, 2004, p. 280).

EU legislation does not include specific legislation on identity theft (Mitchison et al., 2004, p. 23). The member states have conflicting interests and cultural differences in identification, credit card use, political systems and legal cultures (Grossman, 2005, p. 11).

These commodification practices develop due to diversity in legislation and welfare provisions in the member states, which the marginalised members of weak European countries exploit to survive. It is erroneous to assume that these actors are not aware of the risks they take. They can assess the price they might pay for identity commodification, but are also aware of the low risk of getting caught. As long as they receive benefits from the documents, they experience their involvement as profitable. They do not blame the recruiters because it means immediate income for them. Even if some of them have negative experiences with fraudsters, the owners of these IDs keep trying to invest their documents via others familiar with the foreign procedures.

In the classical interpretation, a victim of identity fraud is someone whose identity is abused by a fraudster who is profiting from them. In the transnational mobility context, the roles are fluid and change over time. Individuals who sell their data voluntary and actively participate can be defined as victims and perpetrators at the same time. It is questionable whether biometric technology or other data industry measures can actually reduce the incidence of identity crime. It is argued that instead of making changes in the identification processes, the focus should be on the role of the various actors and altering the processes shaping these activities. The assumption that biometric data is infallible lulls the authorities into thinking they have found a solution to one of the basic problems of modernity, which has acquired a particular salience in today's globalised world, the problem of suspect identities (Cole, 2009). As Lyon (2010b p. 607) suggests, "Showing a token of legitimate ID is now a basic condition for the exercise of freedom" (cited in Aas, 2011). This not only points to how biometric technologies limit movement by producing "disqualified bodies" (Muller, 2004) but also to the advantages this technology can offer to those with the right tokens – the globally mobile "kinetic elites" (Adey, 2004). Identity controls are thus, not only fraud prevention measures, but also techniques of social sorting.

Unlike more inwardly directed national surveillance, in this context, practices of transnational surveillance revolve around alliances between "states like us" and protecting the public, which is no longer defined exclusively as the citizenry of the nation state. At the level of political discourse, these practices seem to aspire to notions of "pan-European and cosmopolitan citizenship" (Aas, 2011, p. 341).

However, unequal positions are held by various social groups (citizens, subcitizens, supracitizens and non-citizens) in terms of the degree of surveillance they are subjected to, ranging from extreme deprivation to great social privilege. This inequality reveals the inadequacy of the traditional liberal notion of citizenship as the springboard for articulating a discourse of rights. Consequently, it is unclear how well equipped the critical surveillance and privacy discourse built on the language of citizenship is to address the unequal social and geopolitical positions of those subjected to surveillance practices at a global level.

The various surveillance measures have different (bio)political objectives and markedly different effects on citizens of the global North, "crimmigrants" (criminal immigrants) and bona-fide global travellers (ibid.). For travellers, they have carved out pockets and corridors of protection and mobility. These practices bring to our attention what Judith Butler (2004, p. 29) calls the "qualitatively differentiated value of life" and the "geopolitical distribution of corporeal vulnerability".

In conclusion, tax benefits are easily accessible but difficult to keep. Different tax credit entitlements trigger different methods of circumventing the system to maintain payments. Parents register the children of their extended family members, hide their changed circumstances, pay for fake addresses, keep their children registered at school while abroad, and participate in benefit fraud. These techniques are constantly changing and have major implications for welfare screening methods, as has been illustrated by the commercial diagnostic software used by HMRC investigators. Still, tax credits are not the only way for employed newcomers to obtain income. Another coping strategy is presented below that confirms a shift from welfare to "debtfare" in neoliberal service provision.

7.5 The commodification of debt

Although the examples demonstrate several innovative strategies for obtaining benefits, not everyone is able to access social provisions. Financial surveillance and mobility control have been seriously impacted by speech acts against the poor, giving debts a new interpretation in risk-oriented geopolitical objectives. As has been illustrated by welfare restrictions, a new shift is forcing welfare-dependent newcomers to take out loans to deal with social inequality. Governing the poor by debt is one of the major critics of geopolitical studies, warning against the criminalisation of newcomers who increasingly slip into debt. Susanne Soederberg explores the illusion of financial inclusion in *Debtfare States and the Poverty Industry* (2014a). She argues that societal structures and processes normalise and naturalise a credit culture by increasing consumer credit at high interest rates, damaging the social fabric of nations by increasing the prevalence of inequality which, in turn, restrains national economic growth.

Under the current economic paradigm, debt accumulation is being utilised as a stopgap to circumvent marginalisation – consumer credit provides households with the ability to mask inequality through consumption, financed by debt accumulation (Hall, 2014). In keeping with his argument, it can be stated that not only has society become dependent on consumer credit, the 'social machinations involved in normalising, depoliticising, legitimising the social necessities compel the working poor to depend on credit to ensure their livelihoods' (Soederberg, 2014a, p. 30).

Focusing on student loans and short-term credit, in the last part of this chapter it will be suggested that newcomers are able to challenge these credit constructions by identity management, allowing the person behind the indebted dividual to avoid being caught.

Newcomer Roma families excluded from social services are regularly trapped in commercial short-term loans that pile debt upon debt. The payday loans favoured by many study respondents are short-term loans for small amounts of money to solve immediate financial problems. They are easily available from high-street shops and internet sites, but interest rates are high. Many contracts include continuous payment authority (CPA). If there is not enough money in the account to repay the loan on the agreed date, the lender may ask the borrower's banks for all or part of the money. Charges are added for late payment. However, the lender is not able to use the CPA more than twice if it has not been able to obtain the money from the borrowers account and cannot try to take a part payment.[4]

Many particiipants threatened with eviction notices or by bailiffs apply for short-term loans. However, the loans come with several preconditions that should be considered. When people are under pressure, they are willing to solve their financial problems by taking out a loan with fake documents. For these loans, the lender must provide a tenancy contract, bank account and referee for proof of income, who is often another self-employed family member. Newcomer families already in debt may need to manipulate addresses to take out another loan or obtain a loan from a usurer to cover living expenses. Due to credit check requirements, indebted newcomers who apply for a loan manipulate addresses and pay for false tenancy agreements,or buy false bank statements from illegal "agencies". Increasing debts are covered with other debts. Sometimes electronic devices bought with credit cards are sold on the black market to spin a quick profit with no intention of paying back the credit card debt. One of the respondents, a young man who used to live in several countries, explains how he copes when he is unable to make enough money to live on:

> *It is easy to sell new bank accounts or gas cards, which you can use to buy products like Tesco cards that can be used to buy GBP 200 or 300 gas, which you can sell for GBP 1:30 a litre. This also makes some profit, but they are not big deals. It's more like to survive when you have no money at all. But how long will this be enough? Like a month? Here, there is nothing anymore – no new businesses, nothing. There was before, like the bank card business. You even used to be able to get credit till about four years ago, but now I can't name any bank that will give you a card with a credit limit. Before, when we went to the bank, we walked out with a bank account and bought four phones for about GBP 300. It*

4 Information of the Citizen Advice Bureau: www.citizensadvice.org.uk/debt-and-money/borrowing-money/types-of-borrowing/loans/payday-loans/payday-loans/

is finished now, this address is shit now [referring to the UK address of his family]. There have been too many applications and stuff registered here.

(HM36)

Similar to bank accounts, loans and credit cards are also becoming restricted. Accordingly, newcomers participate in local credit markets and invest the knowledge and skills acquired in other countries such as Canada about alternative short-term financial solutions. There is hardly any assistance to support newcomers with financial problems. The "responsibilisation" of citizens has become the main principle. In civil society, NGOs are increasingly controlled and threatened by state restrictions and quality claims about service provisions such as licenced advocacy work. As the director of a Roma advocacy group notes, 'advocacy work is criminalised now'. She explains how many legislative restrictions are introduced to control NGOs, for example regarding working conditions, administrative tasks and financial transparency. The director of this NGO suggested that the state is also limiting access to support for vulnerable people, which curbs the ability of poor minorities to access welfare and state-financed services and pushes them into debt.

Although there are many loopholes for short-term loans, these debts restrict the long-term prospects of households, many of which are ruled by debt and ultimately evicted or forced to return to their home country.

7.6 Conclusion – investing in virtual citizenship

Being a migrant is like driving with a GPS that keeps recalculating the path. As is suggested in the theoretical framework, the geopolitical aims are implemented in many internal control measures of nation states, which target the least attractive individuals and force them to move. When targeting algorithms are employed in digitalised selection mechanisms, individuals attempt to bypass the restrictions and trick the system, so they can remain stable in their microenvironment. Based on the collected data of service providers, which can be manipulated, new directions are defined and recalculated to circumvent welfare restrictions.

The capacity of surveillance and dataveillance to deconstruct the individual into a series of discrete parameters that can be scrutinised, assessed and assigned value and intentionality is not limited to the medium of data interpretation. The digital image plays a powerful constructive role in allowing the individual to be captured in the digital system and rendered as an object of interrogation. 'Massing profiles on subject individuals through digital surveillance and dataveillance play a vital role in establishing the parameters on which bureaucratic structures can act' (Jarvis, 2010, p. 14). The cases above illustrate the degree to which this kind of digital profiling has implications for the interactions of individuals with bureaucratic structures and the disciplining of their physical being.

8 Conclusion

> *Imagine a world where all the cities are identical, where people dress uniformly, where you need written permission to travel beyond your immediate environs (and where failure to gain permission leads to enslavement), where you are obliged to travel in groups, where house doors operate automatically so that nothing is private or exclusive, where there are no hiding places outside the home, no spots for secret meetings, and where inhabitants live in full view of each other.*
>
> (Marks, 2005, p. 222)

Is the Brave New World coming of age? The growing popularity of dystopian literature raises the question of whether Western surveillance societies are really moving toward Aldous Huxley's (1932) World State, where geopolitical aims are manifested in extended control measures that are supported by surveillance technologies that govern people on the move. In these surrealistic images of totalitarian control, minorities are defined as uncivilised, traditional and uneconomical, a threat to the happiness of the World Society who should be displaced into "savage reservations". Following the idea of such dystopian social critiques, this study explores the promises of the surveillance society, in particular the side effects of monitoring practices that are used as geopolitical tools of population selection. The central aim of the study was to reveal the limitations of digital surveillance systems and their discriminative nature as well as its impact regarding mobility control and social distrust.

In recent decades, Western European societies have increasingly defined Roma mobility as a welfare concern. They have urged the new EU member states to invest in the socio-economic position of Roma minorities, which they hope will prevent migration. As part of a securitisation process such political speech acts linked the threat of a "Roma flood" with notions of "promising" welfare services in host countries to justify increasing control policies and restrict social benefits for newcomers. In these narratives, the key argument for welfare restrictions is framed in a neoliberal approach of responsibilisation and eligibility for state support, based on labour market participation. These connotations adopted in welfare policies assume that unemployed migrants are responsible for their marginal position and can therefore be legitimately excluded from any entitlement to government support.

This book presents empirical case studies to critically analyse the monitoring and control practices of EU citizens described as the 'Welfare Banopticon' to answer the question: How the interplay between digitalised bureaucracies of welfare providers and the coping strategies of EU newcomers shapes the social sorting of benefit claimants?

As an interdisciplinary analysis of financial surveillance, this study addressed geopolitical incentives in the EU and how recent securitisation of EU transnational migrants is being implemented through digitalised screenings of social service providers. According the examples in the UK welfare system, competitive market relationships are shaping the rules of social inclusion based on economic production and social conformism. Businesslike state bureaucracies are outsourced for corporate companies in order to monitor undesired outsiders, control and sanction them, as part of selective and expulsive governmental incentives. However, the virtual and institutional ethnography on which this study was partly based found that when bureaucracies collect information online, undesired newcomers are able to hide, or manage their identities to fit in.

By combining the subjects of surveillance, mobility and ethnicity, this study contributes to the debate about social sorting in geopolitical governance after the digital turn. In particular, it develops a new understanding of welfare policing as well as how financial circumstances of migrants defined as threats contribute to recent securitisation processes. It can be argued that crime politics and migration control are encompassing new bureaucratic fields and change the tasks of welfare service providers from support to policing.

8.1 Roma migrants under the surveillance gaze

The multi-sited fieldwork explores how some Roma migrants as a response try to hide from the virtual Welfare Banopticon, and how the all-seeing eye of digital surveillance shapes their lives in the United Kingdom. Such a disciplinary control system not only implicate the justification of extraordinary measures, but also a structural exclusion implemented in the 'Funnel of Expulsion', forcing the poor to operate outside the legal framework of the states' bureaucratic system.

As part of a long mobile fieldwork I moved between different realms while pursuing a multi-sited ethnography that crossed social, digital, and legal borders. In two years research period, I interviewed, followed and supported NGO employees, academics, professionals and Roma migrants for the sake of gathering in-depth data about their experiences. By living with several families and visiting others in their home settlements, I was able to build long-term relationships and the trust needed to share sensitive issues and important moments of decision. As I followed families on their way to England, online and offline, they regularly discussed their dilemmas, fears and excitement, as well as the calculated impacts of their choices. Contact was generally facilitated by social media, which allowed me to follow respondents in different localities over time and to maintain contact, so we could discuss their evolving financial situations as relates to debts and entitlements to welfare provisions. Small talks held in Job Centre offices, in

Facebook chats or around kitchen tables gave me a complete view of the surveillance experience and how it plays a role in welfare applications. They also helped to understand how ethnic stigma shapes coping mechanisms in interactions with service providers and NGOs.

However, simply following those who are the targets of profiling and selection based on their financial abilities cannot provide a complete understanding of the dynamics in situational decision-making processes. By spending eight months at a local NGO, I was able to collect information about the role of civil society, how cooperation and conflict shape local service providers' knowledge about Roma and how specific application procedures receive ethnic frames in different London boroughs. Based on the narrative of different stakeholders it has been suggested that these ethnic frames define Roma according to parameters of poverty and welfare dependency. Based on these ethnic connotations described in Chapter 5, it was concluded that the major selection criteria of social sorting are not specifically related to ethnicity, but they are framed by economic productivity and social conformity, in which some parameters are associated with Roma migrants.

Collecting this information had its costs. Ethical issues regarding the possible risks taken by the respondents resulted a selection of data in order to ensure the respondents' confidentiality and prevent their stigmatisation or criminalisation. Therefore, by taking different roles in the field – interpreter, advocacy worker, tenant or teacher – various narratives have been collected and presented based on selected coping strategies in the daily routine of the 'Ban-Opticon'. Being an ethnographer who was exposed to unexpected expectations, conflicts and emotional attachments forced me to get engaged in life situations that provided a better understanding of social transgression based on situational values regarding perceptions on profiling and justification of identity management.

In order to understand 'how securitisation strategies of internal migration control are merging social security and immigration policies in UK surveillance practices', global mobility processes should be analysed, such as the impact of free mobility in the EU. In the recent security narratives threat is defined in terms of migrants' unpredictable mobility. Due to technological developments, the movement of people across borders becomes multilateral and polycentric like flocks of birds, confronting nation states with unpredictable population changes that have intensive economic impacts they cannot control. However, these movements of mobile groups are not occurring randomly. The flow has a definite slope that gives a geopolitical orientation in the European Union.

Consequently, due to lack of mobility control, anxiety is rising as nation states realise they are losing their hold over their own skilled citizens while they are attracting undesired groups, such as 'benefit tourists'. As external control measures are moving towards internal control, technological developments enable an assemblage of new control and surveillance technics to manage population flows. By adapting neoliberal values in population selection, security is defined in economic terms of productivity that forces bureaucratic technologies to screen newcomers based on parameters of financial capability as a precondition of inclusion. As it has been described in Chapter 2, these new selection technologies entitle social service providers to screen the unproductive ones and select them out, as a Welfare Ban-Opticon. Welfare surveillance and restrictive policies on eligibility are justified by speech acts on security, associating threat with newcomers as cultural and economic intruders. As it has been presented in Chapter 6 and 7, the counterstrategies of migrants to combat these bureaucratic measures force local authorities to increase control and financial sanctions to catch a glimpse of those who are slipping through their fingers. As a vicious circle, this process results targeted policies and decrease transparency of state authorities.

In short, this study proves that the dynamics of social sorting are shaped by a conscious dialectic process. Roma mobility illustrates the unintended effects of these geopolitical orientations of population control by presenting how to challange digitalised monitoring of benefit claimants.

8.2 Managing the stranger

Selective incentives of risk management have been introduced in the digitalised bureaucratic strategies of welfare services through screenings of benefit applicants. As it is described in Chapter 4, by increasing the role of screening instruments and profiling of suspicious claimants through algorithms, applicants are constantly under gaze of financial and social monitoring as well as through financial sanctions.

Based on the collected data, I concluded that population control is directed by the economic principles of production in which unproductive citizens are labelled as undesirable. Due to porous intra-European borders, countries have introduced internal control measures in which financial screening has replaced visa restrictions. My observations of Job Centre conversations and Tax Office calls illustrate how social sorting is being conducted by outsourced government bodies that are authorised to screen, control and select foreign welfare applicants. These companies gain increasing power to monitor and sanction vulnerable EU citizens, which turns social provision into security policing, creating fear and distrust among welfare-dependent newcomers. Authorities' strategies are reflected in the disciplinary role of dataveillance, which describes how they manage personal information in public service environments.

Security measures related to welfare services can be compared to obstacles in a computer game: the closer you get to the goal, the more complicated it becomes to achieve it. The real contribution of this study lies in the presentation of different tactics used by Roma newcomers in online and offline bureaucratic interactions. As I noted, the UK service providers greatly underestimate the behaviour modifications of newcomers aimed at avoiding the security mechanisms of welfare services. Automatic screening and algorithm-based selection methods are also biassed and easy to manipulate. Migrants are generally aware of the social sorting mechanisms they are subjected to and most of them proactively profile themselves to succeed. In the case of Roma migrants, identity management and other economic strategies are not only meant to elude ethnic stigmatisation, but also mimic the social expectations of the desired citizen.

In order to answer *how the definition of foreign threat is shaped by the narrative framing of stakeholders, it should be also discussed to what extend are ethnic classifications are represented in financial terms as a threat*?

The social construction of Roma ethnicity is shaped by various actors who are involved into these interactions. Professionals and academics have put forth internally conflicting approaches that cause confusion about the needs and importance of the Roma ethnicity. These connotations have been implemented in European policies, reproducing the social construction of the image of a welfare dependent outsider. This image creates general tensions and increases suspicion toward newcomers.

Digital modalities are present in all bureaucratic practices in EU member states' surveillance practices and these are not only concerning Roma welfare applicants. However, the point of this study is actually, how several profiling mechanisms that have been associated with ethnic discrimination among welfare-dependent Roma groups, are not ethnicity based social sorting mechanisms, but modalities of a digitalised financial discrimination. As it is presented in the last chapters, Roma minorities who have experienced institutional discrimination based on ethnic connotations, explain these financial profiling mechanisms still as ethnic targeting and respond to them according to that. Shortly, welfare surveillance is justified by securitisation narratives in reference to welfare dependent migrants and Roma are interpreting financial policing as ethnic profiling, however, the real social sorting mechansims are based on financial profiling of unemployed claimants.

The new surveillance patterns are not meant "above all" for the Roma as an ethnic minority, but due to their experiences before, Roma newcomers are identifying it as such and anticipate these surveillance measures accordingly. Financial surveillance is of course a practice to screen all welfare applicants, but the algorithms programmed to profile high-risk applicants are clearly based on parameters that are justified by the welfare-magnet theory. Shortly, profiles are based on parameters of migrants who have weak labour history, limited financial resources, low education, suspected of fraud etc. These parameters are also used in cases of ethnic discrimination in sending countries that make Roma associate these profiling algorithms of service providers with ethnic discrimination. This increase mutual distrust and new control measures to ensure the legitimacy of sanctions.

While service provisions build barriers for new unemployed migrants, those who search for the fringes get past them. As a result, those migrants who are more self-sustaining and are unwilling to take high risks move forward, while others who have nothing to lose or are not able to return to their home countries stay in host countries and get involved in illicit activbities and exploitation. Based on the selected cases, I conclude that geopolitical screening and social sorting through welfare provisions generates the opposite of what was expected: the expulsion of those migrants who have more potential to participate in society while the least productive newcomers stay and are forced into informal economic strategies.

Accessing welfare provisions is a stressful, time-consuming, unpredictable process that requires a well-informed network, language skills, internet literacy and financial capital to complete the application procedure. Applicants also need to stay updated about the changing rules of eligibility.

The coping mechanisms of Central European Roma migrants can only be understood through an in-depth knowledge of historically constructed prejudices and a recognition of Roma ethnic diversity in different countries. In the post-transitional societies of the Visegrad group, it is social acceptable to cheat the government and to manipulate or select information about personal circumstances. Their experience in other countries makes these newcomers to the UK more aware of the power relationships and dysfunctions of a bureaucratic system. They also know how to use these relationships and dysfunctions to become eligible for support.

Roma migrants use their relationships with others to cope with life and bureaucracy in the UK. Brokers are often unseen mediators who have a major impact on the success of welfare applications. They can also affect dependence relations with landlords and employers by providing services in confined business networks. Many newcomers who hope to settle in the UK cannot survive on irregular low-paid agency jobs, so they apply for basic benefit entitlements. Due to previous experiences with social servants, Roma applicants use different types of identity management mechanisms in interactions with service providers. As described in Chapter 7, they use various techniques to avoid, rectify or conflate ethnic sigma and to prevent discrimination by self-censorship.

Selection for social service eligibility is an interactive process between service providers and claimants. Migrants apply various strategies to reproduce or imitate characteristics of the "desired citizen". Although Roma are often described as creative pioneers in circumventing monitoring mechanisms, my observations and interviews led me to conclude that applicants who want to become eligible for social benefits learn about the limitations of government data systems and application forms from others. Most of the strategies they apply are learned from others who are familiar with the system, such as settled minorities in their direct environments. Pakistani landlords, employment agency workers and NGO advocacy workers also educate newcomers about how to adapt to screening policies and facilitate documents to make them appear entitled to welfare provisions.

Migrants who consciously construct the identity of a "deserving citizen" also change their coping strategies in line with changes in family circumstances. This development was illustrated by cases in which marital status changed and by shifts from unemployment benefits to tax credits. As it was concluded, virtual identity construction is supposed to ensure the economic and social rights of newcomers, but its behaviour-modification effects are unpredictable.

Policy restrictions targeting EU citizens have led to an increasing shift from unemployment benefits toward tax credit claims, even though this is riskier for applicants. Although tax credit claims often lead to tax fraud and require compliance with an extended digital monitoring system, applicants feel less observed since they feel hidden behind the digital procedures. Choosing to use these tax credit applications is another type of coping strategy, one in which interactions take place in digitalised identification processes.

Although I began this study with a dystopian idea of the European control society, I am ending it with a more optimistic notion of hope. The information-based power relations of surveillance societies are being constantly challenged by innovative ideas from excluded populations who aspire to inclusion, access and recognition. Targeting undesired migrants, who are seen as a financial or security threat, has led Western governments to implement new selective mechanisms in social policies as a mobility control. However, these restrictions are temporary solutions since those migrants who are familiar with the loopholes of the administrative structures can easily find the back doors and invest their knowledge in their networks.

8.3 Virtual bureaucracies and the rise of the "dividual"

This study was based on the hypothesis that intra-European mobility control is taken new forms in digitalised state bureaucracies based on neoliberal values of deservingness. As it was explained by the concept of social sorting, policies on accessing welfare has been included into intra-European control measures based on data surveillance of benefit-dependent migrants. These data collections shall serve to objectively and efficiently select applicants based on parameters of welfare eligibility. However, such selections are representing the neoliberal values of productivity and in place of support, these profiling systems are excluding the poor unemployed applicants based on their financial capabilities. Such a selection method based on the suspicion of welfare claimants has been defined as a new geopolitical measure, the funnel of expulsion, to keep the undesired migrants away. However, such mobility control is overestimated, since the targeted ones are able to challenge such a mechanism and adapt to the parameters of selection, in particular in a virtual environment.

Surveillance is an active process with different levels of interaction between the surveyor and the survey object. The choice to apply for tax credits instead of welfare benefits represents a change from face-to-face interaction to virtual bureaucratic dialogues that shape the techniques of control and selection. Although virtual bureaucracies require internet literacy, they also provide a special identity-making space since the real person is no longer included in the digitalised interactions. This virtual space enables newcomers who are targeted for social exclusion to turn their virtual characteristics into those of a deserving productive citizen.

As a consequence of these cat and mouse games between the claimant and the bureaucracy, there is an increasing reality gap between the real identity of the claimant and the "dividual" who is translated into data based on specific parameters. Databases become filled with the altered personal information provided by those who feel targeted by local bureaucracies. These mutated profiles lead to unpredictability and inconsistency in spatial sorting strategies, increasing the distrust among benefit claimants who, as a result, become even less transparent. Although screening mechanisms like spidergrams are increasingly included in databases, the algorithm that is supposed to filter claimants is cheated. These retargeting and restrictive policies both underestimate the participative skills of applicants and overestimate the capacities of digitalised bureaucracies.

Due to welfarist notions in the media, service providers and applicants are suspicious of one another and therefore keep each other in constant confusion by selecting information in online or offline interactions. I found that not only claimants but also service providers are involved in transgressive actions related to application procedures. The tightened managerialist norms that restrict professional considerations to a risk-screening analysis illustrate how individual considerations still impact decisions about claims. The reality gap facilitated by the digitalisation of welfare services provides a new space of operations for both civil servants and applicants.

Although increasing attention is paid to big data analyses and the reliability of digital surveillance, the impacts of smaller local databases used for local population control on the lives of everyday citizens should not be underestimated. Through welfare application forms, newcomers create a new digital identity that is recycled by governmental statistics, NGO reports and policymakers who believe the data represents their citizens. However, with increasing awareness of data surveillance, those who receive "benefits" from manipulated data will continue their identity management. Criminological studies should pay more attention to digitization and the behaviour-modifying effects of surveillance measures and how awareness of control triggers new incentives to trick Big Brother.

In short, this study proves that benefit tourism is a misconception. Roma newcomers are moving toward Western Europe with a range of aspirations, particularly a search for social dignity. However, ethnic targeting by NGOs and market-oriented advocacy work and policy narratives contribute to existing ideas about marginal Roma groups that justify securitisation. In short, these neoliberal selection methods shift discriminatory practices from ethnic parameters to the financial capabilities of applicants. Roma newcomers who settle abroad are constantly monitored by their environment: they are under high expectations from their family networks and are living under the gaze of welfare surveillance. Theirs is a life of transgression on the edge of moral deservingness and legal eligibility, constructed by a digital identity.

References

Aas, K. F. (2011). 'Crimmigrant' bodies and bona fide travelers: Surveillance, citizenship and global governance. *Theoretical Criminology*, *15*(3), 331–346. doi:10.1177/1362480610396643

Aas, K. F., & Bosworth, M. (2013). *The borders of punishment: Migration, citizenship, and social exclusion*. Oxford, UK: Oxford University Press.

Adey, P. (2004). Surveillance at the airport: Surveilling mobility/mobilising surveillance. *Environment and Planning A*, *36*(8), 1365–1380. doi:10.1068/a36159

Adler, P.A., & Adler, P. (1987). *Membership roles in field research*. Newbury Park, CA: SAGE Publications.

Agamben, G. (1998). *Homo sacer: Sovereign power and bare life*. Stanford, CA: Stanford University Press.

Allmer, T. (2015). *Critical theory and social media: Between emancipation and commodification* (Vol. 144). London, UK: Routledge.

Anderson, B. (2013). *Us and them? The dangerous politics of immigration control*. Oxford, UK: Oxford University Press.

Aradau, C. (2004). Security and the democratic scene: Desecuritization and emancipation. *Journal of International Relations and Development*, *7*(4), 388–413. doi:10.1057/palgrave.jird.1800030

Bank, R. (2000). Europeanising the reception of asylum seekers: The opposite of welfare state politics. In M. Bommes & A. Geddes (Eds.), *Immigration and welfare: Challenging the borders of the welfare state* (pp. 148–169). Abingdon, UK: Taylor & Francis.

Bárány, Z. (1998). Ethnic mobilisation and the state: The Roma in Eastern Europe. *Ethnic and Racial Studies*, *21*(2), 308–327. doi:10.1080/014198798330034

Bárány, Z. (2002). *The East European gypsies: Regime change, marginality, and ethnopolitics*. Cambridge, UK: Cambridge University Press.

Barrett, J., & Sigona, N. (2014). The citizen and the other: New directions in research on the migration and citizenship nexus. *Migration Studies*, *2*(2), 286–294. doi:10.1093/migration/mnu039

Barth, F. (Ed.). (1969). *Ethnic groups and boundaries: The social organization of culture difference*. London, UK: Allen & Unwin.

Bauman, Z. (1998). *Work, consumption and the new poor*. Cambridge, UK: Polity Press.

Bauman, Z. (2013). *Liquid modernity*. Hoboken, NJ: John Wiley & Sons.

Baumann, G. (1996). *Contesting culture: Discourses of identity in multi-ethnic London* (Vol. 100). Cambridge, UK: Cambridge University Press.

Baumgartner, F. R., Breunig, C., Green-Pedersen, C., Jones, B. D., Mortensen, P. B., Nuytemans, M., & Walgrave, S. (2009). Punctuated equilibrium in comparative perspective. *American Journal of Political Science*, *53*(3), 603–620. doi:10.1111/j.1540-5907.2009.00389.x

BBC. (2013a, April 1). *Iain Duncan Smith: Reforms 'make work pay'*. Retrieved from www.bbc.com/news/uk-21993453

BBC. (2013b, April 8). *Disability living allowance replaced by PIP scheme*. Retrieved from www.bbc.com/news/uk-22058059

Beneito-Montagut, R. (2011). Ethnography goes online: Towards a user-centred methodology to research interpersonal communication on the internet. *Qualitative Research*, *11*(6), 716–735. doi:10.1177/1468794111413368

Berk-Seligson, S. (1990). Bilingual court proceedings. In J. N. Levi & A. G. Walker (Eds.), *Language in the judicial process* (pp. 155–201). New York, NY: Springer.

Best, K. (2010). Living in the control society: Surveillance, users and digital screen technologies. *International Journal of Cultural Studies*, *13*(1), 5–24. doi:10.1177/1367877909348536

Bigo, D. (2006. *Illiberal practices of liberal regimes: The (in)security games*. Paris, France: L'Harmattan.

Bigo, D. (2006) 'Security, Exception, Ban and Surveillance', in D. Lyon (ed.) *Theorizing Surveillance: The Panopticon and Beyond*, pp. 46–68. Cullompton: Willan Publishing.

Bigo, D. (2008b). Globalized (in)security: The field and the ban-opticon. In D. Bigo & A. Tsoukala (Eds.), *Terror, insecurity and liberty: Illiberal practices of liberal regimes after 9/11* (pp. 5–49). London, UK: Routledge.

Bigo, D., & Tsoukala, A. (Eds.). (2008). *Terror, insecurity and liberty: Illiberal practices of liberal regimes after 9/11*. London, UK: Routledge.

Bigo, D., & Walker, R. B. J. (2002). Security and migration. *Special Section of Alternatives*, *27*(1), 1–92.

Bigo, D., & Walker, R. B. J. (2007). Political sociology and the problem of the international. *Millennium – Journal of International Studies*, *35*(3), 725–739. doi:10.1177/03058298070350030401

Böcker, A., & Havinga, T. (1998). *Asylum migration to the European Union: Patterns of origin and destination*. Luxembourg: Office for Official Publications of the European Communities. Retrieved from www.researchgate.net/publication/254865228_Asylum_Migration_to_the_European_Union_Patterns_of_Origin_and_Destination

Borja, J., & Castells, M. (2013). *Local and global: The management of cities in the information age*. Abingdon: Routledge.

Borjas, G. (1999). The economic analysis of immigration. In O. Ashenfelter & D. Card (Eds.), *Handbook of labor economics* (Vol. 3, Part A, pp. 1697–1760). Amsterdam, the Netherlands: Elsevier.

Bovenkerk, F. (2014). *Marokkaan in Europa, crimineel in Nederland. Een vergelijkende studie* [Moroccan in Europe, criminal in the Netherlands: A comparative study]. Amsterdam, the Netherlands: Boom Lemma Uitgevers.

Bovenkerk, F., Siegel, D., & Zaitch, D. (2003). Organized crime and ethnic reputation manipulation. *Crime, Law & Social Change*, *39*(1), 23–38.

Bovenkerk, F., & Yesilgöz, Y. (2004). Crime, ethnicity and the multicultural administration of justice. In J. Ferrell, K. Hayward, W. Morrison, & M. Presdee (Eds.), *Cultural criminology unleashed* (pp. 81–96). London, UK: Routledge-Cavendish.

Broeders, D., & Engbersen, G. (2013). *Digital fortress Europe: Policies on irregular migration and the weapons of the weak.* Unpublished manuscript. Retrieved from www.inclusionexclusion.nl/Ereader/Art.%20%20Engbersen.twee.doc

Brown, P. (2012). *Interim research report – Roma SOURCE.* Retrieved from www.romasource.eu/userfiles/attachments/pages/167/romasourceinterimresearchreport-en.pdf

Brown, P., Scullion, L., & Martin, P. (2013). *Migrant Roma in the United Kingdom: Population size and experiences of local authorities and partners.* Manchester, UK: University of Salford. Retrieved from www.salford.ac.uk/__data/assets/pdf_file/0004/363118/Migrant_Roma_in_the_UK_final_report_October_2013.pdf

Brubaker, R. (2004). *Ethnicity without groups.* Cambridge, MA: Harvard University Press.

Brubaker, R., Loveman, M., & Stamatov, P. (2004). Ethnicity as cognition. *Theory and Society, 33*(1), 31–64. doi:10.1023/b:ryso.0000021405.18890.63

Burke, A. D. (2007). *Beyond security, ethics and violence: War against the other.* London, UK: Routledge.

Burke, R. R. (2002). Technology and the customer interface: What consumers want in the physical and virtual store. *Journal of the Academy of Marketing Science, 30*(4), 411–432. doi:10.1177/009207002236914

Butler, J. (2004). *Precarious life: The powers of mourning and violence.* London, UK: Verso.

Buzan, B., Wæver, O., & DeWilde, J. (1998). *Security: A new framework for analysis.* Boulder, CO: Lynne Rienner Publishers.

Cahn, C., & Guild, E. (2010). *Recent migration of Roma in Europe* (2nd ed.). Council of Europe. Retrieved from www.osce.org/hcnm/78034?download=true

Caplan, J., & Torpey, J. (2001). Introduction. In J. Caplan & J. Torpey (Eds.), *Documenting individual identity. The development of state practices in the modern world* (pp. 1–12). Princeton, NJ: Princeton University Press.

Cârstocea, A. E. (2012). *'Ethno-business': The unexpected consequence of post-1989 policies for the political representation of national minorities in Romania* (Doctoral dissertation). University College London, London, UK.

Carter, D. M. (2004). Living in virtual communities: Making friends online. *Journal of Urban Technology, 11*(3), 109–125. doi:10.1080/10630730500064448

Cerny, P. G. (2000). Structuring the political arena: Public goods, states and governance in a globalizing world. In R. Palan (Ed.), *Global political economy: Contemporary theories* (p. 21). London, UK: Routledge.

Chen, P., & Hinton, S. M. (1999). Realtime interviewing using the world wide web. *Sociological Research Online 4*(3). doi:10.5153/sro.308

Cherkezova, S., & Tomova, I. (2013). An *option of last resort? Migration of Roma and non-Roma from CEE countries.* UNDP Europe and the CIS, Bratislava Regional Centre. Retrieved from www.scribd.com/doc/197718148/Migration-of-Roma-and-Non-Roma-from-Central-and-Eastern-Europe#page=25

Chunn, D. E., & Gavigan, S. A. (2004). Welfare law, welfare fraud, and the moral regulation of the 'never deserving' poor. *Social & Legal Studies, 13*(2), 219–243. doi:10.1177/0964663904042552

Clark, C. (1998). Counting backwards: The Roma 'numbers game' in Central and Eastern Europe. *Radical Statistics, 69.* Retrieved from www.radstats.org.uk/no069/article4.htm

Clark, C., & Campbell, E. (2000). Gypsy invasion: A critical analysis of newspaper reaction to Czech and Slovak Romani asylum seekers in Britain, 1997. *Romani Studies*, *10*(1), 23–47. doi:10.3828/rs.2000.2

Clarke, J. (2005). New Labour's citizens: activated, empowered, responsibilized, abandoned? *Critical Social Policy*, *25*(4), 447–463. doi:10.1177/0261018305057024

Clarke, R. (1999). Introduction to dataveillance and information privacy, and definitions of terms. *Roger Clarke's Dataveillance and Information Privacy Pages*.

Clifford, J. (1997). Spatial practices: Fieldwork, travel, and the disciplining of anthropology. In A. Gupta & J. Ferguson (Eds.), *Anthropological locations: Boundaries and grounds of a field science* (pp. 185–222). Berkeley, CA: University of California Press.

Cohen, S. (2002). *Folk devils and moral panics: The creation of the mods and rockers*. Abingdon, UK: Psychology Press.

Cole, S. A. (2009). *Suspect identities: A history of fingerprinting and criminal identification*. Cambridge, MA: Harvard University Press.

Commons Select Committee. (2015, March 24). *MPs call for full independent review of benefit sanctions*. Retrieved from www.parliament.uk/business/committees/committees-a-z/commons-select/work-and-pensions-committee/news/benefit-sanctions-report/

Cresswell, T. (2006). *On the move: Mobility in the modern Western world*. Abingdon, UK: Taylor & Francis.

Dalakoglou, D., & Harvey, P. (2012). Roads and anthropology: Ethnographic perspectives on space, time and (im)mobility. *Mobilities*, *7*(4), 459–465. doi:10.1080/17450101.2012.718426

Davies, V., Hartfree, Y., Kellard, K., & Taylor, J. (2004). *Delivering the Jobcentre plus vision: Qualitative research with staff and customers (Phase 3)* (DWP Research Report No 222). Retrieved from http://webarchive.nationalarchives.gov.uk/20130128102031/http://research.dwp.gov.uk/asd/asd5/rports2003-2004/rrep222.pdf

Dean, H. (1998). Benefit fraud and citizenship. In P. Taylor-Gooby (Ed.), *Choice and public policy*. Basingstoke, UK: Macmillan.

Dee, M. (2013). Welfare surveillance, income management and new paternalism in Australia. *Surveillance & Society*, *11*(3), 272–286. Retrieved from http://ojs.library.queensu.ca/index.php/surveillance-and-society/issue/view/Surveillance%20Textualism

De Giorgi, A. (2012). Punishment and political economy. In R. Sparks & J. Simon (Eds.), *The SAGE handbook of punishment and society* (pp. 40–59). London, UK: SAGE Publications.

Dekker, R., & Engbersen, G. (2014). How social media transform migrant networks and facilitate migration. *Global Networks*, *14*(4), 401–418. doi:10.1111/glob.12040

Deleuze, G., & Guattari, F. (1987). *A thousand plateaus: Capitalism and schizophrenia*. Minneapolis, MN: University of Minnesota Press.

Denhardt, R. B., & Denhardt, J. V. (2000). The new public service: Serving rather than steering. *Public Administration Review*, *60*(6), 549–559. doi:10.1111/0033-3352.00117

De Parle, J. (2004). *American dream*. New York, NY: Penguin Books.

Department for Work and Pensions (2010, October 5). *The secretary of state for work and pensions, the Rt Hon Iain Duncan Smith, today announced the introduction of a Universal Credit*. Retrieved from UK Government website: www.gov.uk/government/news/universal-credit-introduced

Department for Work & Pensions (2014, February). *Personal independence payment: Management information*. Retrieved from UK Government website: www.gov.uk/government/uploads/system/uploads/attachment_data/file/277986/adHoc-pip-statistics-feb14.pdf

Diefenbach, T. (2009). New public management in public sector organizations: The dark sides of managerialistic 'enlightenment'. *Public Administration*, *87*(4), 892–909. doi:10.1111/j.1467-9299.2009.01766.x

Diller, M. (2000). The revolution in welfare administration: rules, discretion & entrepreneurial government. *New York University Law Review*, *75*. doi:10.2139/ssrn.257482

Dowling, S., Manthorpe, J., Cowley, S., King, S., Raymond, V., Perez, W., & Weinstein, P. (2006). *Person-centred planning in social care: A scoping review*. Retrieved from https://lemosandcrane.co.uk/resources/JRF%20-%20Person-centred%20planning%20in%20social%20care.pdf

Duwell, F., & Wollmer, B. (2009). *Irregular migration in and from the neighbourhood of the EU. A comparison of Morocco, Turkey and Ukraine*. Retrieved from www.hwwi.org/typo3_upload/groups/31/4.Background_Information/4.6.Link_library_InternalDocuments/Transit_report_COMPAS_Sept09.pdf

Džambazovič, R., & Jurásková, M. (2003). Social exclusion of the Roma in Slovakia. Čačipen pal o Roma, 325.

Džambazovič-Jurásková, I. M. (2008). MÉSZÁROS Magdolna: Az állami paternalizmustól az egyéni felelősség felé. Szegénység, jövedelmi egyenlőtlenségek, munkapiaci kirekesztés, jóléti transzferek Szlovákiában. In E. Törzsök, I. Paskó, & J. Zolnay (Eds.), *Cigánynak lenni Magyarországon. Jelentés 2007* (pp. 99–121). Budapest, Hungary: EÖKIK.

Eastwood, L., & DeVault, M. (2001). *Mapping social relations*. Presentation at IE Conference, Syracuse University, Syracuse, NY.

Engbersen, G. B. M., & Broeders, D. W. J. (2011). Immigration control and strategies of irregular migrants: From light to heavy foggy social structures. In M. Bommes & G. Sciortino (Eds.), *Foggy social structures: Irregular migration and the Eastern enlargement* (pp. 169–188). Amsterdam, the Netherlands: Amsterdam University Press.

Ericson, R. V., & Haggerty, K. D. (1997). *Policing the risk society*. Oxford, UK: Oxford University Press.

Erjavec, K. (2001). Media representation of the discrimination against the Roma in Eastern Europe: The case of Slovenia. *Discourse & Society*, *12*(6), 699–727. doi:10.1177/0957926501012006001

Escobar, A. (2011). *Encountering development: The making and unmaking of the Third World*. Princeton, NJ: Princeton University Press.

Espenshade, T. J., Fix, M., Zimmerman, W., & Corbett, T. (1997). Immigration and social policy: New interest in an old issue. *Focus*, *18*(2), 1–10. Retrieved from www.irp.wisc.edu/publications/focus/pdfs/foc182.pdf

EU-LFS. (2008). *EU labour force survey*. Retrieved from http://ec.europa.eu/eurostat/statistics-explained/index.php/EU_labour_force_survey_%E2%80%93_data_and_publication

European Communities. (2005). *Treaty establishing a constitution for Europe*. Retrieved from http://europa.eu/eu-law/decision-making/treaties/pdf/treaty_

establishing_a_constitution_for_europe/treaty_establishing_a_constitution_for_europe_en.pdf

European Dialogue. (2009). *The movement of Roma from new EU Member States: A mapping survey of A2 and A8 Roma in England. Patterns of settlement and current situation of new Roma communities in England*. Retrieved from http://equality.uk.com/Resources_files/movement_of_roma.pdf

Falkiner v. Ontario. (2002). 59 OR (3d) 481 Ont. C.A. Retrieved from www.ontariocourts.on.ca/decisions/2000/september/falkiner.htm

Falzon, M. A. (Ed.). (2012). *Multi-sited ethnography: Theory, praxis and locality in contemporary research*. Farnham, UK: Ashgate Publishing.

Fenton, S., & May, S. (2002). *Ethnonational identities*. London, UK: Palgrave Macmillan.

Ferguson, J. (2007). Power topographies. In D. Nugent & J. Vincent (Eds.), *A companion to the anthropology of politics* (pp. 383–399). Malden, MA: Blackwell.

Ferguson, J., & Gupta, A. (2002). Spatializing states: Toward an ethnography of neoliberal governmentality. *American Ethnologist*, *29*(4), 981–1002. doi:10.1525/ae.2002.29.4.981

Ferrell, J., Hayward, K., Morrison, W., & Presdee, M. (Eds.). (2004). *Cultural criminology unleashed*. London, UK: Routledge.

Fielding, N. G., Lee, R. M., & Blank, G. (Eds.). (2008). *The SAGE handbook of online research methods*. Thousand Oaks, CA: SAGE Publications.

FOGSOC Consortium. (2002). *Foggy social structures in a knowledge-based society – Irregular migration, informal economy and the political system* (Research proposal). Retrieved from www.imis.uni-osnabrueck.de/forschung/abgeschlossene_projekte/foggy_social_structures_in_a_knowledged_based_society.html

Forte, M. C. (Ed.) (2014). *Good intentions: Norms and practices of imperial humanitarianism* (The new imperialism, Vol. 4). Montreal/Quebec, Canada: Alert Press.

Foucault, M. (1975). *Surveiller et punir: naissance de la prison*. Paris: Gallimard.

Foucault, M. (1977). *Discipline and punish: The birth of the prison*. New York, NY: Vintage Books.

Foucault, M. (1979). *Discipline and Punish: the Birth of the Prison*. UK: Peregrine.

Foucault, M. (1982). The subject and power. *Critical Inquiry*, *8*(4), 777–795. doi:10.1086/448181

Foucault, M. (1997a). Security, territory, and population. In P. Rabinow (Ed.), *Michel Foucault, ethics: Subjectivity and truth* (pp. 67–71). New York, NY: The New Press.

Foucault, M. (1997b). The ethics of the concern for the self as a practice of freedom. In P. Rabinow (Ed.), *Michel Foucault, ethics: Subjectivity and truth* (pp. 281–301). London, UK: Allen Lane, The Penguin Press.

Foucault, M. (2007). *Security, territory, population: Lectures at the Collège de France, 1977–1978*. New York, NY: Palgrave Macmillan.

FPEG (the EU Fraud Prevention Expert Group). (2007). *Report on identity theft/fraud* (Brussels, October 22). Retrieved from http://ec.europa.eu/internal_market/fpeg/docs/id-theft-report_en.pdf

Galiţa, R., & Bonta, E. (2013). Gypsies: A linguistic construction of their marginality in English newspapers headlines. *Interstudia (Revista Centrului Interdisciplinar de Studiu al Formelor Discursive Contemporane Interstud)*, *14*, 119–127.

Gandy, O. H., Jr. (1993). *The panoptic sort: A political economy of personal information: Critical studies in communication and in the cultural industries*. Boulder, CO: Westview Press, Inc.

Gandy, O. H., Jr. (1996). Coming to terms with the panoptic sort. In D. Lyon & E. Zureik (Eds.), *Computers, surveillance, and privacy* (pp. 132–155). Minneapolis, MN: University of Minnesota Press.

Gasparini, G. (1995). On waiting. *Time & Society*, *4*(1), 29–45. doi:10.1177/0961463X95004001002

Geertz, C. (1973). *The interpretation of cultures.* New York, NY: Basic Books.

Gellner, E., & Waterbury, J. (Eds.). (1977). *Patrons and clients in Mediterranean societies.* London, UK: Duckworth.

Georgeou, N., & Engel, S. (2011). The impact of neoliberalism and new managerialism on development volunteering: An Australian case study. *Australian Journal of Political Science*, *46*(2), 297–311. doi:10.1080/10361146.2011.567970

Giddens, A. (1985). *A contemporary critique of historical materialism: The nation-state and violence.* Cambridge, UK: Polity Press.

Grill, J. (2015). The Economic Strategies of Roma Migrants in Slovakia and the UK. Gypsy Economy: Romani Livelihoods and Notions of Worth in the 21st Century, 3, 88.

Gill, S. R., & Law. D. (1989). Global hegemony and the structural power of capital. *International Studies Quarterly*, *33*(4), 475–499.

Gilliom, J. (2001). *Overseers of the poor: Surveillance, resistance, and the limits of privacy.* Chicago, IL: University of Chicago Press.

Glasius, M., & Ishkanian, A. (2014). Surreptitious symbiosis: Engagement between activists and NGO's. *VOLUNTAS: International Journal of Voluntary and Nonprofit Organizations*, *26*(6), 2620–2644. Retrieved from http://eprints.lse.ac.uk/60128/

Glick-Schiller, N., Çaglar, A., & Guldbrandsen, T. C. (2006). Beyond the ethnic lens: Locality, globality, and born-again incorporation. *American Ethnologist*, *33*(4), 612–633.

Goddard, T. (2012). Post-welfarist risk managers? Risk, crime prevention and the responsibilization of community-based organizations. *Theoretical Criminology*, 16(3), 347–363.

Goffman, E. (1974). *Frame analysis.* Harmondsworth, UK: The Penguin Press.

Gordon, G. R., and Willox, N. A. (2003). *Identity fraud: A critical national and global threat.* New York, NY: Economic Crime Institute, Utica College.

Gounev, P., Bezlov, T., Dimov, M. & Yordanova, N. (2006). *Police stops and ethnic profiling in Bulgaria*. Sofia: Centre for the Study of Democracy.

Graham, S., & Wood, D. (2003). Digitizing surveillance: Categorization, space, inequality. *Critical Social Policy*, *23*(2), 227–248. doi:10.1177/0261018303023002006

Green, S. (1999). A plague on the panopticon: Surveillance and power in the global information economy. *Information, Communication & Society*, *2*(1), 26–44. doi:10.1080/136911899359745

Greenfields, M., & Smith, D. (2010). A question of identity: the social exclusion of housed gypsies and travellers. *Research, Policy and Planning*, *28*(3), 65–78.

Grey, C., & Willmott, H. (2005). *Critical management studies: A reader.* Oxford, UK: Oxford University Press.

Grijpink, J. H. A. M., & Prins, J. E. J. (2003). New rules for anonymous electronic transactions? An exploration of the private law implications of digital anonymity. In C. Nicoll, J. E. J. Prins, & M. J. M. van Dellen (Eds.), *Digital anonymity and the law. Tensions and dimensions* (pp. 249–269). The Hague, the Netherlands: T.M.C. Asser Press.

Grill, J. (2005). The limits of multiculturalism: What can we learn from the Fadime Sahindal's murder? In *Fieldwork and local communities*. Prague: Prague Occasional Papers in Ethnology No. 7.

Grill, J. (2011). From street busking in Switzerland to meat factories in the UK: A comparative study of two Roma migration networks from Slovakia. In D. Kaneff & F. Pine (Eds.), *Global connections and emerging inequalities in Europe: Perspectives on poverty and transnational migration* (pp. 79–102). London, UK: Anthem Press.

Grill, J. (2012). 'It's building up to something and it won't be nice when it erupts': The making of Roma/Gypsy migrants in post-industrial Scotland. *Focaal*, *2012*(62), 42–54. doi:10.3167/fcl.2012.620104

Grossman, W. M. (2005). *Identifying risks: National identity cards* (Lecture delivered at the University of Edinburgh on January 19, 2005). Retrieved from http://www2.law.ed.ac.uk/ahrc/script-ed/vol2-1/idcards.asp

Hainey, M. (2011). Building and integrating databases for risk profiles in the United Kingdom. *Risk-Based Tax Audits, June 2011*, 65–70. doi:10.1596/9780821387542_CH06

Hajnal, L. E. (2002). The Roma in Canada: Emigration from Hungary from the second half of the 1990s. In A. Kováts (Ed.), *Roma migration* (pp. 42–68). Budapest, Hungary: Research Institute of Ethnic and National Minorities, Hungarian Academy of Sciences.

Hale, S. (2004). *Community interpreting*. New York, NY: Palgrave Macmillan.

Halfmann, J. (1998). Citizenship universalism, migration and the risks of exclusion. *The British Journal of Sociology*, *49*(4), 513–533. doi:10.2307/591286

Hall, P. (2014, December 6). *Review: 'Debtfare States and the Poverty Industry'*. Retrieved from International Policy Digest: http://intpolicydigest.org/2014/12/06/review-debtfare-states-poverty-industry/

Hannah-Moffat, K. (2018). Algorithmic risk governance: Big data analytics, race and information activism in criminal justice debates. *Theoretical Criminology*. doi:10.1177/1362480618763582

Harlow, E. (2003). Information and communication technologies in the welfare services: Wired wonderland or hypertext hell. In E. Harlow and S. Webb (Eds). *Information and communication technologies in the welfare services* (pp. 7–28). Jessica Kingsley: London.

Haythornthwaite, C., & Kazmer, M. M. (2002). Bringing the internet home: Adult distance learners and their internet, home and work worlds. In B. Wellman & C. Haythornthwaite (Eds.), *The internet in everyday life* (pp. 431–463). Oxford, UK: Blackwell.

Hebberecht, P., & Baillergeau, E. (2012). *Social crime prevention in late modern Europe: A comparative perspective*. Brussels, Belgium: VUB Press.

Hemelsoet, E., & Van Pelt, P. (2015). Questioning the policy framing of Roma in Ghent, Belgium: Some implications of taking an insider perspective seriously. *Social Inclusion*, *3*(5), 148–160. doi:10.17645/si.v3i5.236

Henman, P., & Marston, G. (2008). The social division of welfare surveillance. *Journal of Social Policy*, *37*(2), 187–205. doi:10.1017/S0047279407001705

Hier, S. P. (2002). Probing the Surveillant Assemblage: On the dialectics of surveillance practices as processes of social control. *Surveillance & Society*, *1*(3), 399–411.

Hjorth, L. (2007). Domesticating new media: A discussion on locating mobile media. In G. Goggin & L. Hjorth (Eds.), *Mobile Media 2007* (pp. 179–188). Sydney, Australia: The University of Sydney.

Hoag, C. (2011). Assembling partial perspectives: Thoughts on the anthropology of bureaucracy. *Polar: Political and Legal Anthropology Review*, *34*(1), 81–94. doi:10.1111/j.1555-2934.2011.01140.x

Humphris, R. (2013). European Union enlargement and Roma migrants' welfare: The role of changing migration status in UK education policy and practice. *Human Welfare*, *2*(1), 26–35.

Huxley, A. (2008). *Brave new world*. Stuttgart, Germany: Ernst Klett Sprachen.

Huysmans, J. (2000). The European Union and the securitization of migration. *JCMS: Journal of Common Market Studies*, *38*(5), 751–777.

Huysmans, J. (2006). *The politics of insecurity: Fear, migration and asylum in the EU*. London, UK: Routledge.

Hyndman, J. (2012). The geopolitics of migration and mobility. *Geopolitics*, *17*(2), 243–255. doi:10.1080/14650045.2011.569321

ICF GHK. (2013). *A fact finding analysis on the impact on the Member States' social security systems of the entitlements of non-active intra-EU migrants to special non-contributory cash benefits and healthcare granted on the basis of residence*. Retrieved from http://ec.europa.eu/employment_social/empl_portal/facebook/20131014%20GHK%20study%20web_EU%20migration.pdf

Ilcan, S., Oliver, M., & O'Connor, D. (2007). Spaces of governance: Gender and public sector restructuring in Canada. *Gender, Place & Culture: A Journal of Feminist Geography*, *14*(1), 75–92. doi:10.1080/09663690601122333

Jarvis, T. (2010). The digital cage: Digital surveillance and bureaucratic governance. *On Politics*, *1*(1), 5–16. Retrieved from https://journals.uvic.ca/index.php/onpolitics/article/view/547

Jiang, L. (2007). From 'community interpreting' to 'discourse interpreting': Establishing some useful parameters. *MuTra 2007 – LSP Translation Scenarios: Conference Proceedings*. Retrieved from www.euroconferences.info/proceedings/2007_Proceedings/2007_Jiang_Lihua.pdf

Jones, J. A. (2012). Ethical considerations in criminal justice research: Informed consent and confidentiality. *Inquiries Journal/Student Pulse*, *4*(08). Retrieved from-www.inquiriesjournal.com/a?id=674

Jones, T., & Newburn, T. (1998). *Private security and public policing*. Clarendon Press.

Kabachnik, P. (2010). England or Uruguay? The persistence of place and the myth of the placeless Gypsy. *Area*, *42*(2), 198–207. doi:10.1111/j.1475-4762.2009.00910.x

Kaboolian, L. (1998). The new public management: Challenging the boundaries of the management vs. administration debate. *Public Administration Review*, *58*(3), 189–193. doi:10.2307/976558

Kade, O. (1967). Zu einigen Besonderheiten des Simultandolmetschens [Some special features of simultaneous interpretation]. *Fremdsprachen*, *1967*(1), 8–17.

Kapoor, D. (2005). NGO partnerships and the taming of the grassroots in rural India. *Development in Practice*, *15*(2), 210–215. doi:10.1080/09614520500041864

Kazmer, M. M., & Xie, B. (2008). Qualitative interviewing in internet studies: Playing with the media, playing with the method. *Information, Communication and Society*, *11*(2), 257–278. doi:10.1080/13691180801946333

Kertesi, G. (2000). A cigány foglalkoztatás leépülése és szerkezeti átalakulása 1984 és 1994 között. Munkatörténeti elemzés [The degradation of Roma employment and structural transformation from 1984 to 1994. Work history analysis]. *Közgazdasági Szemle*, *47*(5), 406–443. Retrieved from http://econpapers.repec.org/scripts/redir.pf?u=http%3A%2F%2Fwww.kszemle.hu%2Ftartalom%2Fletoltes.php%3Fid%3D320;h=repec:ksa:szemle:320

Kierkegaard, S. (1844)*The concept of dread* (Walter Lowrie, Trans. (1946).). Princeton, NJ: Princeton University Press.

Kilger, M. (1994). The digital individual. *The Information Society*, *10*(2), 93–99. doi:10.1080/01972243.1994.9960161

Kinket, B., & Verkuyten, M. (1997). Levels of ethnic self-identification and social context. *Social Psychology Quarterly*, *60*(4), 338–354. doi:10.2307/2787094

Kirkpatrick, I. (2006). Taking stock of the new managerialism in English social services. *Social Work & Society*, *4*(1), 14–24. Retrieved from www.socwork.net/sws/article/view/173/564

Kistermann, F. W. (1991). The invention and development of the Hollerith Punched Card: In commemoration of the 130th anniversary of the birth of Herman Hollerith and for the 100th anniversary of large scale data processing. *Annals of the History of Computing*, *13*(3), 245–259.

Kligman, G. (2001). A "másság" társadalmi felépítése: A "roma" azonosítása a posztszocialista közösségekben [The 'other' social structure of the Roma: Identifying the post-socialist communities]. *Szociológiai Szemle*, *4*, 66–84.

Klímová, I. (2002). Romani political representation in Central Europe. An historical survey. *Romani Studies*, *12*(2), 103–147. doi:10.3828/rs.2002.5

Klimova, I. & Pickup, A. (2003) 'Romani Migration: Strangers in Anybody's Land?', *Nationalities Papers*, 38(1): 7–10. in Vidra (ed.) (2013) Roma Migration to and from Canada: the case of the Czech Republic, Hungary and Slovakia. Central European University, Center for Policy Studies.

Klímová, I. – Pickup, A. (2003) Introduction: Romani migrations – Strangers in Anybody's Land? Further Reviewed. *Nationalities Papers: The Journal of Nationalism and Ethnicity Studies*, *31*(1), 7–10. http://dx.doi.org/10.1080/0090599032000058866.

Kóczé, A., & Rövid, M. (2017). Roma and the politics of double discourse in contemporary Europe. *Identities*, *24*(6), 684–700.

Kóczé, A., & Rövid, M. (2012). Pro-Roma global civil society: Acting for, with or instead of Roma? In S. Selchow, M. Kaldor, & H. L. Moore (Eds.), *Global Civil Society 2012* (pp. 110–122). London, UK: Palgrave Macmillan.

Kohler-Hausmann, J. (2007). 'The crime of survival': Fraud prosecutions, community surveillance and the original 'welfare queen'. *Journal of Social History*, *41*(2), 329–354. doi:10.1353/jsh.2008.0002

Kostka, J. (2015). Implementation of Roma inclusion policies: Why defining the problem matters. *Social Inclusion*, *3*(5), 78–89. doi:10.17645/si.v3i5.231

Kováts, A. (2002). Migration among the Roma population in Hungary. In A. Kováts (Ed.), *Roma migration* (pp. 9–32). Budapest, Hungary: Hungarian Academy of Sciences Institute of Minority Research – Centre for Migration and Refugee Studies.

Kovats, M. (2001). The emergence of European Roma policy. In W. Guy (Ed.), *Between past and future: The Roma of Central and Eastern Europe* (pp. 93–116). Hatfield, UK: University of Hertfordshire Press.

Lacey, D., & Cuganesan, S. (2004). The role of organizations in identity theft response: The organization-individual victim dynamic. *Journal of Consumer Affairs, 38*(2), 244–261. doi:10.1111/j.1745-6606.2004.tb00867.x

Lau, M. H. (2006). *Research on the relationship between risk perception, risk propensity and risk-reducing decision-making in an e-government environment* (Unpublished master's thesis). Erasmus University Rotterdam, the Netherlands. Retrieved from www.pvib.nl/download/?id=6391917&download=1

Lazaridis, G., & Wadia, K. (Eds.). (2015). *The securitisation of migration in the EU: Debates since 9/11.* London, UK: Palgrave Macmillan.

Lemke, T. (2001). 'The Birth of Bio-Politics' – Michel Foucault's lecture at the Collège de France on neo-liberal governmentality. *Economy & Society, 30*(2), 190–207. doi:10.1080/03085140120042271

Levi, M. (2008). Organized frauds and organising frauds: Unpacking the research on networks and organization. *Criminology and Criminal Justice, 8*(4), 389–419. doi:10.1177/1748895808096470

Liégeois, J. P. (1998). *School provision for ethnic minorities: The gypsy paradigm* (Vol. 11). Hatfield, UK: University of Hertfordshire Press.

Lindlof, T. R., & Shatzer, M. J. (1998). Media ethnography in virtual space: Strategies, limits, and possibilities. *Journal of Broadcasting & Electronic Media, 42*(2), 170–189.

Lipsky, M. (2010). *Street level bureaucracy: Dilemmas of the individual in public service* (30th anniversary expanded edition). New York, NY: Russell Sage Foundation.

Little, L. E. (1998). Hiding with words: Obfuscation, avoidance, and federal jurisdiction opinions. *UCLA Law Review, 46*(1).

Lyon, D. (Ed.). (2003). *Surveillance as social sorting: Privacy, risk, and digital discrimination.* Abingdon, UK: Psychology Press.

Lyon, D. (Ed.). (2006). *Theorizing surveillance: The panopticon and beyond.* London, UK: Routledge.

Lyon, D. (2010a). Liquid surveillance: The contribution of Zygmunt Bauman to surveillance studies1. *International Political Sociology, 4*(4), 325–338. doi:10.1111/j.1749-5687.2010.00109.x

Lyon, D. (2010b). Surveillance, power and everyday life. In P. Kalantzis-Cope & K. Gherab-Martin (Eds.), *Emerging digital spaces in contemporary society* (pp. 107–120). London, UK: Palgrave Macmillan.

Lyon, D. (2013). *The information society: Issues and illusions.* Hoboken, NJ: John Wiley & Sons.

MacDonald, R., Shildrick, T., & Furlong, A. (2014). In search of 'intergenerational cultures of worklessness': Hunting the Yeti and shooting zombies. *Critical Social Policy, 34*(2), 199–220. doi:10.1177/0261018313501825

Mann, C., & Stewart, F. (2000). *Internet communication and qualitative research: A handbook for researching online.* Thousand Oaks, CA: SAGE Publications.

Marcus, G. E. (1995). Ethnography in/of the world system: The emergence of multi-sited ethnography. *Annual Review of Anthropology, 24*(1), 95–117. doi:10.1146/annurev.anthro.24.1.95

Marks, P. (2005). Imagining surveillance: Utopian visions and surveillance studies. *Surveillance & Society, 3*(2/3), 222–239. Retrieved from http://ojs.library.queensu.ca/index.php/surveillance-and-society/article/view/3503/3457

Marshall, I. H. (Ed.). (1997). *Minorities, migrants, and crime: Diversity and similarity across Europe and the United States.* London, UK: SAGE Publications.

Marushiakova, E., & Popov, V. (2004). The Roma – A nation without a state? Historical background and contemporary tendencies. In B. Streck (Ed.), *Segmentation und Komplementarität. Mitteilungen des SFB "Differenz und Integration"* (pp. 6–100). Halle, Germany: Centre for Oriental Studies (OWZ) of the Martin Luther University of Halle-Wittenberg.

Marushiakova, E., & Popov, V. (2015). European policies for social inclusion of Roma: Catch 22? *Social Inclusion*, *3*(5). doi:10.17645/si.v3i5.241

Marx, E. (2013). *Bedouin of Mount Sinai: An anthropological study of their political economy*. Oxford, UK: Berghahn Books.

Marx, G. T. (2002). What's new about the 'new surveillance'? Classifying for change and continuity. *Surveillance & Society*, *1*(1), 9–29. Retrieved from http://ojs.library.queensu.ca/index.php/surveillance-and-society/article/view/3391/3354

Mason, I. (1999). *Dialogue interpreting: Translator studies in intercultural communication* (Vol. 5, No. 2). New York, NY: Routledge.

Mason, J. (2002). *Qualitative researching* (2nd ed.). London, UK: SAGE Publications.

Massey, D. (1994). Double articulation, a place in the world. In A. Bammer (Ed.), *Displacements: Cultural identities in question* (pp. 110–119). Bloomington, IN: Indiana University Press.

Matei, S., & Ball-Rokeach, S. J. (2001). Real and virtual social ties connections in the everyday lives of seven ethnic neighborhoods. *American Behavioral Scientist*, *45*(3), 550–564. doi:10.1177/00027640121957213

Matras, Y. (2003). Mixed languages: Re-examining the structural prototype. In Y. Matras & P. Bakker (Eds.), *The mixed language debate: Theoretical and empirical advances* (pp. 151–176). Berlin, Germany: Mouton de Gruyter.

Matras, Y. (2015). Expert frames: Scientific and policy practices of Roma classification. *Social Inclusion*, *3*(5), 167–169. doi:10.17645/si.v3i5.423

Matras, Y. (2015). Expert Frames: Scientific and Policy Practices of Roma Classification. By Mihai Surdu. Budapest: Central European University Press, 2015, 267 pp., ISBN 978-963-386-113-4. *Social Inclusion*, *3*(5), 167–169.

Matras, Y., Leggio, D. V., Constantin, R., Tamase, L., & Sutac, M. (2015). The immigration of Romanian Roma to Western Europe: Causes, effects, and future engagement strategies (MigRom). Year 2 Report on the Extended Survey. University of Manchester. Retrieved from http://romani.humanities.manchester.ac.uk/migrom/docs/Yr2report_Mcr.pdf

Matras, Y., Leggio, D. V., & Steel, M. (2015). 'Roma education' as a lucrative niche: Ideologies and representations 1. *ZEP: Zeitschrift für Internationale Bildungsforschung und Entwicklungspädagogik*, *38*(1), 11–17..

Mayer, M. (2003). The onward sweep of social capital: Causes and consequences for understanding cities, communities and urban movements. *International Journal of Urban and Regional Research*, *27*(1), 110–132. doi:10.1111/1468-2427.00435

McAdam, D., McCarthy, J. D., & Zald, M. N. (1996). *Comparative perspectives on social movements: Political opportunities, mobilizing structures, and cultural framings*. Cambridge, UK: Cambridge University Press.

McDonald, M. (2008). Securitization and the construction of security. *European Journal of International Relations*, *14*(4), 563–587. doi:10.1177/1354066108097553

McDonald, M. (2013). Discourses of climate security. *Political Geography*, *33*, 42–51. doi:10.1016/j.polgeo.2013.01.002

McDonald, S. (2005). Studying actions in context: A qualitative shadowing method for organizational research. *Qualitative Research, 5*(4), 455–473. doi:10.1177/1468794105056923

McGarry, A. (2011). The Roma voice in the European Union: Between national belonging and transnational identity. *Social Movement Studies, 10*(3), 283–297. doi:10.1080/14742837.2011.590030

Mead, L. M. (1997). Citizenship and social policy: TH Marshall and poverty. *Social Philosophy and Policy, 14*(2), 197–230.

Merlini, R., & Favaron, R. (2003). Community interpreting: Re-conciliation through power management. *The Interpreters' Newsletter: Trieste, 12*, 205–229.

Mikkelson, H. (2008). Controversies over the role of the court interpreter. In C. Valero Garcés & A. Martin (Eds.), *Crossing borders in community interpreting: Definitions and dilemmas* (pp. 81–97). Amsterdam, the Netherlands: John Benjamins Publishing Company.

Mirga, A. (1992). Roma territorial behavior and state policy: The case of the socialist countries of East Europe. In M. J. Casimir & A. Rao (Eds.), *Mobility and territoriality: Social and spatial boundaries among foragers, fishers, pastoralists, and peripatetics* (pp. 259–278). New York, NY: Berg.

Mirga, A. (2009). The extreme right and Roma and Sinti in Europe: A new phase in the use of hate speech and violence? *Roma Rights Journal, 1*, 5–9.

Mirga, A., & Gheorghe, N. (1997). *The Roma in the twenty-first century: A policy.* Project on Ethnic Relations. Retrieved from www.per-usa.org/1997-2007/21st_c.htm

Mitchell, K. (2006). Neoliberal governmentality in the European Union: Education, training and technologies of citizenship. *Environment and Planning D: Society and Space, 24*(3), 389–407. doi:10.1068/d1804

Mitchison, N., Wilikens, M., Breitenbach, L., Urry, R., & Portesi, S. (2004). *Identity theft: A discussion paper* (Joint Research Centre of the European Commission). Retrieved from bookshop.europa.eu/ . . . /identity-theft. . . / LBNA21098ENC_002.pdf

Mohan, G. (2002). The disappointments of civil society: The politics of NGO intervention in northern Ghana. *Political Geography, 21*(1), 125–154. doi:10.1016/s0962-6298(01)00072-5

Moran, J. (2004) *November in Berlin: The end of the everyday, History Workshop Journal, 57*, pp. 216–234.

Moroşanu, L., & Fox, J. E. (2013). 'No smoke without fire': Strategies of coping with stigmatised migrant identities. *Ethnicities, 13*(4), 438–456. doi:10.1177/1468796813483730

Muller, B. J. (2004). (Dis)qualified bodies: Securitization, citizenship and 'identity management'. *Citizenship Studies, 8*(3), 279–294. doi:10.1080/1362102042000257005

Munger, F. (2003). Poverty, welfare, and the affirmative state. *Law & Society Review, 37*(3), 659–686. doi:10.1111/1540-5893.3703007

Nacu, A. (2012). From silent marginality to spotlight scapegoating? A brief case study of France's policy towards the Roma. *Journal of Ethnic and Migration Studies, 38*(8), 1323–1328. doi:10.1080/1369183x.2012.689192

Nagel, J. (1994). Constructing ethnicity: Creating and recreating ethnic identity and culture. *Social Problems, 41*(1), 152–176. doi:10.1525/sp.1994.41.1.03x0430n

National Audit Office. (2008, January 23). *Department for work and pensions: Progress in tackling benefit fraud* (Report by the Comptroller and Auditor

General, HC 102 Session 2007–2008). Retrieved from www.nao.org.uk/report/department-for-work-and-pensions-progress-in-tackling-benefit-fraud/

Nayar, P. K. (2015). *Citizenship and identity in the age of surveillance*. Cambridge, UK: Cambridge University Press.

Newman, G. R., & McNally, M. M. (2005). *Identity theft literature review* (National Institute of Justice Focus Group Meeting, NCJ 210459). Retrieved from www.ncjrs.gov/pdffiles1/nij/grants/210459.pdf

Novoselsky, V. (2015). *Internet as a tool of change and the role of Roma virtual network in a process of Roma empowerment*. Retrieved from www.academia.edu/19448417/Internet_as_a_tool_of_change_and_the_role_of_Roma_Virtual_Network_in_a_process_of_Roma_empowerment

Nuijten, M. (2004). The 'hope-generating machine' and the positionality of the anthropologist. *The Development of Religion, the Religion of Development, Eburon Delft*, 51.

Oakley, M. (2014). *Independent review of the operation of Jobseeker's Allowance sanctions validated by the Jobseekers Act 2013*. Retrieved from UK Government website: www.gov.uk/government/uploads/system/uploads/attachment_data/file/335144/jsa-sanctions-independent-review.pdf

O'Hara, M. (2015). *Austerity bites: A journey to the sharp end of cuts in the UK*. Bristol, UK: Policy Press.

Okely, J. (1983). *The traveller-gypsies*. London, UK: Cambridge University Press.

O'Malley, P., Weir, L., & Shearing, C. (1997). Governmentality, criticism, politics. *Economy and Society*, *26*(4), 501–517. doi:10.1080/03085149700000026

Open Society Foundation. (2004). *Who is afraid of migrating Roma? EU Accession Monitoring Programme*. Retrieved from www.eumap.org/journal/features/2004/migration/pt2/whoafraid

O'Reilly, K. (2007a). Intra-European migration and the mobility – Enclosure dialectic. *Sociology*, *41*(2), 277–293. doi:10.1177/0038038507074974

O'Reilly, T. (2007b). What is web 2.0: Design patterns and business models for the next generation of software. *Communications & Strategies*, 1(17).

Osborne, D., & Gaebler, T. (1992). *Reinventing government: How the entrepreneurial spirit is transforming government*. Reading, MA: Addison-Wesley Publishing Company.

OSCE. (2000). *Report on the situation of Roma and Sinti in the OSCE Area*. Organization for Security and Co-operation in Europe, High Commissioner on National Minorities. Retrieved from www.osce.org/hcnm/42063?download=true

Osler, M., Lund, R., Kriegbaum, M., Christensen, U., & Andersen, A.- M. N. (2005). Cohort profile: The Metropolit 1953 Danish male birth cohort. *International Journal of Epidemiology*, *35*(3), 541–545.

Packer, J. (2006). Becoming bombs: Mobilizing mobility in the war of terror. *Cultural Studies*, *20*(4–5), 378–399. doi:10.1080/09502380600711105

Palomera, J. (2014). Reciprocity, commodification, and poverty in the era of financialization. *Current Anthropology*, *55*(S9), S105–S115. doi:10.1086/676420

Panchev, D. (2013). *'Othering' and the criminalization of Bulgarian Roma in the social media* (Unpublished master's thesis). University of Kent, Canterbury, UK. Retrieved from www.academia.edu/12296661/Othering_and_the_Criminalisation_of_Bulgarian_Roma

Pap, A. L. (2014). Is there a legal right to free choice of ethno-racial identity: Legal and political difficulties in defining minority communities and membership boundaries.

Columbia Human Rights Law Review, *46*(2), 152–232. Retrieved from http://papers.ssrn.com/sol3/papers.cfm?abstract_id=2712435

Parkin, J. (2013). The criminalisation of migration in Europe: A state-of-the-art of the academic literature and research (CEPS Paper in Liberty and Security in Europe, No. 61). Retrieved from www.ceps.eu/system/files/Criminalisation%20of%20Migration%20in%20Europe%20J%20Parkin%20FIDUCIA%20final.pdf

Pascoe, T., Owen, K., Keats, G., & Gill, M. (2006). *Identity fraud: What about the victim? Research findings.* CIFAS – Perpetuity Research. Retrieved from www.cifas.org.uk/secure/contentPORT/uploads/documents/External-Identity%20Fraud%20-%20What%20About%20the%20Victim%20Research%20Findings.pdf

Pasquetti, S. (2013). Legal emotions: An ethnography of distrust and fear in the Arab districts of an Israeli city. *Law & Society Review*, *47*(3), 461–492. doi:10.1111/lasr.12028

Paul Rabinów and William M. Sullivan, eds.,(1979) *Interpretive Social. Science: A Second Look.* Berkeley: University of California Press.

Payes, S. (2005). *Palestinian NGOs in Israel: The politics of civil society.* London, UK: I. B. Tauris.

Petintseva, O. (2014). De 'taboes' binnen criminologie: het academisch discours mbt etniciteit/migratie en criminaliteit [The taboos within criminology: The academic discourse with regards to ethnicity/migration and criminality]. In *Update in de Criminologie VII: actuele ontwikkelingen inzake EU-justitiebeleid, cannabisbeleid, misdaad en straf, jongeren en jeugdzorg, internationale vrede, veiligheid en gerechtigheid, gewelddadig extermisme & private veiligheid en zelfregulering* (pp. 192–220). Retrieved from http://lib.ugent.be/catalog/pug01:4316807

Phelan, M., & Martín, M. (2010). Interpreters and cultural mediators – different but complementary roles. *Translocations*, *6*(1). Retrieved from http://doras.dcu.ie/16481/

Piasere, L. (1992). Roma and Roma in north-east Italy: Two types of territorial behavior in the same larger territory. In M. J. Casimir & A. Rao (Eds.), *Mobility and territoriality: Social and spatial boundaries among foragers, fishers, pastoralists, and peripatetics* (pp. 279–291). New York, NY: Berg.

Pickup, F., & White, A. (2003). Livelihoods in postcommunist Russia: Urban/rural comparisons. *Work, Employment & Society*, *17*(3), 419–434. doi:10.1177/09500170030173001

Piven, F. F., & Cloward, R. A. (1971). *Regulating the poor: The functions of social welfare.* New York, NY: Vintage.

Poptcheva, E. M. (2014). Freedom of movement and residence of EU citizens. Access to social benefits. *European Parliament Research Service*, *10*(06), 2014.

Pogány, I. (2006). Minority rights and the Roma of Central and Eastern Europe. *Human Rights Law Review*, *6*(1), 1–25. doi:10.1093/hrlr/ngi034

Pogány, I. (2012). Pariah peoples: Roma and the multiple failures of law in Central and Eastern Europe. *Social & Legal Studies*, *21*(3), 375–393. doi:10.1177/0964663911429152

Pogonyi, Sz (2013) After democratic transition. https://www.eurozine.com/after-democratic-transition/

Poster, M. (1991). *The mode of information: Post structuralism and social context.* Chicago, IL: University of Chicago Press.

Postle, K. (2002). Working 'between the idea and the reality': Ambiguities and tensions in care managers' work. *British Journal of Social Work*, *32*(3), 335–351.

Prónai, C. (2006). *Cigány Világok Európában. Zigeunerwelten in Europa. Kulturanthropologie.* Budapest, Hungary: Nyitott Könyv.
Pusca, A. (2014, November 20). Roma migrants in the UK: Why cautiously welcoming them is a more effective strategy. *British Politics and Policy blog of the London School of Economics.* Retrieved from http://blogs.lse.ac.uk/politicsandpolicy/roma-migrants-in-the-uk-why-cautiously-welcoming-them-might-be-a-more-effective-strategy/
Putnam, R.D. (2000). *Bowling Alone.* New York: Simon & Schuster.
Puxon, G. (2000). The Romani movement: Rebirth and the First World Romani Congress in retrospect. In T. Acton (Ed.), *Scholarship and the Gypsy Struggle* (pp. 94–113). Hatfield, UK: University of Hertfordshire Press.
Pykett, J. (2013). *Governing through pedagogy: Re-educating citizens.* London, UK: Routledge.
Ramage, S. (2008). Covert surveillance. *Criminal Lawyer, 181.*
Rankin, K. N. (2002). Social capital, microfinance, and the politics of development. *Feminist Economics, 8*(1), 1–24. doi:10.1080/13545700210125167
Ringold, D. (2000). *Roma and the transition in Central and Eastern Europe: Trends and challenges.* Washington, DC: World Bank Publications.
Ringold, D., Orenstein, M. A., & Wilkens, E. (2005). *Roma in an expanding Europe: Breaking the poverty cycle.* Washington, DC: The World Bank.
Romani Studies Network. (2015). *Compiling data on Roma: Discussions on Roma migrants in the UK and the number games.* Retrieved from http://romanistudies.eu/documents/email-list-archive/
Rose, N. (1999). *Powers of freedom: Reframing political thought.* Cambridge, UK: Cambridge University Press.
Rose, N., & Miller, P. (1992). Political power beyond the state: Problematics of government. *The British Journal of Sociology, 43*(2), 173–205. doi:10.2307/591464
Russell, S. (2008, September 9). *Presentation at Council of Europe experts meeting on Roma migration.* FCPNM; Council of Europe. Pavee Point, Ireland.
Rutledge, D. (2014a, January 13). The political row over benefits and EU migrants. *Free Movement Immigration law blog of Garden Court Chambers.* Retrieved from www.freemovement.org.uk/the-political-row-over-benefits-and-eu-migrants/
Rutledge, D. (2014b, November 25). Existing EEA migrants at risk of destitution following the removal of Housing Benefit. *Free Movement Immigration law blog of Garden Court Chambers.* Retrieved from www.freemovement.org.uk/existing-eea-migrants-at-risk-of-destitution-following-the-removal-of-housing-benefit/
Rutledge, D. (2014c, March 14). New habitual residence test and the impact on returning UK nationals. *Free Movement Immigration law blog of Garden Court Chambers.* Retrieved from www.freemovement.org.uk/new-habitual-residence-test-and-the-impact-on-returning-uk-nationals/
Rutledge, D. (2014d, March 21). Removal of entitlement to housing benefit for EEA jobseekers. *Free Movement Immigration law blog of Garden Court Chambers.* Retrieved from www.freemovement.org.uk/removal-entitlement-housing-benefit-eea-jobseekers/
Rutledge, D. (2015). Benefits to be withdrawn from EEA jobseekers previously unaffected by the January 2014 changes. *Free Movement Immigration law blog of Garden Court Chambers.* Retrieved from www.freemovement.org.uk/benefits-to-be-withdrawn-from-eea-jobseekers-previously-unaffected-by-the-january-2014-changes/
Sainsbury, R. (1998). Putting fraud into perspective, *Benefits, 21*, 2–6.
Salaff, J. W. (2002). Where home is the office. *The internet in everyday life*, 464–495.

Sampson, S. L. (2002). Weak states, uncivil societies and thousands of NGOs: Benevolent colonialism in the Balkans. In S. Resic & B. Törnquist-Plewa (Eds.), *The Balkans in focus: Cultural boundaries in Europe* (pp. 27–44). Lund, Sweden: Lund University Press.
Sasse, G. (2005). Securitization or securing rights? Exploring the conceptual foundations of policies towards minorities and migrants in Europe*. *JCMS: Journal of Common Market Studies*, *43*(4), 673–693. doi:10.1111/j.1468–5965.2005.00591.x
Sassen, S. (2002). Towards post-national and denationalized citizenship. In E. F. Isin & B. S. Turner (Eds.), *Handbook of citizenship studies* (pp. 277–292). London, UK: SAGE Publications.
Schild, V. (2007). Empowering consumer-citizensor governing poor female subjects? The institutionalization ofself-developmentin the Chilean social policy field. *Journal of Consumer Culture*, *7*(2), 179–203.
Schinkel, W. (2010). The virtualization of citizenship. *Critical Sociology*, *36*(2), 265–283. doi:10.1177/0896920509357506
Schulzek, N. (2012). *Migration Studies Unit*. London School of Economics and Political Science.
Schumpeter, J. (1942). Creative destruction. *Capitalism, Socialism and Democracy*, 82–85.
Sellin, T. (1938). Culture conflict and crime. *American Journal of Sociology*, *44*(1), 97–103. doi:10.1086/217919
Shaw, C. R., & McKay, H. D. (1942). *Juvenile delinquency and urban areas*. Chicago, IL: University of Chicago Press.
Sheldrick, G. (2016, April 5). REVEALED: How YOU pay for Roma gypsy palaces – UK benefits funding Romanian mansions. *Sunday Express*. Retrieved from www.express.co.uk
Sheller, M., & Urry, J. (2006). The new mobilities paradigm. *Environment and Planning A*, *38*(2), 207–226. doi:10.1068/a37268
Shover, N., Coffey, G. S., & Hobbs, D. (2003). Crime on the line: Telemarketing and the changing nature of professional crime. *The British Journal of Criminology*, *43*(3), 489–505. doi:10.1093/bjc/43.3.489
Siegel, D. (2014). *Mobile banditry: East and Central European itinerant criminal groups in the Netherlands*. The Hague, the Netherlands: Eleven International Publishing.
Sigona, N., & Trehan, N. (Eds.). (2009). *Romani politics in contemporary Europe: Poverty, ethnic mobilization, and the neoliberal order* (pp. 272–292). Basingstoke: Palgrave Macmillan.
Sigona, N., & Vermeersch, P. (2012). Editors' introduction. The Roma in the new EU: Policies, frames and everyday experiences. *Journal of Ethnic and Migration Studies*, *38*(8), 1189–1193. doi:10.1080/1369183x.2012.689174
Simandi, S. (2015, December 29). 12 results in 2015 that will make Europe a better place for Roma. *European Roma Rights Centre*. Retrieved from www.errc.org/article/12-results-in-2015-that-will-make-europe-a-better-place-for-roma/4441
Smith, M. J. (2010). From big government to big society: Changing the state-society balance. *Parliamentary Affairs*, *63*(4), 818–833. doi:10.1093/pa/gsq023
Sobotka, E. (2003). Romani migration in the 1990s: Perspectives on dynamic, interpretation and policy. *Romani Studies*, *13*(2), 79–121. doi:10.3828/rs.2003.4
Sobotka, E., & Vermeersch, P. (2012). Governing human rights and Roma inclusion: Can the EU be a catalyst for local social change? *Human Rights Quarterly*, *34*(3), 800–822.
Soederberg, S. (2014a). *Debtfare states and the poverty industry: Money, discipline and the surplus population*. London, UK: Routledge.

Spicker, P. (2005). Five types of complexity. *Benefits, 13*(1), 5–9. Retrieved from https://openair.rgu.ac.uk/handle/10059/853
Spicker, P. (2011). *How social security works: An introduction to benefits in Britain.* Bristol, UK: Policy Press.
Špidla, V. (2009). *Launch of the EU platform for Roma inclusion* [European Commission press release]. Retrieved from http://europa.eu/rapid/press-release_SPEECH-09-192_en.htm?locale=en
Srinivas, N. (2009). Against NGOs? A critical perspective on nongovernmental action. *Nonprofit and Voluntary Sector Quarterly, 38*(4), 614–626. doi:10.1177/0899764009334308
Staniewicz, T. (2011). Negotiating space and contesting boundaries: The case of Polish Roma and Polish migrants. Migration and adaptation as viewed via a social capital lens. *Studia Migracyjne-Przeglad Polonijny, 37*(1 (139)), 259–289.
Stenson, K. (2005). Sovereignty, biopolitics and the local government of crime in Britain. *Theoretical Criminology, 9*(3), 265–287. doi:10.1177/1362480605054811
Stewart, M. (2013). Roma and Gypsy 'ethnicity' as a subject of anthropological inquiry. *Annual Review of Anthropology, 42*(1), 415–432. doi:10.1146/annurev-anthro-092010–153348
Stewart, M., & Rovid, M. (Eds.). (2011). Multi-disciplinary approaches to Romany studies: Selected papers from participants of Central European University's Summer Courses 2007–2009. Retrieved from www.ucl.ac.uk/anthropology/people/academic_staff/m_stewart/multidisciplinary_approaches_to_romany_studies_.pdf
Strange S. (1988) States and Markets, London: Pinter.
Stroschein, S. (2002). NGO strategies for Hungarian and Roma minorities in Central Europe. *Voluntas: International Journal of Voluntary and Nonprofit Organizations, 13*(1), 1–26. Retrieved from http://link.springer.com/article/10.1023%2FA%3A1014793712223#page-1
Summers, S. J., Schwarzenegger, C., Ege, G., & Young, F. (2014). *The emergence of EU criminal law: Cyber crime and the regulation of the information society.* London: Bloomsbury Publishing.
Surdu, M. (2015). *Expert frames: Scientific and policy practices of Roma classification.* Budapest, Hungary: Central European University Press.
Surdu, M., & Kovats, M. (2015). Roma identity as an expert-political construction. *Social Inclusion, 3*(5). doi:10.17645/si.v3i5.245
Swank, D., & Betz, H.-G. (2003). Globalization, the welfare state and right-wing populism in Western Europe. *Socio-Economic Review, 1*(2), 215–245. doi:10.1093/soceco/1.2.215
Swift, K. J., & Birmingham, M. (2000). Location, location, location: Restructuring and the everyday lives of 'welfare moms'. In S. M. Neysmith (Ed.), *Restructuring caring labour: Discourse, state practice, and everyday life* (pp. 93–115). Oxford, UK: Oxford University Press.
Szuhay, P. (2002). Self-definitions of gypsy ethnic groups. In E. Kállai (Ed.), *The Gypsies/The Roma in Hungarian society* (pp. 24–28). Budapest, Hungary: Teleki László Foundation.
Szuhay, P. (2011). The plight of Hungary's Roma. *The Hungarian Quarterly, 202–203*, 86–102. Retrieved from www.ceeol.com/search/article-detail?id=200480
Tanner, A. (2005). The Roma of Eastern Europe: Still Searching for Inclusion. Migration Policy Institute.
Taylor, L. (2017). What is data justice? The case for connecting digital rights and freedoms globally. *Big Data & Society*, 4(2), 1–14. doi: 10.1177/2053951717736335.

Taylor, R. (1977). The local health system: An ethnography of interest-groups and decision-making. *Social Science & Medicine (1967)*, *11*(11–13), 583–592.

Terry, L. D. (1998). Administrative leadership, neo-managerialism, and the public management movement. *Public Administration Review*, 194–200.

Terry, L. D. (1993). Why We Should Abandon the Misconceived Quest to Reconcile Public Entrepreneurship with Democracy: A Response to Bellone and Goerl's" Reconciling Public Entrepreneurship and Democracy". *Public Administration Review*, *53*(4), 393–395.

Themelis, S. (2009). Questioning inclusion: The education of Roma/Traveller students and young people in Europe and England – A critical examination. *Research in Comparative and International Education*, *4*(3), 262–275. doi:10.2304/rcie.2009.4.3.262

Timmer, A. D. (2010). Constructing the 'needy subject': NGO discourses of Roma need. *Political and Legal Anthropology Review*, *33*(2), 264–281.

Titus, R. M. (1999, September). *The victimology of fraud*. Paper presented to the Restoration of Victims of Crime Conference, Melbourne, Australia. Retrieved from www.aic.gov.au/media_library/conferences/rvc/titus.pdf

Tonry, M. (1997). Ethnicity, crime, and immigration. *Crime and Justice*, *21*, 1–29. doi:10.1086/449248

Tóth, J. (2013). Roma migration from a legal perspective. In Z. Vidra (Ed.), *Roma migration to and from Canada: The Czech, Hungarian and Slovak Case* (pp. 23–52). Budapest, Hungary: Center for Policy Studies, Central European University.

Trehan, N. (2001). In the name of the Roma? The role of private foundations and NGOs. In W. Guy (Ed.), *Between past and future: The Roma of Central and Eastern Europe* (pp. 134–149). Hatfield, UK: University of Hertfordshire Press.

Trehan, N., & Sigona, N. (2009). *Romani politics in contemporary Europe: Poverty, ethnic mobilization, and the neo-liberal order*. London, UK: Palgrave Macmillan.

Tremlett, A., & McGarry, A. (2013). Challenges facing researchers on Roma minorities in contemporary Europe: Notes towards a research program (ECMI working paper #62). Retrieved from www.ecmi.de/uploads/tx_lfpubdb/Working_Paper_62_Final.pdf

Tuathail, G.O., & Dalby, S. (1998). *Rethinking geopolitics*. London, UK: Routledge.

UK Government. (2016, May 23). *Jobseeker's Allowance (JSA)*. Retrieved from www.gov.uk/jobseekers-allowance

Urry, J. (2008). *Mobilities*. Malden, UK: Polity Press.

Urry, J. (2012). *Sociology beyond societies: Mobilities for the twenty-first century*. London, UK: Routledge.

Vaidhyanathan, S. (2008, February 15). Naked in the 'nonopticon'. *The Chronicle of Higher Education*. Retrieved from http://chronicle.com

Van Baar, H. (2009, June). *Contesting neo-liberal practices in Central and Eastern Europe: Romani minority governance between activation and activism*. Unpublished paper presented at the Multi-Disciplinary and Cross-National Approaches to Romany Studies-a Model for Europe conference, Budapest, Hungary.

Van Baar, H. (2011a). The European Roma: Minority representation, memory, and the limits of transnational governmentality (PhD thesis). University of Amsterdam, Amsterdam, the Netherlands.

Van Baar, H. (2012b). Socio-economic mobility and neo-liberal governmentality in post-socialist Europe: Activation and the dehumanisation of the Roma. *Journal of Ethnic and Migration Studies*, *38*(8), 1289–1304. doi:10.1080/1369183x.2012.689189 van Baar, H. (2014). The emergence of a reasonable anti-gypsyism in Europe. *When Stereotype Meets Prejudice: Antiziganism in European Societies* (pp. 27–44). Stuttgart: Ibidem.

Van Baar, H. (2015). The perpetual mobile machine of forced mobility: Europe's Roma and the institutionalization of rootlessness. In Y. Jansen, R. Celikates, & J. de Bloois (Eds.), *The irregularization of migration in contemporary Europe: Detention, deportation, drowning* (pp. 71–86). New York, NY: Rowman & Littlefield International.

van Berkel, R., & Knies, E. (2013, June). *Bureaucracy, professionalism and managerialism in a street-level bureaucracy context: A frontline perspective.* Paper prepared for panel 44, 'Street-level policy research: Expanding the boundaries', at the first ICPP conference, Grenoble, France.

Van Broeck, J. (2001). Cultural defence and culturally motivated crimes (cultural offences). *European Journal of Crime, Criminal Law and Criminal Justice*, *9*(1), 1–32. doi:10.1163/15718170120519282

van der Meulen, N. (2006). *The challenge of countering identity theft: Recent developments in the United States, the United Kingdom, and the European Union.* Report Commissioned by the National Infrastructure Cyber Crime program (NICC). Retrieved from www.researchgate.net/publication/238668492_The_Challenge_of_Countering_Identity_Theft_Recent_Developments_in_the_United_States_the_United_Kingdom_and_the_European_Union

Van Poeck, K., & Vandenabeele, J. (2012). Learning from sustainable development: Education in the light of public issues. *Environmental Education Research*, *18*(4), 541–552. doi:10.1080/13504622.2011.633162

Vargas-Silva, C. (2011, September 13). Seven years after the Eastern European enlargement. *Compas blog.* Retrieved from www.compas.ox.ac.uk/2011/seven-years-after-the-eastern-european-enlargement/

Vasecka, I., & Vasecka, M. (2003). Recent Romani migration from Slovakia to EU member states: Romani reaction to discrimination or Romani ethno-tourism? *Nationalities Papers*, *31*(1), 27–45. doi:10.1080/0090599032000058893

Vaughan-Williams, N. (2010). The UK border security continuum: Virtual biopolitics and the simulation of the sovereign ban. *Environment and Planning D: Society and Space*, *28*(6), 1071–1083. doi:10.1068/d13908

Vermeersch, P. (2003). Ethnic minority identity and movement politics: The case of the Roma in the Czech Republic and Slovakia. *Ethnic & Racial Studies*, *26*(5), 879–901. doi:10.1080/0141987032000109078

Vermeersch, P. (2006). *The Romani movement: Minority politics and ethnic mobilization in contemporary Central Europe* (Vol. 4). Oxford, UK: Berghahn Books.

Vermeersch, P. (2011). Roma and mobility in the European Union. In K. Pietarinen (Ed.), *Roma and traveller inclusion in Europe: Green questions and answers.* Retrieved from http://gef.eu/uploads/ media/Roma_and_Traveler_Inclusion.pdf

Vidra, Z. (2013a). Rethinking Roma migration in the light of recent flow of refugees to Canada from three Central Eastern European countries the Czech Republic, Hungary and Slovakia. *International Journal of Arts & Sciences*, *6*(3), 529–540.

Vidra, Z. (Ed.). (2013b). *Roma migration to and from Europe: The Czech, Hungarian, and Slovak case.* Budapest, Hungary: Central European University Press.

Vidra, Zs (2013) *Roma Migration to and from Canada: The Czech, Hungarian and Slovak Case.* Budapest: Central European University, Center for Policy Studies.

Visegrad.info (2010, September 10). Roma minority in Visegrad countries. Factsheet. Retrieved from www.visegrad.info/minorities-social-exclusion-roma-minority/factsheet/roma-minority-in-visegrad-countries.html

Vuolasranta, M. (2015, November 19). *Can Europe afford not to sanction discrimination and racism? A Greens/EFA conference.* Brussels, Belgium. http://www.ungei.org/SaveTheChildren_dafvol2.pdf.

Wæver, O., Buzan, B., Kelstrup, M., & Lemaitre, P. (1993). *Identity migration and the new security agenda in Europe.* London, UK: Pinter Publishers.

White, H. (2014). *On the road to genocide? A critical analysis of the neoliberal narration of the crisis.* Paper presented at the 2014 conference of the European Group for the Study of Deviance and Social Control, Liverpool, UK.

White, J. H. (2014). Prodigal sons and beardless machos: Labor, migration, and masculinity at Itaipú Binacional, Alto Paraná, Paraguay, 1974–1980. *Hispanic American Historical Review, 94*(4), 649–679. doi:10.1215/00182168-2802666

White, A. (2009). Internal migration, identity and livelihood strategies in contemporary Russia. *Journal of Ethnic and Migration Studies, 35*(4), 555–573.

Widerberg, K. (2004). Institutional ethnography – towards a producitve sociology: An interview with Dorothy E. Smith. *Sosiologisk tidsskrift, 12*, 179–184.

Williams, M. C. (2003). Words, images, enemies: Securitization and international politics. *International Studies Quarterly, 47*(4), 511–531. doi:10.1046/j.0020-8833.2003.00277.x

Williams, R. W. (2005). Politics and self in the age of digital re(pro)ducibility. *Fast Capitalism, 1*(1). Retrieved from www.uta.edu/huma/agger/fastcapitalism/1_1/williams.html

Wilson, W. J., & Chaddha, A. (2009). The role of theory in ethnographic research. *Ethnography, 10*(4), 549–564. doi:10.1177/1466138109347009

Wimmer, A. (2008b). The making and unmaking of ethnic boundaries: A multilevel process theory1. *American Journal of Sociology, 113*(4), 970–1022. doi:10.1086/522803

Winter, S., & Nielsen, V. L. (2008). *Implementering af politik* [Implementation of public policy]. Århus, Denmark: Academica.

Wintour, P. (2013, November 27). EU migrants: David Cameron sets out more benefit restrictions. *The Guardian.* Retrieved from www.theguardian.com

Wintour, P. (2014, October 23). Benefit sanctions regime for unemployed to be investigated by MPs. *The Guardian.* Retrieved from www.theguardian.com

Wise, J., M. (2002). 'Mapping the culture of control: Seeing through The Truman Show'. *Television & New Media, 3*(1): 29–47.

Wizner, B. (2000). *Roma vendégmunkások* [Roma guest workers]. Manuscript, Budapest, Hungary.

Woolford, A., & Nelund, A. (2013). The responsibilities of the poor: Performing neoliberal citizenship within the bureaucratic field. *Social Service Review, 87*(2), 292–318. doi:10.1086/671072

Yeatman, A. (1998). Interpreting contemporary contractualism. In M. Dean & B. Hindess (Eds.), *Governing Australia: Studies in contemporary rationalities of government* (pp. 227–241). Cambridge, UK: Cambridge University Press.

Appendix A

Overview of Roma participant informants

Code participant	*Place of first contact*	*Age group*	*Period of contact*
CM1	Presov	25–30	2012 aug
HM2	London	35–40	2013 nov
HF3	London	25–30	2013 nov
PF4	London	40–50	2013 dec
HM5	Borsod	30–35	2012 aug
HM6	London	30–35	2014 febr
HM7	Budapest	25–30	2012 aug
HM8	Baranya	25–30	2012 aug
HM9	London	30–35	2012 aug
HM10	Manchester	35–40	2013 march
HM11	London	30–35	2013 jan
HM12	London	25–30	2013 okt
HF13	Midland	30–35	2013 okt
HF14	London	30–35	2013 nov
HM15	Leeds	30–35	from 2013
HM16	Baranya	25–30	from 2012
HM17	Budapest	35–40	2012 aug
HM18	Miskolc	40–50	2013 aug
HM20	Miskolc	40–50	from 2012
PM21	London	30–35	from 2013
HM22	Budapest	40–50	from 2013
CM23	Brno	25–30	from 2013
PF24	London	40–50	from 2012
CF25	London	30–35	from 2013
PF26	London	25–30	from 1013
CM27	London	30–35	from 2013
HM28	Miskolc	35–40	from 2012
SF29	London	30–35	from 2013
HM30	Manchester	35–40	from 2013
vCF31	Brno	25–30	from 2013
HM32	London	35–40	from 2012
HM33	London	25–30	from 2012
HM34	Manchester	40–50	from 2013
PM35	London	25–30	from 2013
HM36	London	35–40	from 2013
HF37	London	35–40	from 2013
SF38	London	35–40	from 2013
SM39	Liverpool	25–30	from 2013

Code participant	*Place of first contact*	*Age group*	*Period of contact*
SM40	Presov	40–50	from 2012
SF41	Kosice	35–40	from 2012
HF42	Irland	25–30	from 2012
CF43	London	25–30	from 2013
SM44	Bohemia	30–35	from 2013
HF45	Baranya	25–30	from 2012
HM46	Budapest	40–50	from 2012
HF47	Bradford	35–40	from 2013
HM48	Manchester	35–40	from 2013
HM49	Leeds	35–40	from 2013
HM50	London	30–35	from 2013
HF51	Various	30–35	from 2013
HM52	Various	40–50	from 2013
PF53	London	25–30	from 2013
HM54	Baranya	30–35	from 2012
HM55	Budapest	40–50	from 2012
RM56	London	25–30	from 2013
CM57	Ostrava	25–30	from 2012
HM58	Borsod	35–40	from 2012
SM59	London	25–30	from 2013
HM60	Various	30–35	from 2013
HF61	Various	30–35	from 2013
PM62	London	35–40	from 2013
PF63	London	25–30	from 2013
RF64	London	25–30	from 2013
SM65	Various	30–35	from 2013
SM66	London	25–30	from 2013
SM67	London	35–40	from 2013
SF68	London	30–35	from 2013
HM69	Manchester	30–35	from 2012
HM70	Miskolc	35–40	2012 aug
HM71	Miskolc	35–40	from 2012
HF72	Baranya	40–50	from 2013
HF73	Various	40–50	from 2013
SM74	Ostrava	30–35	2013 jun
BR1	London	35–40	2012 nov
BR2	Various	35–40	2012 sept
BR3	Various	30–35	from 2012
BR4	London	35–40	from 2012
BR5	London	30–35	from 2013

Appendix B

Overview of interpreters

Interpreters	*Place interview*	*Language*	*Date of interview*
IN1	London	Hungarian	29/01/2014
IN2	London	Slovak	04/12/2013
IN3	London	Romani	05/02/2014
IN4	London	Hungarian, Romanian	26/03/2014
IN5	London	Hungarian	29/01/2014
IN6	London	Czech	29/01/2014
IN7	London	Hungarian	29/01/2014
IN8	London	Hungarian	29/01/2014
IN9	London	Hungarian	29/01/2014
IN10	London	Slovak	20/02/2014
IN11	Skype	Slovak	27/02/2014
IN12	Leeds	Czech	26/02/2014

Appendix C

Overview of academics

Academics	*Affiliation*	*Place*	*Year contact*
ACCMS1	Institut sociologických studií UK FSV	Prague	07/2013
ACBMC2	Universiteit Gent	Gent	From 2012
ACUKMDS3	PhD London	Skype	06/2013
ACCFDS4	Media	Email	05/2013
ACUKFL5	Law for life	London	02/2013
ACUKM6	University of Greenwich	London	12/2014
ACFL7	ELTE	Budapest	06/2013
ACHFP8	University of Pécs	Budapest	06/2013
ACHFL9	ELTE AJK	Budapest	07/2012
ACHFS10	ELTE TATK	Budapest	02/2013
ACCMM11	Charles University	Email	05/2013
ACHFA12	MTA	Budapest	01/2013
ACRMA13	Romani Academic network	Sibiu	10/2013
ACHMS14	Autonomia	Budapest	08/2012
ACHFL15	ELTE	Budapest	02/2013
ACBMC16	Universit Gent	Gent	10/2012
ACUKFP17	Romany Study Group	London	10/2013
ACCFS18	Masarykova univerzita	Brno	08/2013
ACCMS19	Univerity Brno	Brno	07/2013
ACHMS20	Corvinus University	Budapest	05/2013
ACHME21	SZTE	Skype	05/2013
ACHMSS]22	Demographic Research Institute	Budapest	04/2013
ACHMS23	ELTE TáTK	Budapest	03/2013
ACHML24	ELTE, MTA	Budapest	02/2013
ACBFC25	Gent University	Gent	10/2012
ACIMP26	Central European University	Budapest	07/2013

Academics	*Affiliation*	*Place*	*Year contact*
ACHMP27	Central European University	Budapest	01/2013
ACBFP28	Kent University	Canterbury	09/2012
ACSMP29	Platform for Social Housing, University of Ostrava	Prague	08/2013
ACHMS30	NYU Abu Dhabi	Budapest	05/2013
ACHME31	Kistigris secondary school	Alsószentmárton	04/2013
ACRFA32	University Bukarest Migrom Project	Sibiu	10/2013
ACBFES33	KU Leuven	Gent	09/2013
ACHMM34	Romani teacher	Budapest	09/2013
ACHFDS35	ERRC	Budapest	10/2013
ACCMS36	Fakulta sociálních studií University	Bratislava	07/2013
ACDMES37	Lecturer UvA	Amsterdam	05/2012
ACCMSS38	Secuity Studies University Brno	Brno	07/2013
ACBME39	Roma expert -edu	Gent	08/2013
ACCMS40	University Vienna	Prague	07/2013

Appendix D
Overview of professionals

Professionals	*Affiliation*	*Place*	*Year contact*
PUKM1	Redbridge Children's Services	Redbridge	04/2014
PUKF2	Diversity Programme Manager	Redbridge	05/2014
PUKF3	Education Development Officer	Manchester	02/2014
PHM4	Dr Ámbédkar school	London	03/2014
PUKF5	Sollicitor	London	03/2014
PHM6	Forrásközpont	Budapest	08/ 2012
PHM7	Roma Repr.	Budapest	05/2013
PUKM8	NCA	London	11/2013
PUKM9	Hazelbury School	London	12/2013
PHF10	Közéleti Roma Nők	Budapest	03/2013
PHF11	Kesztyűgyár	Budapest	03/2013
PHF12	Hungarian Child protection service	Budapest	02/2013
PHF13	Hungarian Probation Service	Budapest	02/2013
PSF14	Department of social affairs	Kosice sk	08/2013
PSF15	Social Services Slovakia	Kosice	07/2013
PUKM16	Police	Bradford	03/2014
PSF17	Salvation Army	Ostrava	06/2013
PUKF18	Social Inclusion Case Worker	London	10/2013
PCM19	Czech Government Agency for Social Inclusion	Prague	06/2013
PUKM20	Police	skype	03/2014
PSF21	Dep. of social affairs	Košice	06/2013
PSF22	Social worker	Ostrava	07/2014
PHM23	Police	Skype	03/2014
PNLM24	Police Academy The Netherlands	Amsterdam	08/2012
PCF25	Programy sociální integrace	Prague	06/2013
PCM26	Magistrát města	Brno	09/2013
PCF27	Agentura pro socialni zaclenovani	Prague	07/2013
PUKF28	JCO1	London, Redbridge	03/2014
PUKF29	JCO2	London, Waltham Forest	09/2013
PUKF30	JCO3	London, Newham	11/2013

Appendix E

Overview of non-governmental organisations

NGO workers	*Place*	*Year contact*
NGUSAF1	Skype	2012
NGHM2	Budapest	09/2013
NGRF3	London	01/2014
NGUKF4	London	01/2014
NGCM5	Email	07/2013
NGUKF6	London	11/2013
NGCF7	Brno	07/2013
NGRSF8	Eperjes	07/2013
NGUKF9	London	04/2014
NGUKF10	London	12/2013
NGHF11	Phone	02/2013
NGSRBF12	London	12/2013
NGCM13	Brno	07/2013
NGCF14	Prague	06/2013
NGUKF15	London	04/2014
NGPLF16	London	03/2014
NGUKF17	London	11/2013
NGUKM18	London	05/2014
NGUKF19	Phone	12/2014
NGSF20	Ostrava	07/2013
NGSM21	Moldava nad Bodvou	07/2013
NSUKF22	London	11/2014
NGSM23	Bratislava	06/2013
NGSF24	Ostrava	06/2013
NGUKF25	London	06/2013
NGSF26	Kosice	07/2013
NGCM27	Praga	07/2013
NGUKF27	Redbridge	04/2013
NGUKM28	London	12/2013
NGPLF28	London	01/2014
NGHF29	Budapest	02/2013
NGSM30	Bratislava	08/2013
NGUKF31	Birmingham	11/2013
NGHM32	Budapest	12/2012
NGHM33	Edelény	08/2012
NGUKF34	London	02/2014
NGSM35	Phone	09/2012

NGO workers	*Place*	*Year contact*
NGCM36	Facebook	08/2013
NGUKF37	Conference meeting	11/2013
NGHM38	Phone	09/2013
NGSF39	London	04/2014
NGHM40	Manchester	03/2014
NGSF41	Email	12/2013
NGSF42	Ostrava	07/2013
NGUKM43	London	02/2014
NGUKF44	London	04/2014
NGCM45	Skype	10/2012
NGHF46	Budapest	18/2013
NGHF47	Budapest	08/2012
NGHM48	Budapest	02/2013
NGBM49	Gent	11/2012
NGCHF50	Bratislava	07/2013
NGSM51	Budapest	06/2013
NGBM52	Ghent	08/2012

Overview coding

1, Academics (AC), Non-Governmental org. (NG), OR Professional civil servant (P)
2, Nationality (H)ungarian, (R)omanian, (S)lovak, (C)zech, (P)olish, (UK) British, (B)elgian
3, Gender (M)ale, (F)emale
4, Field of expertise
(M)inority
(C)riminology
(S)ociology
(A)nthropology
(E)uropean Studies
(D)evelopment studies
(S)ecuritu studies
(E)ducation studies
LAWM
(P)olicy Studies

Appendix F

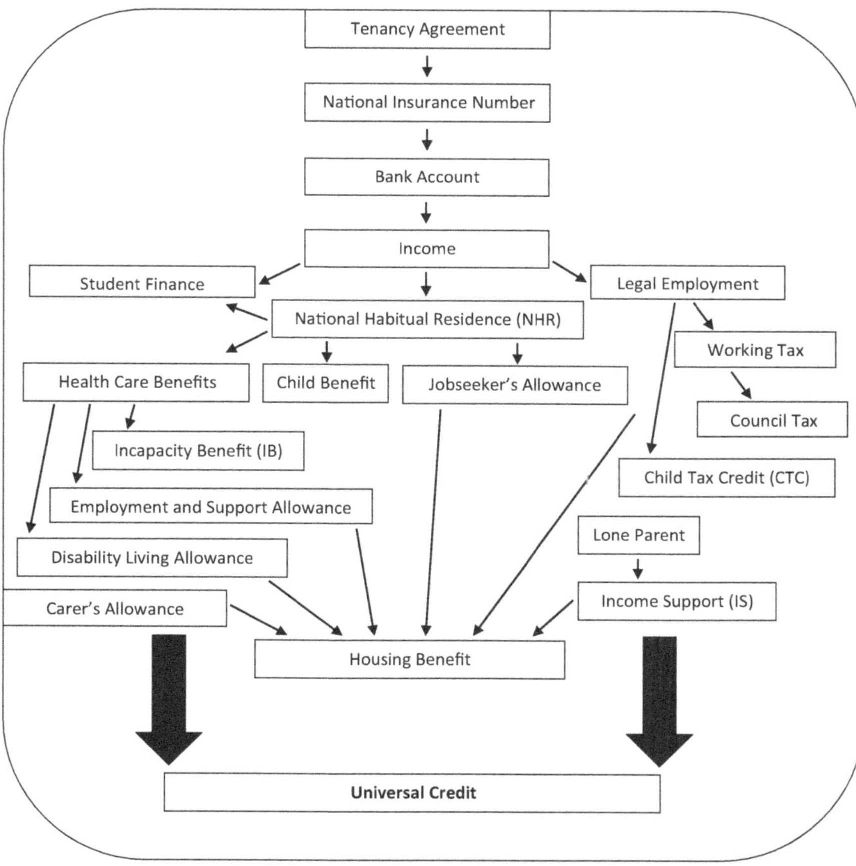

The basic model for application procedures in the UK welfare system.

Index

For Product Safety Concerns and Information please contact our
EU representative GPSR@taylorandfrancis.com Taylor & Francis
Verlag GmbH, Kaufingerstraße 24, 80331 München, Germany